New York City

Also in the series

Buenos Aires by Jason Wilson
Oxford by David Horan
Mexico City by Nick Caistor
Rome by Jonathan Boardman
Madrid by Elizabeth Nash
Venice by Martin Garrett
Lisbon by Paul Buck
Havana by Claudia Lightfoot
Kingston by David Howard
Brussels by André de Vries
Calcutta by Krishna Dutta
Edinburgh by Donald Campbell
Prague by Richard Burton
San Francisco by Mick Sinclair
Athens by Michael Llewellyn Smith
Cambridge by Martin Garrett
Helsinki by Neil Kent

New York City

A CULTURAL HISTORY

Eric Homberger

Interlink Books

An imprint of Interlink Publishing Group, Inc.
Northampton, Massachusetts

To Mark Krupnick

"...my guide, philosopher and friend"—Pope, *An Essay on Man*

This edition first published 2008 by

INTERLINK BOOKS
An imprint of Interlink Publishing Group, Inc.
46 Crosby Street, Northampton, Massachusetts 01060
www.interlinkbooks.com

Library of Congress Cataloging-in-Publication Data

Homberger, Eric.
New York City : a cultural and literary companion / by Eric Homberger.
p. cm.
ISBN 13: 978-1-56656-710-7
1. New York (N.Y.)—Civilization. 2. New York (N.Y.)—Intellectual life. 3. New York (N.Y.)—History. 4. Historic sites—New York (State)—New York. I. Title.
F128.3 .H66 2002
974.7'1—dc21 2002003495

All photographs and illustrations courtesy of Eric Homberger except p. 80 from Unit 1, No. 20, *Armenian Jew, Ellis Island, 1924*. Lewis W. Hine Collection, Nilstein Division of United States History, Local History and Genealogy, The New York Public Library, Astor, Lenox and Tilden Foundations. Photo on page 232, UNIA Convention Parade through Harlem, 1920 is reprinted by kind permission of Schomberg Center for Research in Black Culture.

Cover Images: Eric Homberger, Aquarius Photo Agency
Printed and bound in the United States of America

Contents

ACKNOWLEDGMENTS vii

PREFACE viii

INTRODUCTION: A CITY CHANGED, 9/11/01
Ground Zero xiii

CHAPTER ONE
MANNAHATTA
Names and Naming 1; Port, Harbor, and Sea 5; Traces of the Past 11; Melville, Cooper, and Roosevelt 19; The Grid 25; Flatiron Building 30

CHAPTER TWO
ON THE STEPS OF THE FEDERAL HALL NATIONAL MEMORIAL
J.P. Morgan 38; Trinity Church 43; Federal Hall 50; From City Hall to Federal Hall 52; Wall Street and the New York Stock Exchange 56

CHAPTER THREE
THE IMMIGRANT'S CITY
March or Die 63; The Statue of Liberty 68; Ellis Island 74; The Lower East Side 81; Abraham Cahan and Isaac Bashevis Singer: Finding Voices for the Immigrant World 89; Social Settlements 94; The Tenement 97; The Tenement Museum 103

CHAPTER FOUR
GREENWICH VILLAGE
Symbols and Yellow Fever 108; Washington Square 110;

The New Village, 1912–1917 115; Caroline Ware's Village 121; Village Scenes: Folk Singers, Beats, Hipsters 124; Warhol and the Factory 133

CHAPTER FIVE
Parks

Urban Space and Romantic Landscapes 137; Woodlawn Cemetery 141; Parks and the City 143; The Battery 145; Private Property and Radicalism 147; Olmsted and Central Park 149; Paying for the City's Parks 155

CHAPTER SIX
Broadway

Making Broadway 163; Starting out at Number 1 166; St. Paul's Chapel 169; City Hall 176; City Hall Park 181; Fashionable Ladies, Dandies, Hotels, and Shops 183; Chinatown 192; SoHo 197; Grace Church 201; Union Square 205; Madison Square 208; 42nd Street and Times Square 210; Light and Air 213

CHAPTER SEVEN
Harlem

Old Harlem 220; Toward San Juan Hill 223; The Migration North 227; The New Negro 232; Jazz Age 236; Harlem Reborn 240

CHAPTER EIGHT
More than Manhattan

Brooklyn 243

FURTHER READING 247

INDEX OF PEOPLE 252

INDEX OF PLACES AND INSTITUTIONS 256

Acknowledgments

Having relied on *The Encyclopedia of New York City* (Yale University Press) for seven years, my sense of debt to Professor Kenneth T. Jackson of Columbia University, and latterly of the New York Historical Society, deepens. The staff of the New York Public Library was, as ever, efficient in responding to questions and fulfilling requests. I would like to thank Bill Albert for once again reading my manuscript.

—E.H.

Preface

There are dozens of well-illustrated guidebooks to New York, choc-a-bloc with maps, attractive color photographs, and bits of information largely served up in alarmingly small typefaces. There are also distinguished and readable narrative histories of the city. Edwin G. Burrows and Mike Wallace's award-winning Gotham, published in 1999, takes the city's story to 1898. A second volume will cover the events of the twentieth century. But at 1,383 pages, Gotham is a book for the desk and the library. I hoped that *New York City* might be a book for the backpack and hip-pocket, something to carry around while visiting the city. It is also a book, it seemed to me, that might provide some context, some of the good stories, which visitors often feel are lacking in even the best-intentioned guidebooks.

So this is a book that I imagined might usefully be in the left hand while *New York City for Families* or the *Time Out Guide to New York* or any one of the other New York guidebooks are in the right hand. You will not find here the opening hours of Ellis Island or directions to reach Central Park. But why an immigrant receiving station was created at Ellis Island, and how a museum was created there, is something that readers of this book will find (see pages 74–79.) There is a chapter on parks in the city, and a discussion of the complex problems of who pays for them. This is a topic guidebooks don't tend to dwell on, but the condition of the city's miraculous parks, and their survival, is of concern to most visitors every bit as much as it is to New Yorkers. Each of the chapters begins in a place in the city: Broadway, Greenwich Village, Harlem. In each chapter I have tried to look back, to think through the way the city's past has come to shape its present life. Guidebooks are records of the present, but there is much to be gained from thinking of the many ways the places that a visitor might enjoy (like 42nd Street today) have been shaped by many twists and turns of circumstance. The role of the Disney Corporation in the rebirth of that famous street (see pages 210–213) might serve as a model for the way the "past" and the "present" have a particularly intimate relationship. New York, generally assumed to live in the exuberant present, is a city where the traces of the past, from the experience of slaves in a Brooklyn farmhouse in the early nineteenth century to the labor demonstrations of immigrant workers on Tompkins Square, have deeper and more intriguing resonance.

The impact of the attack on the World Trade Center forms the starting point of the introduction.

—Eric Homberger

Introduction: A City Changed, 9/11/01

This book was written with the idea in mind that New York is a city of incessant change, but that even change has a history, a narrative, that can help us make some sense of change itself and the city that it has created. The events of 9/11/01 or "Nine Eleven"—to Europeans the attack on the Twin Towers came on 11/9/01, but the American preference for ordering dates by month and day inevitably prevailed—fell outside the story that most historians, American or not, have constructed about New York City. Out of the blue, literally, on a warm and sunny morning, a good day to pause over a cup of coffee before going to work, two hijacked, fully loaded passenger planes slammed into the twin towers of the World Trade Center. Within an hour and a half the towers had collapsed into smoking ruins. The calculations, made in hurried ignorance, rapidly settled on a death toll of at least 6,000. It took months before that number came down to 3,000. It was an event unprecedented in scale and conception in American history, and naturally nowhere in the annals of the city has any disaster come close to matching the violence or long-term consequence of Osama bin Laden's attack upon the great symbols of American capitalism and power.

But was 9/11 unprecedented? Washington, D.C. was burned by the British army in August 1814. Atlanta was razed to the ground in the last stages of the Civil War. The great fire of Chicago in 1871 and the earthquakes in San Francisco and Alaska created "ground zero" scenes of utter devastation. New York has been repeatedly devastated by fires. The history of such apocalyptic events is a discontinuous one, each the product of distinctly local circumstances. None had the worldwide impact of 9/11. But it could be argued that 9/11 is not an exceptional event, but comprehensible within the trajectory of the city's history.

New York was a target not because its inhabitants loved freedom ("They hate our freedoms, our freedom of religion, our freedom of speech, our freedom to vote and assemble and disagree with each other," as President Bush suggested in his speech to the joint session of Congress on September 22, 2001), but because the city was more successful than other urban areas at projecting its influence and power, and its rich myths, outward. We do not have a history of New York built upon that notion, of the projection outward of the city's influence, but it might form a powerful basis for the understanding of the ascent of New York from a minor colonial port to a world city, one that is known, admired, and detested across the planet.

New York was created in the seventeenth century by the Dutch as an act of commercial and imperial assertion, and defended against invasion by the British and the Native Americans by a line of earthworks and fortifications that ran from the East River to the Hudson River along the course taken by Wall Street. It was seized at gun point by the British in 1664 and occupied by British soldiers throughout the Revolutionary War. Governor's Island and the Battery contain the surviving structures of the fortifications designed to protect New York from—the British, again. New York has been an object of the competing claims of great powers, and it was only in its *third* century that those fears began to subside.

As well as being the object of the aggressive claims of other people, in the eighteenth century New York merchants began a leap of imagination and ambition that first took the city onto the world stage. It was the determination of sea captains and traders to enter the slave trade—thus creating the famous triangular trade route that brought English goods and West African slaves to New York (the slave auction warehouse was located at the foot of Wall Street)—that brought the city to a new role in the world economy. The China ships that sailed from New York beginning in

EARLY SLAVE MARKET, NEW YORK.

the 1790s with cargoes of beaver pelts and gold bullion, upon which the great fortune of John Jacob Astor was founded, was a further sign that the city's restless merchants accepted no constraints or limits to the serious business of seeking profit. With the opening of the Erie Canal in the 1820s, New York secured privileged access to "the west," effectively seizing a competitive advantage over commercial rivals in Baltimore, Philadelphia, and Boston. The great shipping empire of the Aspinwalls, the railroads of Commodore Vanderbilt, and the dominant position of New York capital, shipping, and manufacturing in the cotton trade extended the city's horizon across the world. As the nation's most important port, and as the center of the publishing and entertainment industries, New York ideas, New York values, were, in 1898, dominant across the vast territory of the United States. The largest state in wealth and population, the greatest port, the leading financial center, the dominant presence in the nation's business and cultural life—no wonder Americans feared New York, and hated it for the changes that capital and the power of a commercial culture imposed upon everywhere else. New York was not thanked for dragging the rest of the country into its commercial sphere of influence. There is, in fact, a long tradition in America of hating New York. It was so *successful.*

The position of the city in 1898, when the four independent municipalities (Staten Island, Brooklyn, the Bronx, and Queens) joined with Manhattan to form Greater New York, could scarcely be sustained. Although it remained the largest city and the center of the financial markets, new industries and sources of wealth, as well as a growing population elsewhere inevitably diminished the dominance of New York in the American republic. But by that time the basic perceptions about New York were established. New York was unlike the rest of the country. It was more diverse in racial composition and religious mix; it had more inhabitants who had been born in foreign countries; it was ten times more Jewish than the rest of the nation, and five times as Catholic. But these demographic differences, however interesting, were not what shaped perceptions, but the way the city conducted its affairs—its reputation for corruption in local government, criminality, licentious vice, and arrogance. New York had not succeeded against its rivals by politeness and a becoming modesty, by being understanding and sensitive, but by a brashly competitive and materialistic spirit. For many

Americans, New York City—with its skyscrapers—stood for all that was modern, and in a conservative and God-fearing Protestant nation, modernity itself was a source of deep anxiety.

New York showed America that modernity was worth embracing, that skyscrapers could be beautiful, that modern art was exciting, that it was jazz and the Charleston, as opposed to the waltzes of the nineteenth century, that captured the imagination of the young. It conveyed a multiplicity of different meanings across the world, meanings in many respects shared with the nation (love of freedom, belief in opportunity and democracy). In other ways the idea of New York was distinctively the creation of the city's wealth-creating power. The migrants who came to New York and the stream of investments that foreign capitalists made in its stock and bond markets were at some deeper level each seeking the same thing. And the appeal of the city, its immense cultural and financial reach, threatened the social stability and the way of life of traditional societies across the globe. Bin Laden was quite right: New York was an enemy—a very proud and resilient opponent—of everything he and his friends hoped to create: a spiritual regime without secular music or kite-flying, and in which women went uneducated and were shrouded in the burqa.

Ground Zero

New York is tense; sirens screaming, flashing lights on speeding unmarked cars; serious men wearing sunglasses are standing in the street, talking into their shirt cuffs. Months after 9/11 the white vans of the bomb squad race down Broadway. Agitated policemen scream at pedestrians, and cordon off the sidewalk. Bystanders ask each other "What is it? A bomb?" A half-hour later the traffic flows as uneasily as ever. Pedestrians bustle and saunter along. The bomb squad has driven sedately off. The calmest place in the city is "ground zero," ominous terminology drawn from the atomic bomb testing program. What was once a large (very large) office development below Vesey Street, a development that had an owner, an architect, and a builder, the location of hundreds of businesses and government offices and the place of employment of thousands of people, has become an abstraction. It will be nice to look forward to the time when it becomes a place with a name and street address again.

In its death the World Trade Center has taken on meanings that it did not possess, or that were not widely held, during its lifetime. Mass death tends to do that. It began life as a large urban renewal project in lower Manhattan. The Port Authority of New York and New Jersey, founded in 1919, was given responsibility to improve facilities for the port and transportation across the two states. It was an efficient, independent body, capable of making decisions and implementing projects beyond the capability of the normal political system in each state. The Port Authority took control of the Holland Tunnel and began work on the Lincoln Tunnel in the 1920s. It eventually became the body that ran the airport in Newark, and the two New York airports (Idlewild, now JFK, and LaGuardia). It constructed the large bus station on the west side of Manhattan, and most of the bridges connecting the boroughs of New York. The Port Authority took over the bankrupt Hudson and Manhattan Railroad, which it reorganized and renamed the PATH (Port Authority Trans-Hudson) commuter rail line. The World Trade Center, commissioned in 1962, was meant to consist of 10 million square feet of space. Amidst a seven-building complex, two 110-story skyscrapers eclipsed the Empire State Building as New York's tallest structures.

The annual gross product of New York City is $500 billion, amounting to five percent of the nation's economic output. The effect of 9/11 across the nation was estimated at 1.8 million jobs lost in 2001, with New York eventually expected to lose 150,000 jobs. Of this gross product, New York's culture industry alone amounts to an annual

product of $13 billion. Since the attack every substantial cultural institution in the city has experienced large drops in attendance. In late 2001, the Metropolitan Museum of Art, for example, was losing $100,000 to $200,000 per week in lost admissions, sales from the museum shops, restaurant proceeds, and garage income. The global estimate of the losses for arts groups across the city (for September 2001 alone) amounted to $23 million. They all reported a sharp drop in donations. The attack destroyed a 16-acre tract in lower Manhattan, creating 260,000 tons of debris. It has been estimated that the removal of the debris alone will cost $5 billion. Thirteen million square feet of office space has been lost. That is the rough equivalent to the central business district of Chicago. The Comptroller, Alan G. Hevesi, estimated that property damage amounted to $34 billion. Economic costs may amount to $60 billion. The medium-term consequences include as many as 100,000 jobs lost. The hole in the city's budget, already hard-hit by a recession that began in 2000, is formidable. It is estimated that in 2002 the budget gap will be between $4 and $6 billion. No city could take a hit like that and recover on its own, though New York found that promises were more readily forthcoming than cash from the Bush administration. Looking at the figures, in the last days of his term Mayor Giuliani imposed a 15-percent budget cut across the many functions of the city government. "The facts are clear," Mayor Bloomberg explained in his inaugural address: "We will not be able to afford all that we want. We will not even be able to afford all that we have."

These are things that can be counted, weighed, estimated. The economic recovery will certainly come. And it will do so out of deep sympathy for New York, and with a spirit of respect for the way the city responded to the disaster. But what of the psychological wounds left by the images of the planes hitting the Twin Towers? And the terrible memories? The stockbroker Gina Lippis worked on the 46th floor of the first tower to be struck: "The screaming, yelling, and the water pouring everywhere. It took us about an hour and a half to get out, and the tower hit the ground right behind me. I will never get that out of my mind." Three months after the attack, she wrote:

> *My mind isn't all together. I can't concentrate. I can't read. It just goes. It's just not me. I'm a strong person. I focus. But now everything is very bad. Physically I feel bad. My body hurts, maybe because of the stress. I'm a person who goes to the gym four or five times a week and now I can't do that.*
>
> *What I really hope is that I can get back on track, back to the way I was before and live my life like I used to. It seems very far away. It's like something I can't reach right now.*

In other ways, some of the consequences for the city have been unexpectedly positive. Public opinion polls and informal journalistic surveys revealed that the American public felt closer to New York than at any time in living memory. There were many signs after 9/11 that the rancorous racial tension in New York was sharply reduced. Communities that formerly defined themselves in terms of their conflicts with the police have been able to feel a common sense of civic identity. The city's firemen are heroes in the eyes of everyone. Across the nation, Robert Putnam, author of *Bowling Alone*, found that there was more trust in government and the police and greater interest in politics. Cynics disregard such reactions, and anticipate the resumption of tensions-as-usual. But that is to ignore the deep psychological wound experienced by the city, and the profound need for healing. The idea of community, so powerful in American life, has traditionally played a healing role. In New York, that most divided and polarized of cities, strong leadership and a strong feeling of community have helped begin the process of recovery. For many New Yorkers meaning is given to 9/11 through a rejection of revenge and detestation of the languages of crusade and war. Peace symbols remembered from the Vietnam War sprung, like some long-hidden desert plant, into vigorous life in the makeshift memorial parks created in Union Square. But for others, perhaps a majority, the prospect of swift and violent retribution provided redress for the terrible imbalance of suffering. People of "foreign" appearance, from Sikhs to Africans in traditional dress, found New York a more hostile environment, as did Arabs.

The transformation of the public standing of Rudy Giuliani, from a combative, moralistic, and deeply partisan figure into the much-admired embodiment of the city's resolve, its morale-booster and *Time* magazine's "Man of the Year," surprised his friends and foes alike. There was a powerful groundswell of opinion to overturn the city's constitution and

allow Giuliani to remain as mayor for an additional term. He emerged from the ugly controversies that had accompanied him through two terms in office as a true leader, and someone—in an age of scripted and robotic politicians—who spoke from the heart and for the whole community. It will be a hard act for his successor, Michael Bloomberg, to follow.

The WTC was one of the city's leading tourist destinations. Even after the destruction, tens of thousands of people have made visits to the site, and in December 2001 viewing towers were erected. Queues reached as far back as Broadway and City Hall for a brief view of the site. It was a recognition that the meaning of the site was perceptibly changing. But the thousands who sought out ground zero, and those who visited the unofficial memorial in the burial ground of St. Paul's Chapel, were not tourists in the customary sense. They came as though pilgrims to a holy shrine, and were not, yet, buying souvenirs. Local businesses, hard-hit by the immense dislocation of the attack, reported little trade from the visitors. There have been requests for organized tours to the site. A memorial will be erected, and like the Vietnam Memorial in Washington, it will become a sacred ground for the city, and the nation. It will have to be connected to the machinery that moves tourists around the city. It will, that is, have to be marketed. That will not be a profanation of a holy shrine, but a recognition that the WTC has acquired meanings that transcend the locality, and indeed now belongs to everyone who cares to visit New York. The stream of visitors is an unwanted but inevitable distraction for the residents of Battery Park City, trying to rebuild their disrupted community. They are far from the only ones so preoccupied in the city.

—*Eric Homberger*

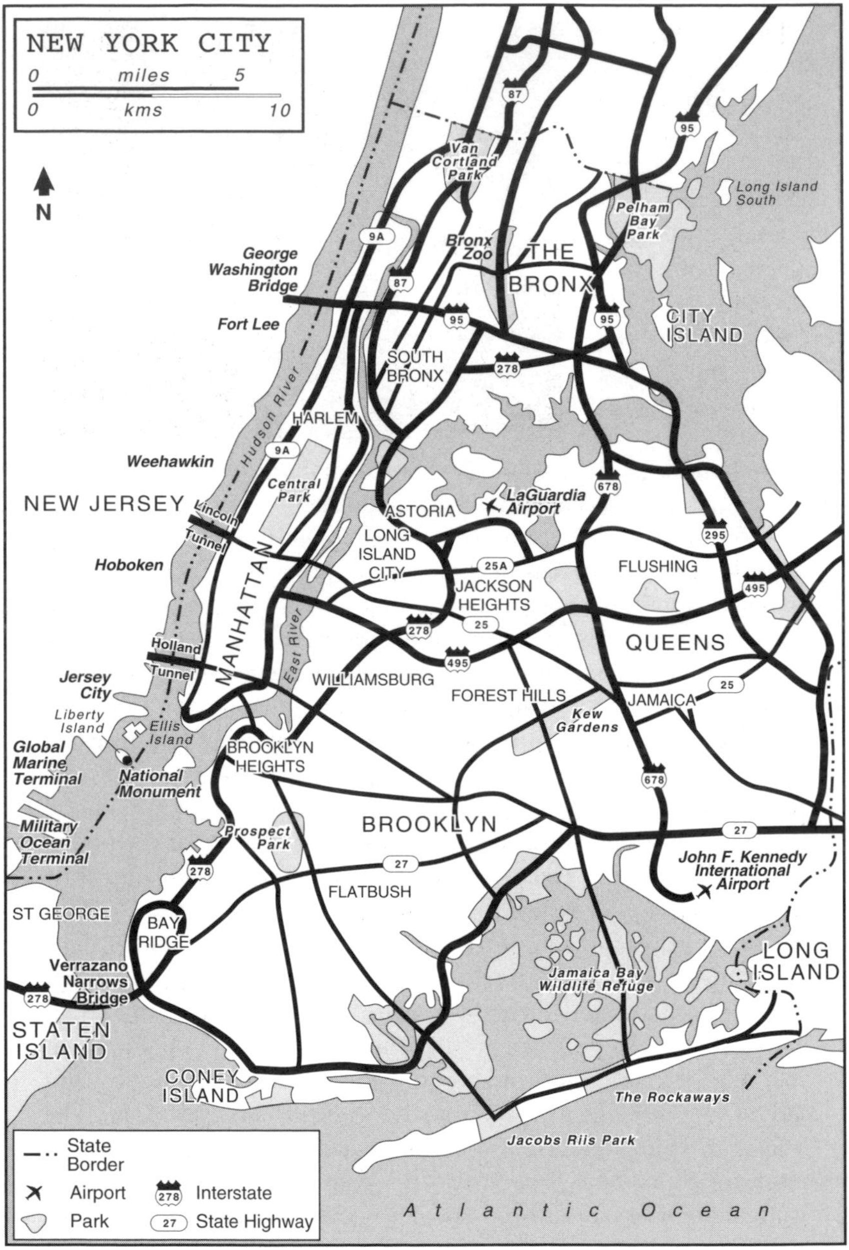
NEW YORK CITY
0 miles 5
0 kms 10
N
George Washington Bridge
Fort Lee
Weehawkin
NEW JERSEY
Lincoln Tunnel
Hoboken
Holland Tunnel
Jersey City
Liberty Island
Ellis Island
Global Marine Terminal
National Monument
Military Ocean Terminal
ST GEORGE
Verrazano Narrows Bridge
STATEN ISLAND
Hudson River
MANHATTAN
HARLEM
Central Park
East River
Van Cortland Park
Bronx Zoo
THE BRONX
SOUTH BRONX
Pelham Bay Park
Long Island South
CITY ISLAND
ASTORIA
LaGuardia Airport
LONG ISLAND CITY
JACKSON HEIGHTS
FLUSHING
QUEENS
WILLIAMSBURG
FOREST HILLS
JAMAICA
Kew Gardens
BROOKLYN HEIGHTS
BROOKLYN
Prospect Park
FLATBUSH
BAY RIDGE
CONEY ISLAND
John F. Kennedy International Airport
Jamaica Bay Wildlife Refuge
LONG ISLAND
The Rockaways
Jacobs Riis Park
Atlantic Ocean
State Border
Airport
Park
Interstate
State Highway

CHAPTER ONE

Mannahatta

Names and Naming

Walt Whitman, the great poet of democratic America, occasionally used the term *Mannahatta* for New York. He thought it was a name fit for "America's great democratic island city! The word itself, how beautiful! how aboriginal! how it seems to rise with tall spires, glistening in sunshine, with such New World atmosphere, vista and action!" The earliest European settlers were told by the native Delawaran inhabitants that the traditional name of the island was Mannahatta ("the island") and *Manhattan* ("hilly island"). Whitman had his own preferred translation, "the place encircled by many swift tides and sparkling waters." A passionate and devoted observer of the texture of New York life, by using the "aboriginal" term (he also used *Paumanok* for Long Island) Whitman wanted to remind New Yorkers of their remote origins. "All aboriginal names sound good," he wrote. "They are honest words—they give the true length, breadth, depth—they all fit."

Place names in New York State like Troy, Rome, and Ithaca could happily be replaced, he thought, by aboriginal names. It was all part of his disdain for artificial forms and congealing traditions. Stripping away the name "New York" would in a manner do justice to the island's original peoples. It would also reconnect the contemporary city with its past, its etymological root identity. It was Theodore Roosevelt in his little history of New York, written in 1890 when he was Civil

Service Commissioner, who added an inflection to Whitman's discontent about the city's name. Following the English seizure of the colony in 1664, New York became the proprietary possession of the Duke of York, afterwards James II. Roosevelt wrote that New York "perpetuates the memory of the dull, cruel bigot with whose short reign came to a close the ignoble line of the Stuart kings." But few New Yorkers have shared Roosevelt's memory or his Whiggish indignation at the many failings of the Stuarts.

Development of what the Dutch optimistically called New Amsterdam, was shaped by the plans drawn up by Crijn Fredericks, an engineer sent from Holland in 1625 with instructions to build a fort and lay out surrounding streets and footpaths. The Dutch names often drew upon vernacular descriptions of the location: Brouwer-Straat (Stone Street) and Peral-Straat (Pearl Street, so named from the oyster shells discarded along the shoreline). The memory of the Dutch inhabitants, and sometimes the continued presence of their descendants in the city, left a legacy in place names like Stuyvesant Street and Cherry Street, formerly the site of a seven-acre cherry orchard owned by Goovert Loockermans, New Amsterdam representative of a Dutch trading company. Cortlandt Street, west of Broadway, and Van Cortlandt Park in the Bronx, are on property once owned by the Van Cortlandts, a family of wealth and substantial influence who made a seamless transition from Dutch to English rule, providing several mayors under the British crown. John Street bears the name of a prosaic Dutch shoemaker who lived on that street. Peter Stuyvesant's farm or *bouwerij* gave a name to the Bowery, which became a center of entertainment for the growing immigrant population of the Lower East Side.

Almost as soon as they arrived in 1664 the English took over and translated Dutch street and place names, replacing De Heere Straat with Broadway, and Heere Gracht with Broad Street. When the British left the city in 1783, another round of changes took place in the city's street names. Between Trinity Church and St. Paul's Chapel, at the heart of the fashionable city, streets with Loyalist names like Crown, Queen, and King Street were given good Patriot names like Liberty, Cedar, and Pine Street. King George Street in the Fifth Ward became William Street.

The growth of the city provided an ongoing need to come up with new names for new streets, and many opportunities to honor real estate developers (Rockefeller Center), military figures, including some of great obscurity (streets and squares named after Wooster, Thompson, Sullivan, Sherman, Chrystie, Perry, and Pershing). John Broome, the merchant who played a large role in opening the China trade after the Revolutionary War, had Broome Street named after him. Straus Park was named after Isidor Straus, one of the brothers who owned Macy's department store beginning in the 1890s. Financiers and philanthropists were often memorialized. Bethune Street in Greenwich Village was named after the school proprietor and benefactor who ceded land to the city for the street. Politicians of all persuasions are recalled in the city's streets, public housing projects, airports, and so on: Clinton Street (south of Houston Street, named after the George Clinton who served as governor of the state for eighteen successive years in the late eighteenth century), LaGuardia Place (below Washington Square, after Fiorello La Guardia, mayor of New York City 1934–1945, the first Italian-American to hold that office), and Tompkins Square (between Avenues A and B and 7th and 10th Streets, named after Daniel D. Tompkins, four-term governor of New York State for a decade beginning in 1817). Racial and ethnic politics have left important traces upon the city's map: Lenox Avenue in Harlem is now Malcolm X Boulevard; a stretch of Seventh Avenue has been renamed in honor of Adam Clayton Powell. Mount Morris Park at Fifth Avenue and 120th Street in Harlem has been renamed Marcus Garvey Park in honor of the leader of the Back-to-Africa movement in the 1920s. Certain acts of renaming have permanently established themselves, such as Columbus Circle. But other acts of cultural, ethnic, and political piety, however worthy the recipient, have a shorter lifespan: Verdi Square (Broadway at 73rd Street), Peretz Square (after the Yiddish writer, at East Houston Street and First Avenue), Taras Shevchenko Place (after the Ukrainian patriot and author, between Second and Third Avenues at 6th Street). Some street names have distinctive literary and cultural associations: Waverley Place, after Sir Walter Scott's novel; Irving Place, after the New York writer Washington Irving; and Duke Ellington Boulevard (West 106th Street). Sara Delano Roosevelt Parkway in the Lower East Side was created in the 1930s when some particularly nasty slums were demolished. Sara Delano Roosevelt came from an old and distinguished New York family, but was honored principally for being the mother of the President, Franklin D. Roosevelt. Other re-namings, such as the attempt to transform Sixth Avenue into the Avenue of the Americas, in honor of the membership of the Organization of American States, were greeted with widespread public indifference and have not truly entered the way New Yorkers name their city.

Whitman was perhaps alone in the importance he attributed to the city's original name. In the 1860 edition of his *Leaves of Grass*, he published a poem titled "Mannahatta" in which he enumerates a place and a people. From line to line he shifts from the man-made city of crowded streets to the swift tides and sailing clouds, inviting us to connect the two:

Rich, hemm'd thick all around with sailships and steamships, an island sixteen miles long, solid-founded,
Numberless crowded streets, high growths of iron, slender, strong, light, splendidly uprising toward clear skies,
Tides swift and ample, well-loved by me, toward sundown,
The flowing sea-currents, the little islands, larger adjourning islands, the heights of the villas,
The countless masts, the white shore-steamers, the lighters, the ferry-boats, the black sea-steamers, well-model'd,
The down-town streets, the jobbers' houses of business, the houses of business of the ship-merchants and money-brokers, the river-streets,
Immigrants arriving fifteen or twenty thousand a week,
The carts hauling goods, the manly race of drivers of horses, the brown-faced sailors,
The summer air, the bright sun shining, and the sailing clouds aloft…
The mechanics of the city, the masters, well-form'd, beautiful-faced, looking you straight in the eyes,
Trottoirs throng'd, vehicles, Broadway, the women, the shops and shows,
The parades, processions, bugles playing, flags flying, drums beating;
A million people—manners free and superb—open voices—hospitality—the most courageous and friendly young men;
The free city! no slaves! no owners of slaves!

The beautiful city! the city of hurried and sparkling waters! the city of spires and masts!
The city nested in bays! my city!
The city of such women, I am mad to be with them! I will return after death to be with them.
The city of such young men, I swear I cannot live happy, without I often go talk, walk, eat, drink, sleep with them!

When he revised the text of the poem in the early 1870s, Whitman dropped the final seven lines, and substituted an encomium less politically and sexually explicit. His love for Mannahatta was luxuriant, caressing, profuse. What makes Whitman so striking a lover is the connection he insists upon between the natural landscape of river, tide and "clear skies," so easily forgotten amidst the growing mid-nineteenth century city, and the rich urban life of "parades, processions, bugles playing, flags flying, drums beating." Whitman wants to embrace all of New York.

The shape of the island, and its location, were primal facts that determined much of its future. Whitman shows that the port, harbor, and the sea, as well as the tight grid of its streets, have strongly shaped New York.

Port, Harbor, and Sea

The history of New York has, until modern times, been dominated by the sea. Immigration, trade, communication, politics, social relations, crime, and even the way the city was first described and visually represented, have been shaped by the physical relationship of the city to the sea, the harbor, and its two rivers, the large North or Hudson River on the west, and the smaller East River, which separates Manhattan from Brooklyn. The most popular visual portrayal of New York, from the days of its early settlement, was the tip of Manhattan as viewed from a ship in the harbor. It was a viewpoint charged with variety and endless possibility. This is the way you fall in love with New York:

From my point of view, as I write amid the soft breeze, with a sea-temperature, surely [wrote Whitman in *Specimen Days*] *nothing on earth of its kind can go beyond this show. To the left the North river with its far vista—nearer, three or four war-ships, anchor'd peacefully—*

> *the Jersey side, the banks of Weehawkin, the Palisades, and the gradually receding blue, lost in the distance—to the right the East river—the mast-hemm'd shores—the grand obelisk-like towers of the* [Brooklyn] *bridge, one on either side, in haze, yet plainly defin'd, giant brothers twain throwing free graceful interlinking loops high across the tumbled current below… with here and there, above all, those daring, careening things of grace and wonder, those white and shaded swift-darting fish-birds…*

With Whitman's lyrical passage in mind, the Staten Island Ferry is one of the briefest and most magical short sea rides in America. The ferry service across the 5.2 miles of New York Harbor linking the southern tip of Manhattan to the north shore of Staten Island is as old as the European settlement in New York. A biweekly service existed as early as 1745, and the sixteen-year-old Cornelius Vanderbilt began his commercial empire by establishing a ferry service in 1810. The city took over operation of the ferry service in 1905, and for 70 years the fare was 5¢, rising to 25¢ in 1975 and 50¢ in 1990. It has been a free ride for pedestrians since 1997. The ferries were painted "boat orange" in the 1960s, for enhanced visibility in fog. The Department of Transport attributes to the ever-fecund urban legend machine the

notion that the ferries are slightly differentiated by color. They are repainted on a revolving schedule, and the impact of sun and salt water fades the orange paint to an attractive golden mango. As the ferry approaches the Battery, the skyscrapers seem to rise, as though miraculously from the harbor itself.

An oft-reproduced watercolor of New Amsterdam (in the Dutch government archives in the Netherlands) portrays the city in the 1650s, just before the English captured the colony. It is a small settlement of gable-ended buildings, looking out over a handful of ships in the harbor. The Dutch presence is modest: there is a little wharf, weighing beam, crane, windmill, various storehouses, a fort, and the former tavern, which served as the *Stadt Huys*, the city hall, home of the city's first municipal government.

Some seventy years later, in 1717, William Burgis drew a large panorama of New York, as seen from the Brooklyn side of the East River. Large is perhaps an understatement: the panorama is six feet wide, and every structure included by Burgis is clearly visible. With a population of 7,000, New York was then the third largest city in the North American colonies. Many of the older Dutch structures had been torn down and replaced by newer buildings, in accord with Georgian ideals of symmetrical design, Palladian sash windows and ready employment of pilasters. Larger structures of three and four stories line the shore, creating the city's first real skyline. The steeple of the first Trinity Church is the tallest structure in the colonial city.

By Burgis' time, the waterfront had begun to be expanded outward into the East River, a process of landfill that eventually changed and expanded the shape of Manhattan, and narrowed the East River. The streets in lower Manhattan running down to the river (Coenties Slip, Old Slip, Burling Slip, Peck Slip) bear the names of colonial residents, merchants, and entrepreneurs whose warehouses, shipbuilding yards or taverns made use of small inlets where ships' cargoes could readily be loaded and unloaded. Trading vessels of all sizes and ships of the Royal Navy fill the river in Burgis' view. The Navigation Acts denied access to any but British ships to North American ports, but Burgis, by including a superabundance of Union Jacks and Red Ensigns on ships in the East River, strikingly out of scale, goes further in stressing the Englishness of the scene. The abundant growth and enterprise presented in his panorama vindicates British commercial policy. Burgis records four shipyards in New York. Where there was once a wharf there is now a great dock, with three piers extending into the river. The meaning of this view of New York is clear: the growth and prosperity of the city are linked to the crowded harbor.

The prosperity that Burgis represents in the early eighteenth century was largely due to the sugar trade. Plantations in Barbados, Jamaica and the Windward Islands, formed a crucial market for the high-quality flour, corn, pork, beef and naval stores produced in New York. Vessels carrying goods for the rich West Indian planters brought sugar, rum, molasses and cotton back to New York, where brown West Indies sugar was refined in large "sugar houses" in New York into the white loaf sugar preferred by consumers. White sugar and tea were central ingredients in a more civilized way of life that tea-drinking New Yorkers had begun to enjoy. New York distilleries turned West Indies molasses into rum, and imported tobacco was converted into snuff. The export trade for such goods made New York an important colonial trading port. The shipyards on the East River, and the nearby coopers, blacksmiths, tanners, and butchers found steady work in meeting the needs of the West Indies trade. Half of all ships entering or leaving the port of colonial New York were engaged in Caribbean commerce, and one resident in four in New York earned their precarious living as mariners.

Production to meet the rapidly growing West Indies trade was largely made possible by an equally rapid growth in the number of slaves in the city. In 1746, when New York had a population of 11,720, just over one out of five inhabitants were slaves, the highest concentration of slaves north of Virginia. The growth of slaveholding proceeded so rapidly that at mid-century at least half of the city's households included one or more slaves. New York farmers had an even greater involvement in the institution of slavery. The fear of a "servile uprising" was widespread in New York, and two slave revolts, in 1712 and 1741, were fiercely repressed. Nonetheless, the demand for labor in the shipyards, rope-walks, and the artisanal crafts was met largely by slaves, not indentured servants. In a 1730 map of New York a large covered slave-market appears at the foot of Wall Street. Excavations at the African Burial Ground (see pp.14) have shed valuable light on the lives of the city's substantial slave population. It is necessary even now to stress that slavery was integral to the development of New York. It was not something regrettable happening elsewhere, as the shed used for slave auctions at the foot of Wall Street makes very clear.

For most of the city's history, the shores of Manhattan were lined with wharves and docks. Streets were crowded, as Whitman recalled, with "carts hauling goods, the manly race of drivers of horses, the brown-faced sailors." John Lambert, an Englishman who visited New York in 1807–8, was impressed by the bales of cotton, barrels of merchandise and sacks of rice piled high in the streets. Everywhere there was a feeling in New York of commercial energy and enterprise. "All was noise and bustle," Lambert remarked,

> ...*Everything was in motion; all was life, bustle and activity. The people were scampering in all directions to trade with each other, and to ship off their purchases for the European, Asian, African and West Indian markets. Every thought, word, look and action of the multitude seemed to be absorbed by commerce, the welkin rang with its busy hum, and all were eager in the pursuit of its riches.*

Arrivals and departures, commodity prices, and the varying fortunes of mercantile firms filled the city's newspapers. Growth and increasing commercial prosperity encouraged a demand for portrait painters, trained in Europe, who would produce decorative family scenes for the wealthier families. Concerts and public subscription dances, called Assemblies, were held at hotels and taverns in New York. French dancing masters taught young fashionables the latest European dances. Tailors and seamstresses could be found who would copy the current fashions from Paris and London. Booksellers imported the newest novels by Sir Walter Scott and Maria Edgeworth. Despite the presence of John Scudder's American Museum featuring natural history curiosities (which P.T. Barnum took over in 1841), and the opening of the American Academy of Fine Arts in 1802, New York was not yet a cultural rival to Philadelphia or Boston, far less London, but it had emerged with growing self-confidence as a purveyor of style and luxury. Word of the latest fashions, dances, and works of literature reached out from New York to small towns and villages in upstate New York, Connecticut, New Jersey, and Pennsylvania. The cultural influence of

New York grew because it was the place to partake of sophisticated imports, luxury goods, and the fashionable world. Its role as a port made it a powerful dispenser of culture to the sleepy hinterland.

New York possessed a strongly commercial view of the world. The city's merchants were on balance more cosmopolitan and less parochial than their rivals in Boston and Philadelphia, and more attuned to the quicksilver changes of taste and the terms of trade. Prices in London, the conditions of trade in Barbados and Hong Kong, shipping rates in Liverpool, directly concerned the city's merchants.

Something of the feel of New York as a seaport survives today on South Street, in the block north of Fulton, where the city's fish market may be found. It's best to arrive early, before 9 o'clock, for the best view of a timeless scene of every imaginable variety of fish piled on hillocks of ice, and workmen with large curved fishhooks. Unlike the South Street Seaport Museum around the corner, the fish market is for real. The South Street Seaport Museum, at the intersection of Water and Fulton Streets, is the creature of the preservationist movement in New York City. The museum, founded in 1967, the purchase of Schermerhorn Row by the state in 1974, and the sale of "air-rights" to developers, successfully preserved a large group of older commercial structures, some dating back to the eighteenth century, from certain demolition in the city's superheated real estate market. Ann Taylor, a Yankees Clubhouse, United Colors of Benetton, and the Body Shop occupy prime retail frontage on Schermerhorn Row.

The sea was everywhere present in the life of the city. Before the arrival of electric lighting after the Civil War, New York homes were lit by sperm oil. (Ambrose Kingsland, mayor of New York in 1851–2, made a considerable fortune as an importer and shipper of sperm oil and sperm candles. New Yorkers had another reason to remember Kingsland with fondness: he was the first public figure to propose the usefulness of a large public park in New York.) Some of the greatest New York fortunes were built upon trade. In the early nineteenth century John Jacob Astor's ships reached the coast of Oregon (the failure of his attempt to create a trading settlement on the Columbia River in Oregon, and its subsequent loss to the British, was described in Washington Irving's *Astoria* in 1839), Hawaii, China, and all the ports of Europe.

The careers of the Aspinwall brothers, Gilbert and John, prominent importers of dry goods and general commission merchants in New York, followed the same pattern. They received consignments of goods from merchants in foreign ports, and also purchased American goods for foreign buyers. They owned several ships, and ran direct trading voyages to St. Petersburg, Liverpool, and other European ports. John Aspinwall's son William Henry continued the family's interest as commission merchants. In partnership with cousins, by the 1840s he had a large fleet of merchant vessels, which regularly sailed to Havana, Tampico, Callao, and Valparaiso as well as to European and Chinese ports. Aspinwall ordered the first of the American clipper ships, which set new records for speed between China and New York. He won the government contract to carry the mail to Panama, San Francisco, and Oregon, and ordered three steamboats for the route. The first voyage in 1848 coincided with the discovery of gold in California. His Pacific Mail Steamship Company held a virtual monopoly of the carrying trade between New York and California for the two decades before the completion of the transcontinental railroad. Aspinwall was also heavily involved in the building of the railway across Panama. His story is one of the greatest in the mercantile history of New York.

It is what Aspinwall did with his great wealth that suggests the complex link between commerce and culture in New York. Living in an elegant home on University Place near 10th Street, Aspinwall was a lavish supporter of many of the benevolent groups created during the Civil War and a founder of the Society for the Prevention of Cruelty to Animals. He was among the leading men behind the Metropolitan Museum of Art, and was a major financial backer of the Lenox Library, founded by James Lenox in 1870. John Jacob Astor's chief act of benevolence was the foundation of a public library for the city in 1852. The Astor Library, the Lenox Library, and a very large bequest left by the politician and railroad lawyer Samuel J. Tilden, were consolidated in 1895 to form the New York Public Library. Erected in 1911, the Carrère & Hastings structure that houses the library (Fifth Avenue, between 40th and 42nd Streets) is one of the city's finest neoclassical buildings.

Traces of the Past

The past in New York, a city notable until recent times for its indifference to the chocolate box ideals of heritage and conservation, is preserved, like geological strata, in names. Without living memory, the names of places soon enough lose meaning. How nice that a major street in New York is named after the Texan patriot, Sam Houston—except that it was a certain William Houstoun, delegate from Georgia to the Continental Congresses in the 1780s, who happened to marry a New Yorker, Mary Bayard. It was the lady's pleased father Nicholas Bayard, through whose land the street was laid, who chose to name it after his son-in-law. Wall Street acquired its name from a palisaded and rather half-hearted defensive works, complete with stone bastions erected along the northern line of New Amsterdam in 1653. The Dutch, who arrived 1624, felt that they were surrounded by enemies. The Native Americans of the Algonquian tribes, the Upper Delawaran or Munsee, from whom they bought fish and beaver pelts and to whom they sold guns, alcohol, and trinkets, were feared and scorned by the Dutch. The large and rapidly growing English settlements in Connecticut posed a threat of a different magnitude. There were 1,500 inhabitants of New Amsterdam, and perhaps no more than 10,000 Dutch in the whole of the Hudson River valley. Ten times that many English colonists were living in Virginia and New England in 1664.

The English were at war, as was usually the case in the seventeenth century, with the Dutch, and the arrival in 1647 of Petrus Stuyvesant as Director-General signaled the determination of the Dutch West India Company to defend the colony. North of the wall stood the *bouweries* (farms, smallholdings, pastures, and country homes of the Dutch settlers), which spread higgledy-piggledy northward toward the small villages of Haarlem and Bloemendael. When the English finally seized the colony in 1665, beginning over a century of colonial rule, the palisade was allowed to decay and was eventually torn down in 1699. The ditch was filled in, which made northward development of the city somewhat easier, but the name Wall Street was retained, preserving the civic memory of the city's vulnerability. Stones from its bastions were reused in the foundation of the City Hall. In the 1790s New Yorkers could look at their City Hall and feel pride that this new expression of civic importance stood upon the foundations of the earliest settlers. We have no record of what the surviving Dutch residents in the city felt about the matter. No one asked. They were not the only group in the city to feel that they had been steamrollered by history.

In 1979 when a new building was erected at 85 Broad Street, a few doors down from the Stock Exchange, the increased height of the structure required deeper foundations. The excavation was halted—for the first time in the city's history—to allow for a proper archeological excavation of the site. Artifacts from Lovelace's Tavern dating back to the eighteenth century and other structures were uncovered. That year an archaeological dig at the site of the Stadt Huys on Pearl Street, the headquarters of Goldman Sachs, failed to find any remains of the original structure. In 1984–6, when the Broad Financial Plaza at the corner of Whitehall Street and Pearl Street was erected, portions of August Heerman's seventeenth-century warehouse, and tens of thousands of artifacts from Dutch domestic life were found. The wall of the tavern has been preserved in a glass-covered ditch as a monument to the archaeologists' work.

Sometimes it is sheer luck, and amateur persistence, that have reconnected the city to its past. An amateur historian named James Kelley was foreman of the dig in 1916 for the Interborough Rapid Transit subway tunnel at the corner of Greenwich and Dey Streets. One of the workmen turned up burned fragments of wood, and the solid oak beams of a ship's prow, keel, and frame, preserved under eleven feet of tidal silt in the Hudson River. Kelley thought they were old, and at such a location they might go back to the city's earliest settlement. The wood was preserved in a tank at the city's old aquarium in the Battery. When that building was partly demolished in 1943, the 82-foot long wooden remains were given by the Parks Department to the Museum of the City of New York, where they are on display in the Marine Gallery. Modern techniques have dated the wood back to the sixteenth or early seventeenth centuries. Kelley, who later became Kings County Historian, had found the remains of Adriaen Block's *Tijger*, a Dutch-built ship that Block had captained on a fur-trading voyage to New Amsterdam. The *Tijger* burned in the mouth of the Hudson in 1613, while fully laden with furs. Block returned to Amsterdam in 1614, submitted a report to the owners of the *Tijger*, and assisted in the drawing of a map, the so-called Figurative Map of 1614, which was the first to correctly identify Manhattan as an island. On the foundation of Block's map, and his account of his voyages in New Netherland, a charter was granted to the United New Netherland Company ensuring a trade monopoly. It was upon Block's report and his advocacy that the Dutch turned, with some seriousness, to making a colony out of the wilderness at the mouth of the "Noort Rivier," what would later be called the Hudson River.

When City Hall Park was reconstructed in the 1990s, a team of archaeologists were present throughout the excavation to salvage artifacts and to ensure that no burial sites were disturbed. The park is built on the site of the "commons," where farmers grazed their cattle, and where the city's almshouse, jail, and military barracks were located. The cascade of artifacts delighted and astonished the teams working on the site. There were coins and buttons, shoe buckles, musket balls, and bits of fine tea sets and bottles of French wine left by the British troops who inhabited the city during the Revolutionary War. Each artifact was sealed in its own plastic envelope, boxed, and carted off to Fairfax, Virginia, awaiting the city's decision about how to organize and pay for this hoard to be cleaned, stabilized and preserved. The cost of preservation is considerable, and without determining how the city would fund the work, the materials held in 349 boxes were collected from Virginia in April 2001, and hauled back to a Parks Department complex in Flushing Meadows-Corona Park, near Shea Stadium, where they presently sit. Money has been set aside to have archaeology students at the City University study the artifacts. But even that outcome is far from secure at a time when budgets are under savage pressure.

Those interested in what lies below the streets should visit New York Unearthed, a small archaeology museum devoted to the long and fascinating history of the city. Dutch clay pipes, delicate china bowls, silversmith's tools, children's toys, and many other artifacts are all on display. The entrance is on Pearl Street, between Whitehall and State Streets, near Battery Park.

A far more explosive discovery was made in the early 1990s. For years the west side of Broadway between Reade and Duane Streets, two blocks north of City Hall, had been used as a parking lot. Excavations by a team of archaeologists on the site designated for the Federal Office Building at 290 Broadway revealed a plot of common land twenty feet below street level that had been set aside by the colonial government for use as a cemetery for African slaves and freemen. The cemetery remained in use into the 1790s. Some 20,000 blacks were buried on the site, a reminder that in the early national period one New Yorker in ten was non-white, and of that number seven percent were slaves. Working one step ahead of the construction crews, archaeologists identified hundreds of individual graves. The existence and location of the African Burial Ground had been known only to a handful of scholars of early New York history, but the reverberations of its rediscovery made big waves.

The city's Landmarks Preservation Commission voted to designate the burial ground as an historic landmark. A similar National Historic Landmark designation was also granted. Details, such as the presence of filed teeth, coins in the hands of the dead, a female buried with a girdle of beads, or a shell placed next to the head of a buried man, linking the dead to the sea, shed new light upon a population which had largely been forgotten. Skeletal remains were measured, documented and exhumed for further detailed study. There was a prolonged struggle between scientific camps over the remains. The Metropolitan Forensic Anthropology Team based at Lehman College in the Bronx was meant to conduct the cleaning and study of the remains, but were edged out in a struggle with historically black Howard University. The predominantly white MFAT team was outgunned in this kind of empowerment struggle, and the research contract to study the artifacts and remains of some 408 individuals was awarded to Howard University. One half of the excavated burials were of infants under the age of two, confirming other evidence of fearfully high levels of infant mortality in the African population of colonial New York.

Public reaction to the discovery of the oldest African-American cemetery in America was instantaneous. Such discoveries were immediately swallowed up in the insistent racial politics of the city. In 1998, after spending nearly $12 million on the research project at Howard University, and a substantial program of public education, the federal government began to draw back from open-ended support. The General Services Administration, the government agency funding the excavation and research, was accused of being insensitive to the site's importance for African Americans. An unseemly struggle for control of the bones and management of their study between the self-appointed "descendant community," the academic institutions, civic preservation bodies, and the GSA dragged on for years. Among the high (or low) points of the undignified squabble over funding was the changing of the locks on the archaeology laboratory in the World Trade Center early in 2000 (the fate of the laboratory after the terrorist attack on September 11, 2001, is uncertain), Howard University's refusal to accept an extension of the research contract, and a decision by the GSA to borrow money to pay for the reburial of the ancestral skeletal remains. The memorial space is located on Duane Street, on the corner with Elk Street, one block east of Broadway. No date for re-burial has been agreed.

The publication of a history of Central Park by Roy Rosenzweig and Elizabeth Blackmar in 1992 reminded the city of the existence of Seneca Village, a black community living between 83rd and 88th Street, on the west side of what today is Central Park. Seneca Village aroused a similar debate about African-American life in New York. The casual way Seneca Village had been removed in 1853, to make way for the park, and the way the village had for more than a century been misrepresented by historians of the park or simply forgotten, had uncomfortable echoes of other disgraceful episodes in the American past. An elderly retired Parks Department employee, Robert Stockett, whose great-grandfather was buried in the village in 1842, was the only living New Yorker who could point to a family link to Seneca Village.

Everywhere across the city traces of the past are being uncovered. The newly discovered stories, as well as the artifacts, are changing New Yorkers' sense of their history. Consider the story of James Weeks, a black longshoreman from Virginia, believed to have once been a slave, who purchased a tract of land in Brooklyn from the Lefferts family in 1838. Slavery in New York had only been abolished in 1827. In time African Americans from Manhattan—some fleeing the draft riots in 1863—built the little clapboard cottages that were known as Weeksville, in the Brownsville district, near the intersection of King's Highway and East New York Avenue. Schools, churches, an orphanage, workshops, and a home for the elderly made Weeksville, like Seneca Village, a community of extraordinary interest to the city's African Americans. The remains of that community were lost to memory, and the houses decayed; some just vanished. The first understanding that there had once been a distinctive community on the site came in 1968, when a historian and a pilot noticed, from aerial photographs, the surviving cottages. The Landmarks Preservation Commission designated the site, named the Hunterfly Road Historic Houses, and they were added to a National Register of Historic Places. Title to the houses has been acquired by the Society for the Preservation of Weeksville, and more than $10 million has been raised to restore the buildings and create a museum and education center. An award of $400,000 was made by Save America's Treasures, the federal agency that funded the preservation of the home of Harriet Tubman, and Edith Wharton's country home in Massachusetts. The major budgetary cuts announced in the aftermath of the attack on the World Trade Center have thrown plans for the education center into disarray. But the survival of Weeksville is secure.

In 1989 an elderly woman named Ella Suydam died at her home in the Marine Park neighborhood in Brooklyn. The old wooden farmhouse was landmarked, but would have succumbed to the weather and old age if residents had not taken an active interest in the oldest building, and the largest private home, in their neighborhood. In 2000 a Brooklyn College archaeological team, led by Professor H. Arthur Bankoff, conducted a study of the house, which had been erected in 1800 by Hendrick I. Lott (1760–1840), of an old farming family that had once owned more than 200 acres in Marine Park. The Lotts were, by the standards of New York, fairly large slave owners. In 1803 they reported owning twelve slaves. But the passage of the state's gradual emancipation law in 1799, which granted freedom to slaves who were born after that date, and who agreed to serve their masters until their twenties (28 for men, 25 for women), sharply reduced the commercial value of slaves, who were in any event unwilling to prolong their servitude so long. There were many early emancipations, and Lott seemed to have freed his slaves by 1810. When two Ph.D. candidates, Christopher Ricciardi and Alyssa Loory, conducted a close examination of the Lott farmhouse, they unexpectedly discovered a trapdoor in the ceiling of a closet. Crawling through the narrow opening, they found under the eaves two small rooms that had been the slave quarters, and when they pulled up the floorboards in the passageway they found corncobs that had been left—for two centuries—in an unusual star pattern. Archaeologists in the American South have found such ritual items, and they identified it as a cosmogram, a symbolic representation

of the boundary between the living and the dead, and on its other axis the path of force that connects these worlds. Along with other objects that had served ritual purposes, the scholars were able to see, in a farmhouse in Brooklyn, how traditional African religious practices persisted. It was the first such discovery in New York, and opened an extraordinary window upon the spiritual life of the city's slave population. There is a lively report on discoveries made at the Lott House on the Web at:
www.archaeology.org/online/features/lott/index.html

Occasionally the artifacts are something other than buttons, coins, and broken teacups. And sometimes they are not all that old. In the 1980s restoration work began at the Eldridge Street Synagogue, home of Congregation K'hai Adath Jeshurun, whose ornate façade designed by Herter Brothers in 1887 has been praised by White and Willensky in the *AIA Guide to New York City* as the finest of any of the Lower East Side synagogues. An empty lot at 5 Allen Street was acquired to assist work on the restoration, and possibly with a view toward its subsequent use as an education center connected to the synagogue. A tantalizing piece of gossip, otherwise known as oral history, came to the ears of the restoration team. A man who had owned the tenement that had stood at 5 Allen Street until it was torn down in 1958 claimed to have instructed the demolition crew to leave intact the ritual bath (or *mikveh*) that stood in the basement. There had been a bathhouse in the Allen Street tenement (the Allen Russian Baths), whose proprietor had been a member of the Eldridge Street congregation. Some long-term neighbors recalled the bathhouse, but no one had any memory of a *mikveh* on the site. Acting on no more than a hunch, a caterpillar hydraulic excavator set to work opening a three-foot trench. White ceramic tiles were soon uncovered, and further digging revealed a twenty-foot swimming pool lined in hexagonal colored tiles. Another trench revealed a small shallow pool which, when excavated by hand, was conclusively identified as a *mikveh*, a small pool used for ritual purification by orthodox Jewish women after menstrual periods. No other mikveh has been identified on the lower East Side, and the absence of such a structure strengthened arguments that the Jewish immigrants had begun to lead increasingly secular lives in America. The newly-discovered *mikveh* offers a glimpse into a previously undocumented aspect of Jewish religious observance, and may lead to a reconsideration of the persistence of traditional rituals in the New World. And it is possible that the swimming pool may have been used for ritual communal immersions.

Archaeology and the study of the past had become serious politics in the 1980s and 1990s. There is today only a very modest sign marking the site of the African Burial Ground on Duane Street (a design competition for a proper memorial is underway), and nothing beyond a sign to mark the site of Seneca Village. Yet both places reverberate in the city's sense of its own past, constructed of many layers of claim, evidence, and memory, however small are the tangible traces remaining on the surface of the city. The role of historical memory is always intensely political, and the burial ground and Seneca Village affirm the stake that African Americans have in the city. The presence of the graves, far beneath the street level of Broadway, and the rediscovery of the site of the razed village, carries with it a claim: This is our city, too. Every group, every ethnicity and race, makes a similar assertion as part of their claim to be New Yorkers. To engage in that kind of archaeology, as I am attempting to do here, perhaps is to make another kind of claim to a share in this world city*.

Melville, Cooper, and Roosevelt

The city's writers were powerfully drawn to the sea. Herman Melville made his first sea voyage to Liverpool as a young man of eighteen in 1837, and later wrote a semi-autobiographical novel, *Redburn* (1849), about his experiences. Wellingborough Redburn's father had been

> *...an importer in Broad-street. And of winter evenings in New York, by the well-remembered sea-coal fire in old Greenwich-street, he used to tell my brother and me of the monstrous waves at sea, mountain high; of the masts bending like twigs; and all about Havre, and Liverpool...*

* In Trow's Directory, in the 1880s, there is an Alexander Homberger who sold "trimmings" and lived at 348 East 57th Street in New York. Bernhard and Robert Homberger lived at the same address. My father Alexander supposes that the trimmings merchant who shares his name, which is a fairly uncommon one, may be his grandfather. Genealogy is a claim of possession, granting him permission to say "I'm a New Yorker, too."

The letters of Melville's father Allan, a New York merchant, are in the New York Public Library, and offer a moving account of hopes and fears fixed upon the uncertainties of trans-Atlantic trade. Frequent voyages to Europe gave Allan Melvill (the "e" was later added to the family name) a metaphor for the changeability of man's condition: the sea "is at best a most capricious & deceitful element, one moment decked in smiles & the next foaming with rage." For his son Herman, going to sea was a way to escape his family's poverty. It promised adventure. "As I grew older," recalled Redburn,

> *my thoughts took a larger flight, and I frequently fell into long reveries about distant voyages and travels, and thought how fine it would be, to be able to talk about remote and barbarous countries; with what reverence and wonder people would regard me, if I had just returned from the coast of Africa or New Zealand; how dark and romantic my sunburnt cheeks would look…*

Melville's greatest novel, *Moby Dick* (1851) begins with the moody Ishmael, sunk in "a damp, drizzly November in my soul," reflecting upon the importance of the sea for New Yorkers.

> *Right and left, the streets take you waterward. Its extreme down-town is the Battery, where that noble mole is washed by waves, and cooked by breezes, which a few hours previous were out of sight of land. Look at the crowds of water-gazers there.*
>
> *Circumambulate the city of a dreamy Sabbath afternoon. Go from Corlaers Hook to Coenties Slip, and from thence, by Whitehall northward. What do you see?—Posted like silent sentinels all around the town, stand thousands upon thousands of mortal men fixed in ocean reveries. Some leaning against the spiles; some seated upon the pier-heads; some looking over the bulwarks of ships from China; some high aloft in the rigging, as if striving to get a still better seaward peep.*

Melville was far from the only New York writer to be drawn to the sea. James Fenimore Cooper's worldwide fame was based upon his Leatherstocking novels, set on the American frontier. But Cooper found the sea and the freedoms it offered every bit as engaging. He had served as a midshipman in the United States Navy, and made a considerable reputation as a master of sea fiction, publishing *The Pilot* (1823), a sea tale recounting a naval raid on the English coast, and the long-forgotten *Mercedes of Castille* (1840), about the first voyage of Columbus. Cooper's *The Two Admirals* (1842), with a thinly disguised portrait of Nelson, recounted a tale of adventure and rivalry in the British Navy. Cooper also published a polemical history of the US Navy in 1839, and other books about naval matters.

If Cooper's histories of the navy and sea tales were minor notes in a long career, the sea became one of the dominant themes in the political and literary life of Theodore Roosevelt, the first New Yorker to become president of the United States. Roosevelt's 1882 history of the naval war of 1812 between Great Britain and the US was an exceptional achievement for a young historian of twenty-three. It was the first military history of the conflict to be solidly based upon original archival research. Roosevelt turned to his uncle James D. Bulloch, an experienced naval officer, for help with the technical complexities of warfare in the age of sail, and in return assisted Bulloch with his memoirs, an account of his adventures as head of the Confederate Secret Service in Europe during the Civil War.

Roosevelt was among the first politicians in America to recognize the importance of the writings of Alfred Thayer Mahan, whose lectures on *The Influence of Sea Power Upon History, 1660–1783* (1890), argued that there was a connection between naval power and the projection of national power across the globe. Mahan's doctrines were used by advocates of "big navy" strategies. Roosevelt's meteoric political career included a term as assistant secretary of the Navy in 1897–8, at the moment when the rebellion of Cubans against Spanish rule reached its culmination. In Washington and across the nation, at a time when high tariff walls and a tiny standing army reflected a national isolationist sentiment, Roosevelt was a belligerent advocate of military preparedness and imperial expansion. "I wish to see the United States the dominant power on the shores of the Pacific," he wrote, and to that end urged the building of an inter-ocean canal. When he became president in 1900, he accelerated the construction of new battleships. In 1907 he sent the "Great White Fleet" across the world. After a voyage lasting fourteen months, and covering 46,000 miles, it was an impressive demonstration that the United States was now among the world's great sea powers. Interested in power, not colonies, and with incomparable energy and a bullying self-confidence, Roosevelt dragged the nation into the new century. Roosevelt's scorn for "respectable men in easy circumstances" made enemies among his own class, the wealthy old New York families of Dutch and English descent, but he articulated a view of the world that prevailed among the merchants and financiers of the city. Isolationism was never a cause that made much sense to New Yorkers, so thoroughly had the life of the city been shaped by international finance and foreign commerce.

Ernest Poole, the son of a wealthy Chicago grain broker, lived in the University Settlement in New York after graduating from Princeton in 1902. While doing research for articles about the New York harbor scene, he came across a dusty warehouse in Brooklyn where he found ledgers surviving from the city's old sea-faring past. "As I read I saw the sails speed out along those starlit ocean roads, stately East Indiamen bearing such names as Star of Empire, Daniel Webster, Ocean Monarch, Flying Cloud." The harbor in 1912 had lost some of its old romance. The railroads and the big shipping companies had driven the last of the small ship owners out of business. Nonetheless, there was about the harbor an unmistakable life. "In gangs at every hatchway," he wrote in his autobiography *The Bridge* (1940), "you saw men heaving, sweating; you heard them swearing, panting. That night they worked straight through till dawn. For the pulse kept beating, and the ship must sail on time! Quickly I could feel this place yielding up its inner self, its punch and bigness, endless rush, its feeling of a nation young and piling up prodigious wealth." Meeting a Wobbly labor organizer working for Big Bill Haywood's Industrial Workers of the World, Poole found his hero, and in *The Harbor* (1915) he wrote a novel of labor struggles set amidst the world of New York's docks and harbor. In the novel the old ledgers belong to the narrator's father, who as a young man before the Civil War had come to New York to sail on the clipper ships. There was revolution in the air in 1915, and the city was alive with immigrants, poverty, industrial conflict—enough romance and harsh reality, thought Poole, to form the basis of an epic novel of the making of modern New York.

It was the poets Walt Whitman and Hart Crane who responded most intensely to the physical interaction of the city and its surrounding waters. "Crossing Brooklyn Ferry," published in the 1856 edition of Whitman's *Leaves of Grass*, weaves the river, the passengers on the ferry connecting New York and Brooklyn, his readers, and those who will read his poem in generations to come, into a great affirmation and celebration of the interconnectedness of things.

Just as you feel when you look on the river, so I felt,
Just as any of you is one of the living crowd, I was one of a crowd...

Hart Crane's "The Bridge," written in the late 1920s while the poet was living in Brooklyn, sought to reach back into the mythic past of America, to its explorers and earliest inhabitants, and extend outward to the furthest reaches of human life. With so complex a scope, Crane nevertheless rooted the poem in the life of the city. One section began "I met a man in South Street, tall—." Like Whitman, Crane's poem is rich in memories: of walking across the Brooklyn Bridge, advice about how to get around the city on the subway ("For Gravesend Manor change at Chambers Street"), and commonplace things ("the toothpaste and the dandruff ads") of city life.

More than a third of the total American merchant shipping capacity was destroyed during the Civil War. In the face of the stiff competition offered by the Cunard line (founded 1840), Hamburg-American (1848), the North German Lloyd (1857), Compagnie Générale Transatlantique (1861) and the Holland-America Line

(1872), the wounded American maritime fleet was scarcely able to compete with foreign carriers, and the US flag gradually disappeared from ports across the world. The elimination of the United States from the ranks of the great naval powers inevitably weakened the port of New York. The end of New York's shipbuilding industry followed remorselessly. The number of ships launched from the city's shipyards and total tonnage declined. It was in British and German shipyards that the important technological innovations were made. The Blue Riband, the prestigious speed record for the North Atlantic run, was seldom in American hands for long. Foreign ships dominated passenger and commercial shipping to and from New York. Though New York remained the leading US port, handling half of the entire imports and exports for the nation in the 1860s, mostly foreign carriers were carrying American passengers and American exports. And of the lucrative passenger trade in the age of mass immigration, American ships carried but a minuscule proportion. By 1914 only some ten percent of American cargo was carried by American ships.

The city's natural advantages of location and harbor were nullified by the lack of space for freight movements, and changes taking place in the pattern of travel. The first steps toward the creation of the Port Authority came when the US entered the First World War in 1917. The lack of unified control of port facilities in New York and New Jersey hampered wartime development. In 1921 the Port Authority, formally agreed between the two states, formulated a program to halt the relative decline of the port. A self-sustaining public corporation ratified by Congress, the Authority had the power to develop modern facilities at Newark and Hoboken, on the New Jersey side of the Hudson River. Additional powers were given to improve waterways, tunnels, highways, bridges, and terminals.

The Port Authority constructed virtually the entire infrastructure of the city. However you enter or leave New York, or travel between boroughs, the facilities were constructed and operated by the Port Authority, and other authorities pursuing similar ends. The Port Authority controls the Lincoln Tunnel, George Washington Bridge, all three bridges linking Staten Island with New Jersey, the regional system of four airports, the bus station, marine shipping terminals, hotels, PATH trains (taken over from the defunct Hudson

& Manhattan Railroad, connecting New Jersey and Manhattan, and—until Republican governors of New York and New Jersey pressed for privatization and downsizing—the 95 million square feet of rentable office space at the World Trade Center, which opened in 1971. This imposing edifice was created upon the tolls and fees paid by users of the city's bridges, tunnels, and other facilities. Inevitably, the Port Authority has come under attack by conservatives for its monarchical government, the scale of its activities, and the cross-subsidy of loss-making facilities that its $2 billion annual budget makes possible.

In 1956, a guidebook to New York suggested that "the harbor is the busy core, and at the same time the master, of the city." That observation, or boast, was supported by impressive figures: the port of New York then moved 179 million tons of goods a year. There is a water frontage of 771 miles, and 350 miles of docking facilities. But the long-term decline of New York as a port was unmistakable. The fate of the city's piers was sealed by the rise of international air travel, which precipitated a rapid decline in passenger-ship traffic. Containerization and the increasing use of larger ships that could not easily be maneuvered into the confined harbor reduced the competitiveness of the ports. The Brooklyn Navy Yard, at the end of the Second World War the largest naval construction facility in the United States, closed in 1966. The abject decline of the port became a symbol of the many social and economic woes of the city.

Henry James, who perhaps of all New York writers had the least interest in the port and its fabled role in the city's life, recorded the scene on a return visit to the city in 1904. Writing in *The American Scene* (1907), he found the shores low, "depressingly furnished and prosaically peopled." Absent from New York for twenty years, he could nonetheless see that there was reason to feel a "fine exhilaration" at the approach of the city.

> *There is the beauty of light and air, the great scale of space, and seen far away to the west, the open gates of the Hudson, majestic in their degree, even at a distance, and announcing still nobler things, But the real appeal, unmistakably, is in that note of vehemence in the local life…, for it is the appeal of a particular type of dauntless power.*

The Grid

Below Washington Square, New York feels much like a European city, with winding, narrow streets and irregular sized blocks. North of Washington Square, New York is distinctively, unmistakably, an American city, laid out on a grid pattern, with right-angled corners, regular-sized blocks and uniform street widths. The streets are numbered. A visitor, wondering how to get from Hanover Square (say) to Greenwich Street, experiences a navigational problem that is characteristic of Paris or London. The route from East 11th Street (the East-West borderline is marked by Fifth Avenue) to the intersection of 34th Street and Fifth Avenue is simplicity itself. The fact is that it is mostly hard to get lost in New York. But there is another kind of navigational dilemma that the grid has presented to us. "A glance suffices to show you," wrote Jean-Paul Sartre, "that you are on the East Side, at the corner of Fifty-second Street and Lexington. But this spatial precision is not accompanied by any sentimental precision." Time spent walking in the streets of New York alone can give a *feel*, a "sentimental precision," for the differences that mark blocks, streets, neighborhoods, intersections, and the people one sees in different places in the city. New Yorkers acquire such knowledge over time and are puzzled why clever Frenchmen feel so disoriented. Visitors need a crash course in how to read the grid and the way it shapes the urban clutter and diversity of New York.

Set out in 1811, the grid has dominated thinking about the form of the city, and has indelibly shaped its development. Found in every urban setting virtually throughout history, the grid has been the preferred design for absolute dictators, democrats, soldiers, and religious communities. The Puritans in New Haven, Hartford, and Cambridge laid out their plans for a squared, rectilinear settlement following grid principles. William Penn's plan for a Quaker settlement at Philadelphia, a grid of streets and squares laid out between the Schuylkill and Delaware Rivers, was the largest application of the principle in colonial North America. The Mormons in Salt Lake City employed an extended grid, with the Tabernacle at the center. Colonists, whether English or Spanish, Catholic, Protestant or Quaker, employed the grid. Attempts to read simple political meanings or analogies into the grid, attributing to its proponents democratic or egalitarian aspirations, or political virtue, will not wash. As Spiro Kostof argued in *The City Shaped* (1991), the grid, "by far the commonest pattern for planned cities in history," defies attempts to associate any particular form of government or rule with urban design.

The grid remains unloved. Its inflexibility has often been deplored. It had many practical consequences which New Yorkers came to regret. The limited number of north-south streets condemned Manhattan to centuries of traffic congestion. The inadequate provision of public space for parks and plazas in the original plan needed large expenditure and long delays to be corrected. Proponents of the City Beautiful Movement, with their enthusiasm for radial boulevards and scenic parkways, regarded the absence of dramatic vistas in the grid as one of the causes of the drabness and uniformity of modern cities. Suggestions for improvements flowed from the Municipal Arts Society, founded in New York in 1893 and dedicated to the proposition that "To make us love our city, we should make our city lovely." Diagonal Beaux-Arts boulevards, opening up sightlines for new buildings, were proposed by the Society in 1904 as a way to overcome the limitations of the grid.

There is a long tradition of architectural critics going back to Camillo Sitte, who regarded the uniformity of the urban grid as stultifying. Sitte's influential *Der Städtebau* (1889), translated as *City Planning According to Artistic Principles* (1965), repeatedly identified the grid as a deadly enemy of all things "artistic" and imaginative in urban planning. Despite its presence in urban settlements from Japan to Scotland, the grid was viewed by Sitte as the characteristic form of *American* urbanism. Sitte sarcastically noted that the urban grid was most appropriate for places where people lived only for earning money or were concerned merely with colonizing the land, for a society which "lacked a past, had no history, and did not yet signify anything else in the civilization of mankind but so many square miles of land." Lewis Mumford's magisterial and dogmatic *The City in History* (1961) followed Sitte's line of attack. The grid, he argued, was spectacularly inefficient and wasteful, best suited for the capitalist conversion of natural resources into a medium for speculation and exploitation. To Henry James, the grid was a "primal topographic curse," an "original sin," that left New York "of all great cities, the least endowed with any blest item of stately square or goodly garden, with any happy accident or surprise, any fortunate nook or casual corner, any deviation, in fine, into the liberal or the charming."

The grid, then, is a very troubling fact of life in Manhattan. Yet it came about at a time when the city was growing rapidly in population and its mercantile ambitions seemed unbounded. In 1806 the Common Council petitioned the state legislature to appoint commissioners to lay out new streets for the undeveloped part of the island north of Washington Square. The Common Council is the legislative branch of the government of New York, so named as the "council of the commonality" in the city charter granted by Governor Thomas Dongan in 1686. The complex history of local government and charter reform obliged the city to seek authority from the state for civic needs that went beyond those authorized in the various charters going back to the first charter granted to the city by the Dutch West India Company in 1653. The request in 1807 was the only way the city could act coherently to plan its own growth.

The commissioners were instructed by the state legislature to lay out streets and public squares of a size to allow for "free and abundant" circulation of air. When they finally submitted their report in 1811, it was accompanied by a large map extending the grid to 155th Street, and a combative statement of assumptions and principles. Thinking perhaps of Major Pierre L'Enfant's plan for Washington, D.C., with its grand provision for vistas and a hierarchy of streets (see Chapter 2 for more about L'Enfant's significant role in New York), the commissioners dismissed out of hand the benefits of "supposed improvements by circles, ovals, and stars, which certainly embellish a plan." Rather, recalling that New York was to be composed "principally of the habitations of men," they favored "straight-sided and right-angled houses [which] are the most cheap to build and the most convenient to live in." While deploring "the pernicious spirit of speculations," they wanted to ensure the rapid and orderly development of the large quantity of land lying to the north of the existing city. Land in the most desirable locations near the wharves and docks was notoriously in short supply, driving prices up, and forcing inhabitants to seek housing far from their work. The commissioners hoped to improve the supply of land for development. Their intention was to make the city useful to its inhabitants, and by planning the grid in small regularly shaped lots, amenable to development.

The physical location of New York, embraced by the harbor and two rivers, seemed to set a distinctive limit to the extent of the grid. At the banks of the East River, the Hudson, and the Harlem, the city and the grid came to an end. Within decades, as the populations in the Bronx, Queens, and Brooklyn expanded, New York outgrew the "closed grid." Formerly independent townships were drawn into the financial and speculative orbit of New York interests. The Fulton Street Ferry, so beloved of Walt Whitman, made Brooklyn, rather more than upper Manhattan, a convenient place to live. The New York grid was, in practice, without boundary or limits. Wherever there was a growth in population and profit to be made by the purchase and sale of land, the "open grid" became established. The booming capitalist economy of New York went hand in hand with the extension in all directions of the grid across the landscape.

The commissioners argued that the physical situation of New York rendered unnecessary any further provision of open space, either for the benefit of public health or for recreation. Land was set aside for a reservoir, observatory, and a "grand parade." The commissioners expected the greatest criticism of their plans to come not over the modest provision of parks or the absence of "circles, ovals, and stars," but from the astonishing idea that in the future the whole of Manhattan would be covered by streets and houses. "To some it may be a matter of surprise that the whole island has not been laid out as a city. To others it may be a subject of merriment that the Commissioners have provided space for a greater population than is collected at any spot on this side of China." The surface of Manhattan was uneven, and some parts were probably never going to be suitable for housing. In that case, the extension of the grid would compensate for the unbuilt areas. The commissioners assumed the scale of urban property would largely remain what it was in 1811: small lots, with 20- and 25-foot frontages, seemed perfectly adequate to the needs of the city, and would preserve the modesty and republican virtue of the people. The commissioners assumed that large, irregularly shaped lots would act as an inhibition on the real estate market, and thus impede the development of the city.

The commissioners proposed the creation of twelve avenues, each one hundred feet wide, running north–south. At regular intervals of two hundred feet, streets of sixty-feet width would be laid out to run east-west from the East River to the Hudson. Their plan called for the laying out of 2,000 long, narrow blocks. No provision was made to adapt the grid to the existing property boundaries, established by real estate sales and land grants, some dating back to the Dutch colonial period. Nor was there any provision for amending the plan in accordance with existing watercourses or the irregular contours of the land. Broadway was allowed to continue its meandering course across the grid. Development required repeated changes and adjustments of the 1811 plan: squares were laid out at the intersection of Broadway with 14th Street (Union Square) and 23rd Street (Madison Square). The long space between Third Avenue and Fifth Avenue was divided into three avenues (Lexington, Park and Madison). Frederick Law Olmsted and Calvert Vaux's plan for Central Park, adopted in the 1850s, took the irregular terrain north of 59th Street, between Fifth and Eighth Avenues, out of the grid altogether. The aim of the designers of Central Park (see Chapter 5) was to provide a space that turned away from the regularity of the grid and enabled visitors to the park to forget for a time that they were actually in a city of such rigid lines.

The grid played a role, hard to quantify but of some real consequence, in the accelerated development of the city. The career of the great nineteenth-century New York property empires, owned by the Wendels, Astors, Schermerhorns, Costers, and others, suggests that the growth in the value of real estate was an incomparable speculative investment, and one that was not inhibited by the grid that covered the city. But it was far from clear that the city's inhabitants, living in small apartments for which they paid high rents, would have shared the enthusiasm of the large real estate moguls for a system of land ownership and housing that left them so readily exploited by the owners of the land.

Flatiron Building

One of the unintended consequences of the grid was the small, pie-slice-shaped fragments of land created by the angle at which Broadway crosses the major avenues. The possible uses of such spaces were anticipated by the intersection formed where the Bowery, renamed Fourth Avenue, swerves west toward Union Square at 8th Street,

leaving a small plot, an island, where the Cooper Union Foundation Building was erected in the 1850s. This vivid Italianate brownstone building was donated by the wealthy industrialist Peter Cooper to house the Cooper Union for the Advancement of Science and Art. It was at the Cooper Union on February 27, 1860, where Abraham Lincoln delivered a celebrated address on slavery and disunion before an enthusiastic audience of 1,500, who had each paid 25¢ for their tickets. Lincoln's speech was published by Horace Greeley in the *Tribune* on the following day, and circulated across the nation. His eloquent defense of the constitution in the Cooper Union address, and opposition to slavery, did much to win Lincoln the Republican nomination for president. The Cooper Union was designated a historic landmark in 1966. Buildings on V-shaped lots were common enough in the financial district downtown. It was their appearance uptown that aroused such strong reactions.

Where Broadway crosses the line of Fifth Avenue at 23rd Street, the remaining thin slice of real estate seemed to defy ordinary commercial usage. The footprint of such a building would be a right triangle. Despite the unpromising configuration of the site, its location at the heart of fashionable 1890s New York was superb, and the value of the land skyrocketed. The Fuller Company purchased the entire block in 1901 for $2 million, and planned a 300-foot office block, with 120,000 square feet of rentable commercial space. But the site posed striking architectural problems. When in 1890 George B. Post designed a 309-foot tall building to house Joseph Pulitzer's *New York World*, the load-bearing walls were nine feet thick at the base. But when the idea of "Chicago construction"—the use of a cage of structural steel to carry the weight of the building—arrived in New York, the architect Daniel Burnham designed in 1902 an unprecedented 20-story structure of rusticated limestone, brick, and terra-cotta for the strange, unpromising site. Burnham rounded the north-facing prow of the triangle, and created an observation platform (now closed) from which there were remarkable views of New Jersey and the far reaches of Brooklyn.

Burnham had been chief of construction at the World's Columbian Exposition in Chicago in the previous decade, and was a key figure in that orgy of classicism and Beaux-Arts influence that dominated American architecture. In partnership with John Wellborn Root, and then with his own architectural firm, Burnham was one of the leading architects of the age. Daniel Burnham, and Co. specialized in tall office buildings for commercial developers. "Burnham was an artist in business vestments," wrote his biographer, "an artist, indeed, with whom the capitalists could communicate and identify."

The Flatiron was an important entry into the intense New York property market for the Fuller Construction Company, under the management of the founder's son-in-law, Harry S. Black, a young man in a hurry. Black had large ambitions to transform the Fuller Company into a real estate trust. With the support of aggressive capitalists like James Stillman and Henry Morgenthau, Black made Fuller a wholly-owned subsidiary of the $66-million U.S. Realty and Improvement Company. The Fuller Company, which built the Plaza Hotel in 1907, was famous for flamboyant publicity, quick construction methods (as many as four stories a week), and a ruthless willingness to cut corners, and, where necessary, pay off union bosses. U.S. Realty had behind it Wall Street and its unlimited supply of capital.

Daniel Burnham's social skills may have been at full stretch when the floor plan of the structure was discussed. How, indeed, could full rental value be extracted from the fascinating room at the northern tip of the building, an office twelve feet wide at its base, tapering to a six-foot prow, affording a spectacular vantage point for parades and a wonderful view of Madison Square and Broadway? Such a room would be crowded with little more than a roll top desk and a filing cabinet. Along the Broadway side of the building there were eight offices, and not a single one had the same dimensions.

The public responded to the building with apprehension at its height. The tallest structure north of the financial district in 1902, and twice the height of the newest buildings on Broadway, the Flatiron towered over Madison Square. It seemed out of scale for the setting, and critics felt it expressed the overweening will of Wall Street. In 1903 the Municipal Art Society used the Flatiron to attack the builders: "It stands there as an example of the greed of the corporation controlling it and owning it. Architecturally, it is unfit to be in the center of the city." The public decided otherwise. No matter how the owners tried, the public declined to call the building anything but the Flatiron, a term at once familiar, affectionate, and slightly mocking. The bold avant-garde spirits around Alfred Stieglitz and his journal *Camera Work* took the Flatiron to heart. Through a series of brilliant photographs taken from within Madison Square, and along a misty Fifth Avenue at dusk, they taught Americans to think of this startling piece of modern architecture as a picturesque adornment of the city. The photographers were often happy to represent the Flatiron as though it was not in the city at all, but rose amidst the trees in the park. The art critic Sadakichi Hartman predicted that in twenty years the public would pronounce the Flatiron a thing of beauty:

... o'er the nocturnal
City's flickering flame, you proudly tower,
Like some ancient giant monolith
Girt with the stars and mists that lour....
Iron structure of the time...
Emblem staunch of common sense,
Well may you smile over Gotham's vast domain
As dawn greets your pillars with roseate flame,
For future ages will proclaim
Your beauty
Boldly, without shame.

(The term "Gotham," which originally came from a village in Nottinghamshire noted for the eccentricity of its inhabitants, was first used as a jocular nickname for New York by the knickerbocker writer Washington Irving in 1807 in one of the *Salmagundi* essays. In 1830 James Kirke Paulding used Gotham in the title of a collection of short tales, *Chronicles of the City of Gotham*. Whatever ironic or negative associations once attached to the term, it soon acquired a fondness in New York ears. Charles Astor Bristed in his *The Upper Ten Thousand: Sketches of American Society* (1852) wrote of "our beloved Gotham, and in the places to which regular Gothamites—American cockneys, so to speak—are wont to repair.")

The Flatiron was soon dwarfed by larger and more imposing structures, and the ornate terra-cotta decorative style of Burnham, which resembled nothing so much as finely-wrought marzipan, inevitably fell out of fashion in the age of the International Style. Nonetheless, as M. Christine Boyer suggested, "Its great prow, like an ocean liner, sailed up Fifth Avenue unashamedly." Iconic status today inevitably translates into lawsuits, and in 1999 Newmark & Company, the real estate firm that manages the Flatiron, successfully brought a lawsuit preventing a venture capital subsidiary of the Chase Bank from using the building's distinctive appearance as its trademark. Any firm seeking to use the image must now pay for the privilege, and acknowledge Newmark & Company's trademark rights. (Similar attempts have been made to trademark the Chrysler Building, the Guggenheim Museum, Rockefeller Center, Lincoln Center, and the New York Stock Exchange.) The Flatiron, New York's oldest skyscraper, remains one of the most glorious opportunities for the unexpected that the New York grid allowed.

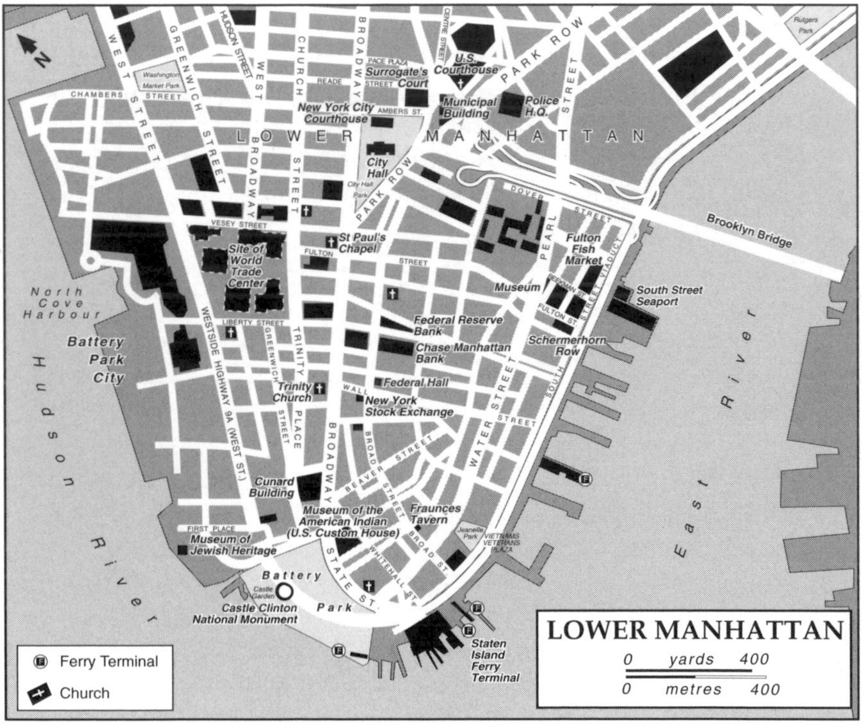
LOWER MANHATTAN
0 yards 400
0 metres 400
Ferry Terminal
Church
N
LOWER MANHATTAN
Hudson River
East River
North Cove Harbour
Battery Park City
Washington Market Park
Chambers Street
West Street
Greenwich Street
Hudson Street
West Broadway
Church Street
Broadway
Centre Street
Park Row
Pearl Street
Pace Plaza
Surrogate's Court
U.S. Courthouse
Reade Street
Municipal Building
Police H.Q.
New York City Courthouse
Ambers St.
City Hall
City Hall Park
Dover Street
Brooklyn Bridge
Rutgers Park
Vesey Street
St Paul's Chapel
Site of World Trade Center
Fulton Street
Fulton Fish Market
Museum
Beekman St.
Fulton St.
South Street Viaduct
South Street Seaport
Federal Reserve Bank
Liberty Street
Chase Manhattan Bank
Schermerhorn Row
Westside Highway 9A (West St.)
Trinity Place
Greenwich Street
Trinity Church
Wall Street
Federal Hall
New York Stock Exchange
Water Street
Broad Street
Beaver Street
Cunard Building
Museum of the American Indian (U.S. Custom House)
Fraunces Tavern
Jeanelle Park
Vietnams Veterans Plaza
First Place
Museum of Jewish Heritage
Battery Park
Castle Garden
Castle Clinton National Monument
State St.
Whitehall St.
Staten Island Ferry Terminal

CHAPTER TWO

On the Steps of the Federal Hall National Memorial

The history of a city leaves traces, sometimes buried deep beneath the streets. At the intersection of Wall Street and Broadway, the past and present of New York meet. The Stock Exchange, Trinity Church, the Morgan Guaranty Bank, and the Federal Hall National Memorial each, in different ways, bear witness to the presence of the past in the midst of the bustling city.

Take a cup of coffee (50¢) and a donut (the glazed crullers are a particularly good buy at 75¢) and sit on the steps of the Federal Hall National Memorial on Wall Street. On sunny days the steps are crowded with tourists, mostly school kids, who like being photographed next to the statue of President George Washington on the steps of the Hall. Office workers, glad to have somewhere to sit, watch the busy street scene. It is the sidewalk life, the "urban ballet" in Jane Jacobs' fine phrase, that catches the eye. Barely a third of a mile long, running from Trinity Church on Broadway down to the East River, Wall Street is lined with the kind of anonymous office buildings that fill every financial district in large cities around the world. But everywhere on this planet there are people, and not just bankers, watching the news from Wall Street, center of the financial district in New York, and thus the central nervous system of the world-wide network of money and news that is capitalism. Wall Street is an icon of the economic system that dominates all of our lives.

On the other side of the street from the Federal Hall, at number 23, stands the headquarters of the Morgan Guaranty Trust Company, formerly the private bank owned by the legendary financier J.P. Morgan. Around the corner on Broad Street appears the neoclassical façade of the New York Stock Exchange. On the west side of Broadway stands the Gothic Revival masterpiece of Trinity Church. This irregular four-sided configuration suggests the meaning of Wall Street. The site of the Federal Hall is sacred ground for the making of the American republic. Where it now stands George Washington was inaugurated president in 1789. This is where the Senate and House of Representatives held their first session. Trinity Church, a Gothic masterpiece built in the 1840s, carries the weighty burden of higher values in the district and city, devoted to the pursuits of material things: power and money. The Morgan Bank and the Stock Exchange between them embody the intangible system of exchange and speculation upon which financial markets depend.

J.P. Morgan

Nowhere else on the planet are God and Mammon so gloriously cheek-by-jowl than on Wall Street. Power and great wealth are close here, and do not seem uncomfortable in each other's company. Power is not set back, surrounded by fences and threatening armed guards. Trinity Church, the Morgan offices, even the Federal Hall, are comparatively modest structures built in accord with nineteenth-century ideas about urban scale. If not intimate, the scale is human. The modest width of Wall Street seldom fails to startle visitors. So famous, and so—well, insignificant. The great financial power that Wall Street represents is far from being merely human in scale.

Of all the great money men in the late nineteenth-century age of the "Robber Barons," J. Pierpont Morgan had the greatest impact upon New York City. The survival of the corporate name "Morgan" in the vast amalgamation of the Morgan Bank with Chase Manhattan, in the rapidly changing financial markets today, is a sign of how strong an impact he made upon American finance. He was notorious for having an imperious temper. Everything about him was florid, decisive, assertive.

Morgan, a Wall Street banker, was behind the creation of financial and industrial amalgamations (the notorious "trusts"), which included virtually the entire rail system, and in 1901, the creation of the United States Steel Corporation. Morgan, who had a wealthy man's disregard for public opinion, scarcely bothered to defend himself against the charge that he exploited the power of capital against the public interest: "I owe the public nothing." In the opinion of many Americans, Morgan was at the heart of everything that was wrong with the capitalist system. Yet he was also a man of fervent piety, a founder of the New York Society for the Suppression of Vice, who also enjoyed being seen in the company of showgirls.

A hymn-singing capitalist predator to his enemies, Morgan was also, according to Aline Saarinen, "the most prodigious private art collector of all time." It is Morgan as a collector who has left the most striking legacy to the city. His loans and bequests to the Metropolitan Museum of Art, between 6,000 and 8,000 objects, were of such high quality that they remain, nine decades after his death, among the Met's most important holdings. The library that Morgan built on 36th Street at the corner of Madison Avenue, a much-admired Italian palazzo designed by Charles McKim of the architects McKim, Mead, and White, houses the Morgan Library. Built to be Morgan's office, it was only at the instigation of his son that the library became a public institution. The "East Room," where the library was originally located, houses an incomparable collection of 10,000 drawings, as well as rare autograph music manuscripts, and important manuscript works of Milton, Keats, Dickens, Byron, and Scott, and a vellum Gutenberg Bible. There is also a Court Café at the Morgan, which, amidst such heavyweight cultural glories, is a place to catch one's breath.

Morgan's taste was fateful for New York as a center for art. Elected president of the board of trustees of the Metropolitan Museum in

1904, he sharply tilted the museum's acquisition policy toward the highest standards of world masterpieces. Visiting the Museum, Henry James wrote in *The American Scene* that there was a new atmosphere about the institution. "There was money in the air, ever so much money." Morgan had a settled indifference to American art, and despite a policy emphasizing the need to expand American holdings, under his presidency the Museum did little in practice to acquire American material. He owned nothing by contemporary artists. No Impressionists, nothing by Courbet, Gauguin, or Toulouse-Lautrec hung on the Morgan walls. One of his advisers was Roger Fry, whose advocacy of Post-Impressionism did so much to persuade contemporaries of the importance of the modern movement. Fry, who did not get on with Morgan, and who had tart things to say about overbearing multimillionaires, could interest Morgan in nothing other than Old Masters. Given the importance of Morgan as a collector, it was an opportunity lost. A year after his death the Armory Show alerted New Yorkers to the importance of avant-garde art.

Morgan, who insisted that "no price is too large for an object of unquestioned beauty and known authenticity," was the leader of a generation of wealthy American industrialists, financiers, and capitalists who engaged in a frenzied competition for "masterpieces," and who also left their mark upon New York. The Frick Collection (Fifth Avenue at 70th Street), housed in a mansion designed in 1914 by Carrère & Hastings, was amassed by an associate of Andrew Carnegie in the Pennsylvania steel industry. Frick's handling of the Homestead strike in 1892, proverbial in the history of American labor relations for its ruthless violence, made him among the most hated men of the late nineteenth century. His art collection, opened to the public as a museum in the 1930s, gives us a powerful glimpse into the dream life of the American super-rich. Furniture owned by Marie Antoinette, Bouchers painted for Madame de Pompadour's chateau near Chartres, and *The Progress of Love* panels by Fragonard, commissioned by Madame Du Barry, are among the *ancien régime* glories of the Frick collection. The Fragonard panels were bought by Morgan in 1899 for $310,000 and sold upon his death. They were later acquired by Frick from a dealer for $1,200,000.

From 1882 Morgan lived in a large brownstone house at the

northeast corner of Madison Avenue and 36th Street (which today houses the Morgan Library bookstore), where some of his collection of valuables were held. Morgan's collection soon outstripped the available space in the collector's home. Many important objects were housed in his London home at 13 Princes Gate in Knightsbridge, facing Hyde Park. He also used his father's country seat outside London to store his growing collection, and loaned many objects to the Victoria & Albert Museum and the National Gallery. When a change in the American tax law allowed him to repatriate his main collections to the United States, he instructed Charles McKim to design a suitable home.

After Morgan's death, large bequests were made by his son to the Metropolitan Museum, but the star items were sold. The Duveens, who had made a fortune selling priceless things to Morgan, made an even bigger killing selling the Morgan collection to others. What remains, principally manuscripts and rare books, is housed in the Morgan Library (the entrance is at 33 East 36th Street, between Madison and Park Avenues). Facing the entry to the East Room is a badly faded sixteenth-century Brussels tapestry depicting King Midas, entitled "The Triumph of Avarice." It was once on display at Hampton Court. Morgan was perhaps guilty of cultural gluttony and other sins, but the hoarding of wealth seems not to be among his most prominent failings.

He liked to live surrounded by beautiful things, and acquired the knowledge and taste to shield himself from the worst of the art "experts," shady dealers and the legion of interested advisors, led by Joseph Duveen, who skinned alive wealthy American collectors with more money than taste or knowledge. Dealers learned to their regret that Morgan could distinguish dross from the real thing. But his was not the exquisite taste of a Gilbert Osmond in Henry James' *Portrait of a Lady* (1881), whose refinement was contrasted so lethally with the naive simplicities of the earnest American Caspar Goodwood. No one who acquired 15,000 or 20,000 art works over two decades of furious collecting, including whole collections each of which might contain several thousand items, could exactly be said to have a *refined* appreciation. There was nothing about Morgan's brusque manner to suggest delicacy of appreciation. But he had gusto, and an invincible belief in art itself. If that art was jewel-encrusted, or had belonged to crowned heads or Renaissance princes, so much the better. Morgan wanted items with a unique provenance, such as John Eliot's Indian Bible, in an Algonquian dialect, published in 1663, and Napoleon's copy of the Paris translation of Goethe's *Werther*. Of the forty-nine copies of the Gutenberg Bible known to exist, Morgan owned three. No other library in the world has so many.

He was no less interested in the eighteenth-century portraits of Reynolds, Gainsborough and Raeburn. His father, Junius Spencer Morgan, walked into the gallery of the art dealer Sir William Agnew in London in 1876 and purchased Gainsborough's *Georgiana, Duchess of Devonshire*, then much discussed after Agnew had bought it at auction for 10,100 guineas, the highest price then paid for an English picture. Morgan senior explained that his son had "begun collecting pictures in New York," and thought the Gainsborough would make a good start. That evening, the American art thief Adam Worth stole the painting from Agnews. J.P. Morgan finally acquired *Georgiana* for $150,000 after it was ransomed by Agnews in 1902. After Morgan's death, his son and heir J.P. Morgan Jr. offered his sisters the choice of anything they liked in their father's collection. Each in turn chose eighteenth-century English portraits. Louisa Morgan, who had married Herbert Satterlee (author of a sycophantic biography of his father-in-law) chose Gainsborough's *Georgiana*. The painting is today at Chatsworth, home of the Devonshire family.

On Wall Street, and there was intense competition, J. Pierpont Morgan was the embodiment of Mammon. The headquarters of J.P. Morgan & Company at 23 Wall Street was the target of a terrorist bomb in 1920, which killed thirty people and injured more than 400. The marks from the explosion are still visible on the building's façade. No one was ever convicted for this bombing, but it was widely assumed to be a response to the heavy-handed "Red Scare" roundup of radicals and the deportation of immigrant radicals. On December 20, 1919, the U.S.S. *Buford*, an old army transport ship that had seen service in the Spanish-American War and in World War I, carried the anarchists Emma Goldman, Alexander Berkman, and 247 other radicals to European exile. "Through the port-hole," Goldman wrote in her autobiography, "I could see the great city receding into the distance, its sky-line of buildings traceable by their rearing heads. It was my beloved city, the metropolis of the New World. It was America, indeed, America repeating the terrible scenes of Czarist Russia! I glanced up—the Statue of Liberty!"

Morgan's role in the formation of United States Steel, and long opposition to union attempts to organize the workforce, made him a hated figure in the eyes of the American labor movement. After the assassination of President McKinley in 1901, threats were made against Morgan and he was given police protection. He was advised to stay on his yacht rather than in his home in Murray Hill. As for Morgan, the only Goldman he was worried about was Marcus Goldman, who in partnership with Samuel Sachs, had formed the great brokerage house of Goldman Sachs in 1885. After 1900 Goldman Sachs began to compete with the great Goliath of J.P. Morgan & Company as an underwriter of securities.

Trinity Church

"And now it is finished, and all complete," wrote a radical bard on the consecration of Trinity Church in 1845,

How happy are they that can purchase a seat;
How important they feel, as they strut down the aisle,
Through the host of bright faces, all wearing a smile;
Here they may come with the utmost propriety,
And mingle among the tip top of society.

Trinity has been a target of radical satire and indignation because it was rich and powerful and because the Episcopal Church was such a central institution of the city's aristocracy.

Richard Upjohn's brownstone Gothic Revival masterpiece, preserved from the ravages of the New York climate by the ingrained soot of a century and a half, embodies the role of the Anglican Church in the city. Trinity Church and its parish were created by royal charter in 1697 during the reign of King William. The original document is on display in the Trinity Museum. A land grant followed, which included the area west of Broadway from Fulton Street to Christopher Street. At the time of the grant it consisted of farmland and pastures running down to the shore of the Hudson River. Rental income from this large tract, which grew astronomically in value as the city expanded northwards, in theory funded the activities of Trinity Church.

Whenever the church entered into relations with the real estate market, it betrayed an other-worldly naïveté, nowhere more vividly demonstrated than in the story of Aaron Burr, John Jacob Astor, and the Richmond Hill district at the northern end of the Queen's Farm.

In 1767 Trinity Church granted a 99-year lease for approximately five hundred lots between Spring and Christopher Streets (just south of Greenwich Village) to Abraham Mortier, paymaster general to the British forces in North America. Mortier agreed to pay the church a rent of $269 a year. He erected a handsome country house on Richmond Hill overlooking the Hudson River, which was later rebuilt as the Richmond Hill Opera House. When Mortier fled with the departing British army in 1783, the matter of his sweetheart leases came under closer official scrutiny. The Richmond Hill mansion was occupied in 1789 by Vice President John Adams and his wife Abigail, who described the estate as a tranquil and private space: "The venerable oaks and broken ground covered with wild shrubs, which surround me, give a natural beauty to the spot which is truly enchanting. A lovely variety of birds serenade me morning and evening, rejoicing in their liberty and security, for I have, as

much as possible, prohibited the grounds from invasion, and sometimes almost wished for game laws, when my orders have not been sufficiently regarded…"

Richmond Hill was afterward the residence of Aaron Burr, an unscrupulous New York lawyer and politician who saw an incomparable opportunity in the Mortier lease. Obtaining the lease in 1797, he promptly mortgaged it for $38,000. Debt piled up on Burr's shoulders and he sold the Trinity lease in 1803 to John Jacob Astor for $62,500. Astor, who made his fortune buying and selling beaver pelts, was among the first New York merchants to open up the lucrative China trade. He plowed his sizable profits into New York real estate. With the Mortier lease to run until 1867, Astor granted tenancies of only 20 years and spent no money developing the land. Leaving that to builders, Astor reaped the benefit of the rise in property values as the city expanded in the following decades. Burr tried unsuccessfully to regain possession of the Richmond Hill estate, and died in poverty. When Astor died in 1848, he was reputed to be the wealthiest man in America. He was certainly the largest owner of real estate in New York City.

The Trinity vestry drew upon its wealthy parishioners to supplement its annual income of $269 from Astor, and continued its energetic missionary and educational work. Trinity School, founded by the church in 1709 and now located on West 91st Street, is the oldest continually operated school in the city. Trinity played a more controversial role in the founding of the city's first university, King's College (now Columbia University). Anglicans dominated the first board of trustees of the new college, chartered in 1754. In exchange for land on which the new college would be located, the Trinity-inspired trustees insisted that the college's presidents should be Anglicans, and that the Anglican liturgy should be used in all formal religious observance. Into the late nineteenth century, when the university moved to its present location on Morningside Heights in northern Manhattan, the university retained its distinctive Episcopalian and upper-class ethos. Lutherans of the Dutch Reformed Church, Presbyterians, Methodists, and Baptists regarded Trinity Church somewhat less benevolently after this transparent power grab, and conflicts between churches remained a powerful factor in New York life.

When the British army occupied New York City in 1776, a fire, which started in a tavern, swept across the port district and burned down Trinity Church. The vestry was able to continue to function in satellite chapels: St. George's, a Romanesque brownstone founded in 1752, where J.P. Morgan later negotiated promissory notes with his maker, and the city's great example of ecclesiastical Georgian, St. Paul's Chapel, founded 1764–6 at the corner of Broadway and Fulton Street. During the British occupation, the burned-out site of Trinity was fenced off, benches were installed, and it became a favorite walk. Military bands gave regular concerts.

Trinity Church was a bastion of "Loyalist" sentiment during the American struggle for independence. There is a painting in the Trinity Museum of a sober cleric named the Rt. Rev. Charles Inglis who was the fourth rector and a devout Loyalist. Inglis ceased to be rector in 1783. His next clerical appointment came in 1787, when he became bishop of Nova Scotia. In the brief text accompanying the painting there is no mention of this gap in the Rector's CV. Unwilling to remain in a city that had rebelled against the Crown, and also perhaps fearing for his life at the hands of Patriot mobs, Inglis joined thousands of New Yorkers who fled with the departing British troops. The majority of Loyalists were re-settled in Nova Scotia, where they uneasily joined a small community of farmers and fishermen of New England Protestant stock. The majority inhabitants, the Acadians, who were French-speaking and Catholics, had been deported in 1755 as part of a long-term scheme to secure the British imperial presence in eastern Canada. To the Acadians this ruthless act of ethnic cleansing is known as the "Grand Dérangement." When passions calmed, some of the Loyalists returned to New York. But the end of the Revolutionary War broke the hold of the Loyalist aristocracy in New York.

"Patriots," who took the side of the colonies against the Crown when the struggle for independence began in the 1760s, regarded Trinity as an implacable enemy, and at the end of the war they took their revenge by disestablishing the Anglican church in 1784 as part of an attack on Tories and their privileges. Later that year, the Episcopal Church of America was formed, with a pledge to remain unswervingly loyal to the doctrines of the Church of England. (Trinity is one of the few places in New York where a smiling photograph of the Archbishop of Canterbury is lovingly displayed, and where there is a plaque to mark the visit of the Queen.)

Trinity was rebuilt and rededicated in 1790. But the new church had structural flaws, and was in danger of collapsing. It was torn down in 1839, and the British architect Richard Upjohn was given the commission to build the third Trinity Church. Upjohn had emigrated to America in 1829. At a time when few American-born architects had ever seen a real Gothic building, Upjohn was influenced by the high Anglican Gothicism of A.W. Pugin. Upjohn was to go on and build many important Gothic churches, and to spread Ecclesiological ideas in America. Ecclesiology was a reform movement within the Anglican Church calling for a return to medieval forms in church design and ritual. St. Paul's Chapel, six blocks north along Broadway, embodied the Enlightenment spirit that the Ecclesiologists deplored. Upjohn's Trinity Church powerfully suggests the spirit of the new movement. Authors of Gothic romances like George Lippard (*The Empire City*, 1850; *New York: Its Upper Ten and Lower Million*, 1853) found Upjohn's Trinity Church an irresistible setting for midnight scenes among ghostly vaults, involving disputed legacies and far-reaching conspiracies.

There are many features of Trinity that catch the eye. Upjohn employed New Jersey brownstone, a popular material easily cut by stonemasons. Its inadequacy as a primary building material became clear in later years, when the climate and environmental pollution of New York produced spalling—a tendency of the surface of the stone to disintegrate into fragments and chips. At 280 feet, the eight-sided spire, supported by flying buttresses, was for decades the tallest structure in the city. A bell, presented to the church in 1704 by the Bishop of London, remains in daily use. The three sets of large bronze doors, designed by Richard Morris Hunt after the Ghiberti doors of the Baptistry in Florence, were presented to the church by William Waldorf Astor in memory of his father John Jacob Astor III.

The burial ground surrounding the church, flanked on either side by large early twentieth-century office buildings remains of considerable historical interest as well as offering visitors and office workers a shaded place of quiet and reflection. Buried here are the usual pious and respectable city merchants and mariners, distinguished citizens like William Bradford, editor of the city's first newspaper and champion of press freedom, and Robert Fulton, who brought steam-propelled navigation to the waters of New York. The Trinity burial ground also has memorials to implacable political opponents like Alexander Hamilton, killed in a duel with his arch-rival Aaron Burr in 1804 (copies of the flintlocks used in the duel are on display in Trinity Museum), and Albert Gallatin, the Swiss immigrant who served two terms as Secretary of the Treasury under Thomas Jefferson.

There is an ornate Gothic memorial in the northern section of the Trinity burial ground, facing Pine Street, dedicated "to the memory of the great and good men who died [during the Revolutionary War] whilst in captivity in the old Sugar House and were interred in Trinity Church yard…" The memorial was suggested at a meeting at City Hall in 1852 chaired by the mayor, Ambrose C. Kingsland. It is one of a number of similar memorials seeking to keep alive the memory of the Revolutionary War. The statues might form an interesting route for a stirring patriotic walk around the city.

- An equestrian statue of George Washington erected to mark Evacuation Day, the anniversary of the withdrawal of the British army from New York in 1783 (Union Square Park, 1854, by Henry Kirke Brown with John Q. A. Ward).
- Benjamin Franklin (Printing House Square, on Park Row at Nassau Street, 1872, by Ernst Plessmann). To celebrate Franklin's early career as a printer and publisher.
- Marquis de Lafayette (near the statue of Washington in Union Square, 1876, by Frédéric Auguste Bartholdi). Offered in gratitude by the French nation to the United States for support during the Franco-Prussian war of 1870–1.

Bartholdi's Statue of Liberty was unveiled in 1886.

• Alexander Hamilton (on the East Drive in Central Park, 1880, by Carl Davids).

• President George Washington (on the steps of the Federal Hall National Memorial on Wall Street, 1883, by John Q. A. Ward). The bronze statue stands 13'2" high on a six-foot granite pedestal. It was erected to mark the centenary of Evacuation Day, on the site where Washington took the oath of office.

• Nathan Hale (on the Broadway side of City Hall, 1893, by Frederick MacMonnies). A bronze statue of the Yale graduate hanged as a spy by the British in 1776. Erected by the Sons of the Revolution in 1893, on the 110th anniversary of the British evacuation, it captures Hale at the moment of uttering his patriotic farewell: "I only regret that I have but one life to lose for my country." MacMonnies' is an imaginary portrait, as no likeness of Hale is known to exist.

• The Washington Memorial Arch (in Washington Square Park, facing Fifth Avenue, 1889 in wood, 1895 in stone, by Stanford White). Erected to mark the centenary of the inauguration of the first president, it proved such a popular success that it was re-erected in stone.

This explosion of patriotic statuary, amidst scores of other statues erected in the city commemorating explorers, politicians, writers, and European luminaries from Dante to Beethoven, is, like the African Burial Ground and Seneca Village, part of New York's politics of memory. The Martyrs' Memorial, the statue of Nathan Hale, and the others were erected at a time when contemporary concerns seemed to distract Americans from their patriotic heritage. Changes in economic life, from the growth of cities to industrialization and mass immigration, threatened to make Americans a more materialistic people, with little time to reflect on the past. The divisions between rich and poor seemed to deepen, decade by decade. Organizations like the Sons of the Revolution feared that their countrymen worshipped the dollar and knew little of American history or traditions. The statues made a claim on behalf of the older families, long settled in New York, who felt their social leadership had been forgotten along with the contributions of their patriotic ancestors. The statues say: This is our city, too.

Federal Hall

The Federal Hall National Memorial at 28 Wall Street, on the northeast corner of Nassau Street, an uncomfortably hemmed-in Parthenon complete with Doric columns, is one of the most important Greek Revival buildings in New York. It was designed by the architectural firm of Ithiel Town and Alexander Jackson Davis, leading practitioners of the Greek Revival style. The building has a long and complex history, but it is the site rather than the building that reaches back to the early history of the city.

The present structure at 28 Wall Street was erected in 1842 by the United States government as a Custom House. The soaring rotunda, sixteen Corinthian columns in the main hall, and marble floor make the interior of the Federal Hall one of the most impressive spaces in the city. It is easy to see why so expensive and grand a structure (it cost over $1 million) was erected for a government office. Before civil service reform in 1891, the Custom House was the greatest source of political patronage, and produced the greatest revenue stream for the government. In 1852, total government receipts amounted to $61 million. Of that sum, $58 million consisted of customs revenue. Some 80 percent of all customs revenue received that year was collected in New York, the largest American port in the nineteenth century. Duty on all foreign goods (silk, woolens, hats, carpets, wine, spices, crystal glass, fine china tea cups, paintings, and books), was collected at 28 Wall Street. The salary of the collector of the Port of New York, the chief officer of the Custom House, was greater than that of the president of the United States.

The novelist Nathaniel Hawthorne worked as an inspector in the Custom House in Boston in 1839–41, and was dismissed when the new Whig administration of General Zachary Taylor demanded its turn at the patronage trough. It was Hawthorne's pleasure in *The Scarlet Letter* (1850) to portray the Custom House as an institution of superannuated ancient sea captains, whiling away their idle days on government salaries. Other writers had less bruising experiences of Custom House work. After his career as a novelist had petered out, Herman Melville worked in the New York Custom House as an inspector. On a salary of $4 a day he examined trunks and other luggage for false bottoms and smuggled goods, and listened to returning

Americans explain how remarkably *little* they had actually paid for a Worth gown, how *terribly* mediocre a painting was. Through one administration after another for nineteen years, Melville held on to his post, and could proudly point to the fact that there had never been a single complaint made against him. In the public mind, however, the Custom House was the seat of the "spoils" system (jobs awarded for political and financial reasons, which required substantial "contributions" to the campaign funds of the party in power). The corruption pervasive in New York City government, especially under the mayoral administrations of Fernando Wood and William "Boss" Tweed in the 1850s and 1860s, was more than matched in the Custom House.

In 1862 the Custom House moved to another site nearby, and 28 Wall Street was taken over by the United States Treasury Department, and functioned as a Sub-Treasury, issuing and receiving bonds and gold certificates, until 1925. It was from the Sub-Treasury on Wall Street that the first of the "greenbacks," legal tender notes, were issued during the Civil War. In the inter-war years the building housed the Passport Agency of the Department of State, and other government agencies, until 1940 when it was granted the status of national memorial. What was being remembered was not a century of tariff duties, tax revenues, and passports, but the events that made this site one of the patriotic shrines of the nation.

From City Hall to Federal Hall

From 1699 until 1812, 28 Wall Street was the location of the second City Hall of New York. The Dutch colonial City Hall, the *Stadt Huys*, was a tavern on Pearl Street looking out on the East River. As late as the 1870s, old timers could point out the warehouse at 71 and 73 Pearl Street where the foundation of the original structure was still visible. Converted into a City Hall in 1653, the Stadt Huys was replaced in 1699 with a brick structure on Wall Street at its intersection with Nassau. This was itself a building with an important historical identity. In addition to housing the Common Council and the provincial assembly, City Hall served as a courthouse and jail. In 1735 it housed the trial of John Peter Zenger, a German immigrant printer whose *New-York Weekly Journal* led opposition to the provincial governor Colonel William Cosby. Zenger was accused of seditious libel (the publication of anything undermining the authority of the government). He was arrested and held in a cell in City Hall for ten months, dictating fierce articles on press freedom through a hole in the prison door to his wife. At his trial, Zenger's defense was led by the famed Philadelphia attorney Andrew Hamilton. Common

CITY TAVERN, NEW AMSTERDAM,
AFTERWARD "THE STADT HUYS,"
BUILT IN 1642.

law then, and for many years after, did not admit evidence on the truth of an alleged libel, but the jury in 1735 thought otherwise. A "Not Guilty" verdict was the first great victory in the long struggle to win freedom of the press.

The New York City Hall was the venue for the Stamp Act Congress in 1765, where a Declaration of Rights and Grievances was drawn up in measured protest against "taxation without representation." The Declaration of Independence was read from the balcony of City Hall on July 18, 1776. During the British occupation, the City Hall served as headquarters of the occupying army. After the conclusion of the Revolutionary War, the Continental Congress met in the New York City Hall in 1785. The structure, then nearly a century old, was showing its age. In September 1788 the Common Council decided to make the building available to the federal government. A plan submitted by the French military engineer Major Pierre L'Enfant called for extensive reconstruction and expansion. Over the next two years the resources and credit of the city, just emerging from a long period of British occupation, were strained to the breaking point to fund the improvements. Costing more than $26,000, and partially funded by lottery, what was now the "Federal Hall" was transformed into the largest building on the continent, with an assertive American eagle on the pediment. There were marble floors and painted ceilings, damask curtains and canopies, and portraits of Louis XVI and Marie Antoinette presented to the United States by the French king in 1785. When Congress first met in March 1789, they found a large chamber for the Representatives on the ground floor, 61 feet deep and 58 feet wide. The ceiling had an imposing height of 31 feet, while the Senate Chamber on the first floor was 40 feet long and 30 feet wide. There was an open gallery on the first floor, looking down Broad Street, and it was on this gallery that President Washington took the oath of office.

The organization of the inauguration in 1789 was the first great public ritual of the new nation, and was planned with meticulous care. Washington traveled from Virginia to New York, arriving on April 23. John Adams, elected vice president, made the shorter journey from Braintree, Massachusetts. Their arrivals were choreographed with precision. The crowds were large. Houses along the route were decorated with flags, silk banners, wreaths of flowers. In the evening it seemed as though every house in the city, except those occupied by Quakers, who did not go in for rejoicing, were illuminated with candles. Wall Street, which had become increasingly prosperous and elegant, had impressive new houses from which to offer greetings to the president. The first Executive Mansion was on Cherry Street, on a site under the present line of the Manhattan Bridge. Demolished in 1856, a chair fashioned from materials rescued from the house is preserved in the New-York Historical Society. In 1790, the president moved into a house on Broadway.

The inaugural oath was taken on Thursday, April 30. Wall Street was so crowded that a witness thought it would be possible literally to walk on the heads of the people. Every window was filled, and even the roofs were lined with respectfully silent people. At 57 and standing six feet tall, Washington was an imposing figure. He wore a deep brown suit of domestic material so fine that everyone was sure it had been made in Europe. Metal buttons with a patriotic eagle design, white silk stockings, and a sword completed his costume. The oath was administered by Chancellor Robert R. Livingston, the chief legal officer of the State of New York.

> *I do solemnly swear that I will faithfully execute the office of President of the United States, and will, to the best of my ability, preserve, protect, and defend the Constitution of the United States.*

When Washington kissed the bible on which he had taken his oath, a flag was raised on the cupola of Federal Hall to signal churches to ring their bells. Artillery in the Battery fired a salute. The crowd cheered and cheered. Washington bowed to the people, and retired to the Senate Chamber, before emerging again to join a procession led by a troop of horse, with "citizens" making up the rear, up Broadway to St. Paul's Chapel, where divine service was led by the Episcopal Bishop of New York. In the evening there was a display of fireworks at the Fort. Transparencies (Fortitude, Justice, and Wisdom) were projected on the walls of prominent structures. On May 7 the president appeared at a ball given in his honor and attended by political and diplomatic leaders, thus initiating another presidential tradition: the Inaugural Ball. (The women with whom the new president danced became celebrities in New York.) Thomas Jefferson wrote a derisive account of the ball, mocking the behavior of several prominent guests. It was yet another reason why he was regarded with such distrust by the president and his party.

It was some time before the Federal Hall became an object of patriotic feeling. The federal government moved to Philadelphia in 1790, and then in November 1800 to its permanent home in Washington, D.C. The New York Common Council once again occupied the building as a City Hall, along with the courts and state legislature. In 1797, when the legislature, state agencies, and offices began to relocate to Albany—the location of the state capital was so controversial that an official legislative designation of Albany as the capital was not made until the 1980s—the adequacy of the building to the needs of the local government of the city, and perhaps its noisy and hemmed-in location, was questioned. The Common Council proposed building a new structure on a larger site. The building where Washington was inaugurated was unceremoniously sold for scrap in 1812, raising $425. The third City Hall (see Chapter 6), completed in 1811, was designed in

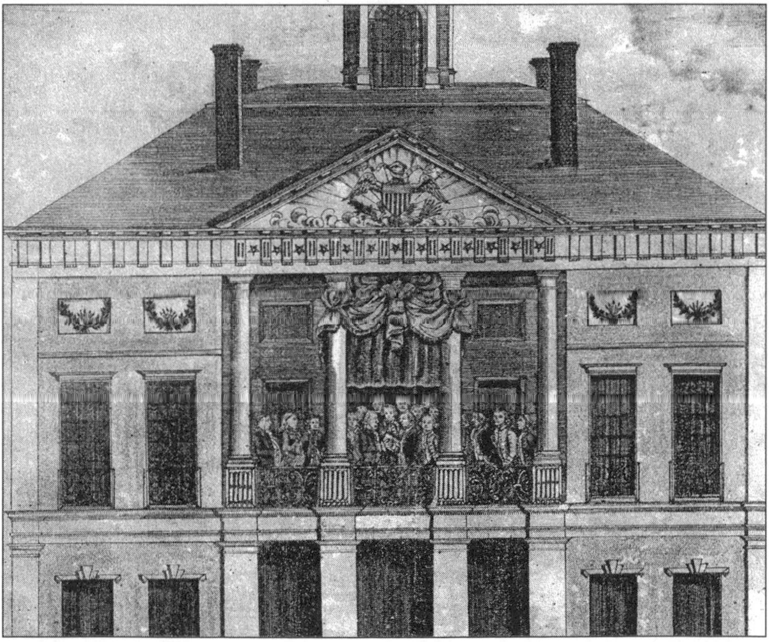

The gallery of Federal Hall, in an early engraving, where George Washington was inaugurated in 1789.

and was located in the wedge-shaped piece of land enclosed by Broadway, Park Row, and Chambers Street. The center of gravity of the city was perceptibly moving uptown.

Wall Street and the New York Stock Exchange

In Tom Wolfe's novel *Bonfire of the Vanities* (1987), Wall Street bond brokers like Sherman McCoy are the "Masters of the Universe," men for whom "There was... no limit whatsoever!" The bond trading room at the high-powered Pierce & Pierce where McCoy works is a place where mysterious things happen, making some men very wealthy. Wolfe's satire, which caught the mood of the great bull market of the 1980s, ends with McCoy in disgrace, staring at the likelihood of prison. His mistress is gone, his Park Avenue apartment now belongs to his wife. In the real world of New York in the 1980s few Masters of the Universe wound up going to jail. As McCoy understands, the purpose of money is to buy space, to create a protection against the city itself: "If you want to live in New York," McCoy says, "you've got to insulate, insulate, insulate." The wealth of Sherman McCoy buys social distance, the rarest of commodities, from the Third World city where he lives. On Park Avenue and the trading floor of Pierce & Pierce, men like McCoy rule. Money, and the men who are its master, is what Wall Street is all about.

Curiously, for all its immense importance in American life, Wall Street has seldom been of interest to American writers. When Herman Melville published "Bartleby the Scrivener: A Tale of Wall Street" in *Putnam's Monthly* in 1853, he was venturing into an aspect of New York that had scarcely been written about. The narrator of Melville's short story is a lawyer, not a broker, and his legal practice on Wall Street is a somnolent affair. In his small office the narrator employs two clerks, and to their number is added a copyist, Bartleby, who in a spirit of quiet determination declines to do what his employer demands. The struggle of wills between the two men gave Melville an opportunity to explore what the "bonds of common humanity" meant in the relations between an employer and employee.

The Stock Exchange has had an occasional figure of literary interest among its members (such as the now forgotten poet Edmund Clarence Stedman, who published a history of the exchange in 1905), but for some Americans at least the worlds of speculation and finance have been regarded as an enemy of the higher life of the imagination. "In Wall-street," wrote the abolitionist Lydia Maria Child, "Mammon, as usual, coolly calculates his chance of extracting a penny from war, pestilence, and famine; and Commerce, with her loaded drays, and jaded skeletons of horses, is busy as ever 'fulfilling the World's contract with the Devil.'" Melville never sought to write about the vivid, larger-than-life figures who dominated Wall Street in mid-century, any more than did Hemingway, Saul Bellow, or John Updike in the twentieth century. With the important exception of Theodore Dreiser, money and the unashamed pursuit of wealth did not stir the imaginations of American writers. For Jay Gatsby in Fitzgerald's *The Great Gatsby* (1925), wealth was a vehicle with which to realize the American dream. But the dream was, as Fitzgerald shows, beyond reach, and perhaps wasn't the real thing anyway. Henry Adams made a similar distinction, writing in *The Education of Henry Adams* in 1918:

> *That the American, by temperament, worked to excess, was true; work and whiskey were his stimulants; work was a form of vice; but he never cared much for money or power after he earned them. The amusement of the pursuit was all the amusement he got from it; he had no use for wealth. Jim Fisk alone seemed to know what he wanted; Jay Gould never did.*

Fisk and Gould were freebooting collaborators in the notorious attempt on Wall Street to corner the market in gold in 1869. There is an ambivalence in American attitudes toward wealth, and the Stock Exchange—embodying as it does the naked chase after riches—is a creature of that ambivalence.

The New York Stock Exchange traces its origin back to the "Buttonwood Agreement" signed on Wall Street in 1792 by the twenty-two brokers and merchants then actively trading government securities. The agreement sought to establish fixed commission levels on transactions, and to favor brokers who were signatories. In other words, the New York markets began with a proud attempt to fix prices and eliminate competition. The buttonwood tree, which stood on Wall Street until it was cut down in 1865, was the symbol of humble origins and of an innocent age when brokers traded securities in the open air on Wall Street and Broad Street. In the succeeding decades brokers did business at several locations before acquiring premises on nearby William Street in the 1860s.

Although only members of the exchange could buy and sell shares and securities on the Regular Board, and there was a steep initiation fee, the conduct of the exchange before the orderly age of electronic transactions was anything but orderly. During the daily trading sessions at 10:30 am and 1 pm, stocks were taken in a set order. The brokers would sit around chatting, desultorily awaiting the call of an exciting stock. Then all hell broke loose.

> *Chairs are abandoned, men rush pell-mell into the cock-pit, and crowd, jostle, push, and trample on one another. They scream out their offers to buy and sell. They speak all at once, yelling and screaming like hyenas. The scene is very exciting. Pandemonium is not wilder, or more disorderly. The presiding officer stands erect, cool, and silent. Several hundred men surge before him, stamping, yelling, screaming, jumping, sweating, gesticulating, violently shaking their fists in each others' faces, talking in a tongue not spoken at Pentecost.*

The Regular Board was gentility itself compared to the Long Room, where trading was continuous and wild:

> *Voices like a church-organ and voices like a bag-pipe; stridulous, whooping, screeching, deep-toned, piping voices,—voices like a trap-hammer crashing through all other cries, and carrying the whole market down by an offer as tremendous as the lungs which gave it birth. Every step and crevice jammed with men. Note-books, arms, fists, dexter-fingers, hats, heads, tossing, swaying, darting hither and thither with nervous eagerness, and suggesting a perpetual explosion of bomb-shells from below.*

Most accounts of nineteenth-century life stress the decorum of "Victorian" America and the emphasis in middle-class life upon correct behavior. Strict notions of etiquette ruled on Fifth Avenue. But on the trading floors of Wall Street the decorum fell away before the eager hunger for profit.

The stock market was also a remarkable linguistic pressure cooker, introducing to America a racy, vivid metaphor-rich discourse of bulls and bears, pools, corners, breaks, covers, margins, longs, and shorts. Investors across the nation needed the mysteries of the market explained: "If you are a *long*, you are a 'bull'; if *short*, a 'bear.'" All too often the hopeful investor in Ohio (or London) was there to be scalped by the professionals. "If a large operation is to be made," suggested one student of the markets, "*Ursa Major* gives the word to some special agent, who distributes the order to A, B, and C; A whispers to D, C instructs F, B commissions G, and so the complication extends. This *finesse* is one of the difficulties of the game which perpetually confront the player. Brokers, however, have eyes like ferrets and the instincts of a Fouché."

The wealth created by market speculation can be seen everywhere in the city, shaping luxury expenditure on top-of-the-line BMWs and Mercedes Benzes, and the wild real estate market in the 1990s. In the 1890s, the conspicuous expenditure of Wall Street speculators might be expressed in mansions on Fifth Avenue and Newport, steam yachts, fast teams of trotters, and champagne suppers for the latest *diva* at the opera.

There is no necessary reason why New York became the center of the nation's securities' trading, but with the rise of the city's trade and growth in population, it has been easy to assume that it was all inevitable. In the 1790s Philadelphia, not New York, was the nation's leading city, with the largest banks, and a functioning stock exchange. Even in New York, there were rival bodies to the Stock Exchange, traders who specialized in gold and petroleum, who functioned outside the regular trading sessions, and even "curbstone" brokers who did business on the sidewalks of Broad Street. The Stock Exchange regularized market transactions, and established norms for members (a "seat" on the Big Board, as it was called, was a form of private property that could be sold). The Stock Exchange also embodied the powerful free-market conservatism that proved, over two centuries, utterly resistant to government regulation and taxation. The Stock Exchange's most heartfelt threats to leave New York City came when the city, near bankruptcy, threatened to tax financial transactions. In that tug of war, the city government invariably backed off.

Until the recent decimalization of quotations, the Stock Exchange conducted its business in fractions. Stock prices were quoted in sixteenths, a charming anachronism going back to the foundation of the exchange. In the early years of the nation, there was complete chaos in currencies. The Spanish-milled "dollar" or piece of eight, which remained legal tender in the United States until the 1850s, could physically be broken into quarters, eighths, and sixteenths, which thus established a norm for transactions that persisted. Other aspects of the business of trading stocks and securities were less resistant to change. The invention of the telegraph in 1844 carried news of stock prices across the nation. When the first transatlantic cable was laid in 1866, prices were in the hands of New York dealers almost as quickly as they reached the London brokerages. The invention of the stock ticker in 1867 enabled real time prices to arrive at the offices of brokers. Ticker machines were installed in banks, men's clubs, hotels, and saloons of the better class.

The accumulating paper tape from the ticker machines was central in the creation of one of the city's most distinctive rituals. The procession accompanying the dedication of the Statue of Liberty was greeted by a spontaneous ticker-tape greeting. The ticker-tape parade became a way to greet visiting heads of state, triumphant baseball teams, athletes, astronauts, politicians, generals, and miscellaneous groups, like the winners of the American Legion Drum and Bugle Corps national championship in 1949. Organized by the Mayor's Reception Committee, often at the request of the US State Department, a ticker-tape parade is as close as America comes to the award of a Triumph to a returning Roman general. The "success" of a parade was measured not in the usual police estimates of the number of people lining Broadway, but by the weight of ticker-tape dumped from skyscrapers. John Glenn, the astronaut and later US Senator, was welcomed to New York in 1962 with 3,474 tons of ticker tape. No one else has ever come close to that total.

When the Stock Exchange moved in 1903 into its present building at 18 Broad Street, the busy sculptor John Q.A. Ward was commissioned to execute statuary for the building's pediment. "Integrity Protecting the Works of Man," carved from white Georgia marble, did not last more than three decades before being so extensively damaged by pollution that the statues had to be removed and replaced by figures cast in copper and lead that had been coated to resemble stone. "Integrity" was not quite what she seemed. It was only in 1975 that the requirement for brokers to offer fixed commissions was abolished. That was the last element of the "Buttonwood Agreement" to be discarded.

The public is invited to experience the New York Stock Exchange by visiting the "Interactive Education Center," a self-conducted tour that ends with a view of the trading floor from a narrow balcony and a little shop, where baseball hats, tee shirts, and other things with the NYSE logo are sold. The plate glass that protects the visitors on the balcony, or the brokers below, is a reminder of one of Abbie Hoffman's better stunts. With a group of co-conspirators on August 24, 1967, he tossed handfuls of dollar bills at the startled brokers. The story of his guerrilla theater took control of the national media on the next day. "The sacred electronic ticker tape, the heartbeat of the Western world," Hoffman wrote in *Revolution for the Hell of It* (1968),

> *stopped cold… The system cracked a little. Not a drop of blood had been spilled, not a bone broken, but on that day, with that gesture, an image of war had begun. In the minds of millions of teenagers the stock market had just crashed.*

On the trading floor there are 3,000 brokers, specialists and clerks, all wearing tasteful cotton jackets in wine red, oyster, tan, green, and navy, indicating the wearer's role and institutional affiliation. Free tickets for the tour are available at 20 Broad Street, with the tour entrance at the rear of the building on New Street. At midday you will enjoy the skilled sniffer dogs checking trucks and cars for bombs, and note the x-ray machines that scan all goods entering the exchange. There is a cute little corral on New Street where delivery boys wait, chatting in Spanish, for brokers to collect their lunches.

CHAPTER THREE

The Immigrant's City

March or Die

Growth—in size, population, and wealth—is the way success works in America. The language of superlatives has a natural home in New York, where you will find the biggest, richest, tallest, most wonderful, and most diverse array of everything under the sun. But like sharks, if American states and cities are still, they die. Perhaps a closer parallel might be with the French foreign legion: march or die.

States that do not grow, or grow more slowly, suffer consequences. They lose political power. In the census of 2000 New York State and Pennsylvania lost two seats each in the House of Representatives. The trend of population movement away from the North and East to the South and West continues. The Sunbelt states of Florida, Georgia, Arizona, and Texas gained two seats each. The population of New York State grew in the 1990s by 5.5 percent, nearly one million additional residents. With a population of 18,976,457 New York nonetheless slipped from second to third place in total state population, behind Texas and California. New York was tenth in the national ranking of growth, behind the breakneck pace of Nevada (over 66 percent), Texas (over 23 percent), Georgia (over 26 percent), and California, the most populous state, with a growth over the decade of nearly 14 percent. New York and Pennsylvania will lose federal funds because the complex social information collected in the census reveals other states have larger problems and more pressing needs.

Out of the heated debate about the way the census was conducted came an estimate that as many as 3.3 million people were omitted from the count. The Census Bureau resisted pressure from cities like New York to adjust the count. As a result, New York is likely to lose $850 million in federal aid between 2002 and 2012, largely in Medicaid funding due to the "undercount."

Nonetheless, the 2000 census was greeted with considerable relief in New York. After the financial crises of the 1970s, and the rising welfare rolls, explosion in crime, and related social problems of a city in decline, New York today looks more self-confident, prosperous, and more able to cope with the future. (The events of September 11, 2001 have shaken the city to its foundations, but, as worried commentators say when the stock market is on the slide, the *fundamentals* are solid.) The city today has a population of just over eight million, the highest figure ever recorded. Social trends, like the decline of the city's non-Hispanic white population, have begun to turn around. In the early 1990s more than two percent of the city's non-Hispanic white population left the city each year for life in the suburbs or retirement to the Sunbelt states. By the end of the decade "white flight" halved to one percent. It will be a long time, however, before people retiring in Ohio move to New York City.

The economic good times of the 1990s, and the decline in crime, persuaded New Yorkers that the city seemed to have a future. Admirers of Mayor Rudy Giuliani point to a decline in the public assistance caseload by 48 percent. These impressive figures are perhaps a function of the city's booming economy. They could (and did) go into reverse when the economy stalled in 2000. Nonetheless, the image of the crisis-laden, graffiti-smeared city has been replaced by a more attractive idea: New York as the city of glitz and "bright lights," a place where the most vibrant things in American life may be found. By 1997 New Yorkers were beginning to feel more positively about their own city, and its mayor, and something of this changed attitude seemed to reach the wider nation. Public opinion polls were reporting in 1998 that a majority of Americans now had a "good image" of New York. Of those polled, 45 percent thought that New Yorkers were "unfriendly"—but that was good news, for similar polls taken since 1991 revealed that the 1998 "unfriendly" rating was the lowest ever recorded. New York was less "unfriendly" than ever before—official. The aftermath of September 11 strengthened this shift of perception.

Theodore Dreiser, with his *Sister Carrie* (1900) and F. Scott Fitzgerald with *This Side of Paradise* (1920) and *The Great Gatsby* (1925) helped shape the view of New York as a city whose glitter and promise—and coldness—inevitably led to disillusionment. Fitzgerald's heirs, like Jay McInerney in *Bright Lights, Big City* (1983) and *The Story of My Life* (1988) reclaimed for contemporary readers a rich sense of contemporary New York as a world of glitz and miserableness. "The electronic buzz of fast money," wrote McInerney in *Brightness Falls* (1992), "hummed between the wired streets, affecting all the inhabitants, making some of them crazy with lust and ambition, others angrily impoverished, and making the comfortable majority feel poorer." In McInerney's New York, the buzz is remorseless, 24/7. The protagonists of *Brightness Falls*, Russell and Corine Calloway, could hear late at night "in between the sirens and the alarms and the car horns" a buzz—"worrying vaguely, clinging to the very edge of the credit limits on their charge cards."

The census of 2000 shows that forty percent of the city's inhabitants today are foreign-born. This represented a return to the way New York was in 1910, at the peak of the "New Immigration," when four New Yorkers out of ten were foreign-born. Changes in immigration policy in the 1920s radically limited immigration, and over time the proportion of foreign-born declined to twenty percent. Even that figure was higher than the proportion of foreign-born in the nation as a whole, but as the twentieth century went on New York undoubtedly became a more "American" city. The flood of new immigrants is once again transforming the city. The city agency responsible for keeping tabs on the changing demography of New York is the seven-person population division of the Department of City Planning, with its chief demographer Joseph J. Salvo. It is upon the Population Division's work that city agencies can address the planning implications of a sharp rise in immigration to New York, and the changing composition of the foreign-born population. If the estimated fertility rates are misjudged, there may be overcrowding in city schools. Estimates of population changes in turn enable the planned provision of maternal healthcare and related services in immigrant communities.

In the decade of the 1990s a million foreigners came to New York, mainly from the Caribbean, Central America, and Asia. (The immigrants of 1910 came from Italy, Russia, and Eastern Europe.) Half the population in the Bronx describes itself as Hispanic. The Asian population in the city has risen from seven to ten percent of the total population over the 1990s. The African-American population remained at a steady ten percent. The Indian population in Queens, largely in Jackson Heights, Elmhurst, and Richmond Hill, nearly doubled to 109,114 in the 1990s. Chinese Americans in Sunset Park (known in Cantonese as "Bat Dai Do," or a more prosaic "Eighth Avenue") and Sheepshead Bay in Brooklyn grew by 77 percent to 120,662. Five mosques have opened in Astoria. The traditional dominance of Puerto Ricans within the Hispanic community and Chinese in the Asian immigrant community has declined as new streams of immigrants arrive from the Dominican Republic and Korea. Hispanics have displaced African Americans as the largest minority group. At more than two millions, the Hispanic population in New York is the largest and most diverse of any American city. With each successive wave of immigrants (Irish, German, Jewish, Italian) the city was remade. The Asian and Hispanic migration of the 1990s will have a similar impact.

In the 1980s and 1990s, the city's immigrant communities made a striking political discovery about themselves. For all their diversity, in America they were seen in the wider society as "ethnics." The separate nationalities (which contained within themselves strong regional and urban-rural divisions) found that they could best function within New York as part of the ethnic politics of the city. Distinct subgroups composed of Asians, Caribbeans, Latinos, Hispanics (the terms were highly fluid) asserted ethnicity as a powerful way to preserve a solidarity that was, in a highly complex urban society, historically something new. As distinct nationalities, they were politically isolated. As Caribbean or Asian ethnics they were empowered. The political leaders, who had been happy to connive at the exclusion of "minorities" from patronage and power, had to take them into account. But the coalition-building that led in 1989 to the election of the city's first black mayor, David Dinkins, fell apart under the weight of racial tension and spiraling crime problems. With the failure of traditional power-brokering routines and no obvious solutions to the city's disorders, the way was open in 1993 for a candidate, Rudy Giuliani, to run full-tilt against the ethnic "mosaic" that brought Dinkins to power.

Unlike California and the Sunbelt states over the past decade, New York failed to attract significant inward migration from elsewhere in the United States. That may be influenced by the way New York, and New

Yorkers, are perceived across the nation (which until the past decade had about it an edge of hostility, which self-satisfied New Yorkers are happy to call envy), and also by the kinds of economic opportunities that were available. The famous Saul Steinberg *New Yorker* cover, with the view from the city out on an empty, uninteresting continent, says it all. Assuming that they are admired, that every superstar wants to play for the Yankees, New Yorkers are sometimes surprised when they learn that they are regarded with suspicion and dislike. "New York is not America," goes the conventional wisdom. In this case, the conventional wisdom is still persuasive.

New York is a city chock-a-block with good stories. The best among these are the epic tales of families: how we knew hard times in the old world or our little village, how we came to America, how we struggled in New York, learned a difficult language, and in time how we made a life for all of us. These family stories of arrival and adaptation are the feel-good narratives of successive generations of New Yorkers. The problem is that "we" is a tribal usage: for all that it celebrates the idea of community, it also narrows and excludes. The warm acknowledgment of diversity is a central element in contemporary democratic life. The wonders of "diversity" sometimes serve to obscure the enduring suspicions, fears, and bigotries at the heart of the way "we" feel about "them." If the idea of social and racial diversity expresses the idealistic aspirations of contemporary New York, it also reminds us that there are social and political alternatives around. Prejudice, nativism, paranoia, and demagoguery are as true to aspects of the spirit of New York as reasonableness and tolerance. And when matters of race are considered, the city takes second place to few other northern urban areas in the urgency of its high-minded liberalism, and the tenacity and rich variety of its hatreds.

Immigration is perhaps the greatest of all the ideas that serve to unite New Yorkers. Ellis Island, where so many immigrants arrived; the Lower East Side, where so many immigrants began their experience of American life; and above all, the great symbol of immigration, the Statue of Liberty—these set New York distinctively apart as the immigrant's city.

The Statue of Liberty

It is the second stanza of the sonnet that caught the eye of contemporaries, and in particular the few oracular words the poet puts in the mouth of a giant statue of a "mighty woman":

THE NEW COLOSSUS

Not like the brazen giant of Greek fame,
With conquering limbs astride from land to land;
Here at our sea-washed sunset gates shall stand
A mighty woman with a torch, whose flame
Is the imprisoned lightning, and her name
Mother of Exiles. From her beacon-hand
Glows world-wide welcome; her mild eyes command
The air-bridged harbor that twin cities frame.

"Keep ancient lands, your storied pomp!" cries she
With silent lips. "Give me your tired, your poor,
Your huddled masses yearning to breathe free,
The wretched refuse of your teeming shore.
Send these, the homeless, tempest-tost to me,
I lift my lamp beside the golden door."

Emma Lazarus

Bartholdi's statue and Emma Lazarus' poem are connected. Visitors to the statue will find the text of the poem on a plaque. It is official: the poem and the statue carry the same meaning. The most memorable lines of the poem, and the gesture of Bartholdi's female embodiment of the spirit of the Enlightenment, convey a message of welcome and uplift to the immigrant. The history of the poem, which was written several years before the statue was unveiled in New York harbor, and while it was only known from photographs taken in the Parisian factory where it was fabricated and assembled, is a fascinating example of the cultural kidnap of a visual object. So successful has the appropriation been that scarcely anyone notices that the poem provides quite a different spin upon the statue.

The French sculptor Bartholdi had brought the idea of a statue celebrating American independence with him on a visit to the United

States in 1871. Emanating from a circle of liberal French aristocrats and politicians, the statue (titled "Liberty Enlightening the World") was conceived as a gift from the people of France to the Americans in celebration of the achievement of independence. The role of the French in the battle of Yorktown and the deep affection Americans had long felt for the French patriots and soldiers, especially Lafayette and Rochambeau, who had fought on the side of the Americans, also served a project of French republicanism and liberalism. Hoping to forge a different kind of political regime from the "Empire" of Louis Napoleon, which had collapsed on the battlefield at Sedan in 1870, and which would be explicitly distanced from the social conflict and radicalism of the Paris Commune, there was a hope behind the gift of "Liberty" to the US to associate France ever more firmly with the American tradition of moderate republican and democratic government.

Carrying letters of introduction to American politicians, writers and public figures, Bartholdi paid calls upon President Grant, who received the young Frenchman politely but declined to support the project. He met with a more enthusiastic reception from Horace Greeley, editor of the New York *Tribune*, and Peter Cooper, one of the city's leading supporters of any and all projects for civic improvement. When the French fundraising campaign was formally launched in 1875, support came from the president of the French Republic and a broad swathe of public opinion. Gala performances were held at the Paris Opéra to raise funds for the statue. On the American side, the call for funds to build the pedestal was soon caught up in domestic politics. If Greeley (who had been the unsuccessful Democratic candidate for president in 1872) had supported the idea, the *New York Times*, a conservative and aggressively Republican rival newspaper, was quick to express doubts. It was sourly suggested that since it was a French statue in the first place, the French had better pay for the pedestal.

Bartholdi was tireless in promoting the project. The torch-bearing hand had been put on display at the Centennial Exhibition in Philadelphia in 1876 and in Madison Square, where visitors could climb inside the structure for 50¢, but nothing further had happened. To raise the funds needed for the pedestal and spur greater interest in New York, "The American Committee on the Statue of Liberty" was formed in 1877 by members of the Century Association, a leading New York gentleman's club known for its cultural interests.

New York's socialites rallied to the cause, supporting benefit performances at the Academy of Music, but fundraising elsewhere among the wealthy showed little dynamism. None of the city's millionaires was prepared to reach into his pocket for the $100,000 that was needed. When Congress rejected an appropriation bill in March 1883, the American fundraising scheme looked on the verge of collapse. "The New Colossus" was written in November 1883 at the request of Mrs. Burton Harrison, novelist and society hostess, who solicited manuscripts from writers for a charity auction in aid of the Bartholdi Pedestal Fund. Longfellow, Twain, and Walt Whitman were also invited to provide manuscripts for the sale. The French, with support from a lottery, seemed far more interested in the project.

Joseph Pulitzer, a baptized Hungarian Jew who emigrated to America in the 1860s and had prospered as a newspaper editor and proprietor in St. Louis, came to New York in 1883, where he bought the *World*. Among his first campaigns was the placing of the Bartholdi

Pedestal Fund on the front page of his paper. If the rich to the "irrevocable disgrace" of New York failed to support Liberty, Pulitzer was certain that the plain people would make the needed response to the magnificent French gift. In the face of sniping from the city's other papers, and the refusal of support from the federal government, the state government, and the city of New York, Pulitzer's first campaign petered out. The cornerstone was laid on Bedloe's Island in 1884, after which the money dried up and work was ordered to stop. Elite leaders in other cities, sensing an opportunity, began to campaign for Liberty to be erected in Philadelphia, Boston, or San Francisco.

In the midst of the acrimonious and sometimes bitter polemics over the French gift, Lazarus at first doubted that she had anything to say about the statue. Mrs. Harrison reminded her friend of their recent discussions about newly arrived Russian immigrants whom Lazarus had visited on Ward's Island (in the East River, now re-named Roosevelt Island). The assassination of Czar Alexander II in 1881, an attack on the Jews of Elizavetgrad that triggered off pogroms across the Russian Empire, and the notorious "May Laws" of 1882, which restricted Jewish business activity, mobility, and rights of residence, launched hundreds and then thousands of Russian Jews toward the United States. Lazarus had been moved by their desperate plight, and hoped to do something about it. She saw the connection between the statue, conceived by the French as a symbolic expression of the triumph of enlightenment over ignorance, with the plight of the Russian Jews. "The New Colossus" was soon forthcoming. James Russell Lowell wrote to Lazarus: "I liked your sonnet about the Statue much better than I like the Statue itself. But your sonnet gives its subject a *raison d'être* which it wanted before quite as much as it wanted a pedestal." What she had actually done was to appropriate the French gift to the plight of Russian Jews.

Lazarus was a new, rather exotic kind of figure in the cultural life of New York. Her father was a sugar manufacturer who belonged to the small, exclusive Sephardic Jewish community of New York. Well-assimilated into the ways of the city's upper class, Moses Lazarus was a founder-member of the Knickerbocker Club, and the family took their summers at Newport. Privately educated, Emma Lazarus received literary encouragement from Emerson. His portrait had a revered place on Lazarus' mantelpiece. Her first volume of verse, *Poems and Translations* (1867), appeared when she was only eighteen. It was followed by further volumes of verse, a novel on the life of Goethe, and translations from Heine. After the outbreak of pogroms in Russia, Lazarus wrote a poetic drama, "The Dance of Death," in her volume *Songs of a Semite* (1882) which, through a portrayal of the plight of twelfth-century Thuringian Jews, was an impassioned response to the pogroms in Russia. Not herself particularly religious, Lazarus was nonetheless intensely moved by the human tragedy of the refugees. "I shall always be loyal to my race," she explained, "but I feel no religious fervor in my soul."

"The New Colossus" was printed in Mrs. Burton Harrison's program, read at the gala opening, and reprinted several times—and then largely forgotten. A further campaign was needed by Pulitzer in 1885 to raise the funds to complete the pedestal. Pulitzer could claim responsibility for the erection of Liberty, where the city's traditional elites had hung back. Determined to keep the memory of his own role fresh in the minds of New Yorkers, he incorporated the figure of Liberty into a redesigned banner for the *World*. When the statue was unveiled in the next year, amidst enthusiastic public ceremonies (300 ships accompanied President Grover Cleveland to Bedloe's Island for the unveiling), Lazarus' poem played no role. Nor was her concern for immigrants much on anyone's mind at the dedication. President Cleveland fully accepted the French meaning of the statue, anticipating that Liberty's torch—an instrument of light and, in the aftermath of the Paris Commune, carrying no hint of incendiary threat—would send forth "a stream of light" to "pierce the darkness of ignorance and man's oppression until Liberty enlightens the world." Thomas Alva Edison, as ever creative with publicity stunts for his latest invention, proposed installing a phonograph in the mouth of Liberty, enabling the statue to speak welcoming words to ships in the harbor.

Bartholdi took his place inside Liberty's crown, and was to release the French flag that covered the statue's face when the speeches were concluded. William Evarts, chairman of The American Committee on the Statue of Liberty, paused in mid-discourse and Bartholdi, misinterpreting the lawyer's pace, released the flag. The public cheered, horns were sounded by ships in the harbor, church bells rang out—and the hapless Evarts could only wait till the next day when his address was printed in full in the city's newspapers. Above the proud words, noise, the clouds of steam and the flags, listless on a wet, foggy afternoon, Liberty rose above the harbor. At 305 feet, she was the tallest structure in New York.

Every year about four million tourists visit Liberty Island and Ellis Island, and of that number perhaps 40 percent actually climb the 354 steps, or take the internal elevator, to view the harbor from Liberty's crown. The view of the city's skyline from Liberty is spectacular. The statue received a $66 million restoration in 1983–6, which included the installation of a new torch, a thorough scrubbing to remove bird droppings, and repairs to the inevitable damage to the thin copper skin of the statue. Workmen found that there were holes as large as five inches in diameter in the skin, and rivets, holding together the 300 pieces of metal that form the statue, had worked loose. The technique of *repoussé*, or pounding metal into intricate shapes, had died out in America, and French *repousseurs* from Reims gilded the new torch—and decided to stay in America, where they hoped to find more work.

Both installations, administered by the National Park Service, were closed to the public on September 11. Access to the island was restored for the Christmas holiday, with security screening carried out before boarding the ferries that dock at the Battery and those which sail from Liberty State Park in New Jersey. But Liberty remains, for the time, closed—another victim of the attack on the World Trade Center.

After her death in 1887, Lazarus' reputation as a writer and spokesperson for the Jewish community was largely forgotten, and it was only in 1903 that a plaque bearing her poem was affixed to the statue. "Liberty" was adopted as an unofficial national symbol, eclipsing "Uncle Sam" during the First World War. One half of the cost of the war was funded by the sale of Liberty bonds. It was at the 50th birthday celebrations of the unveiling in 1936 that President Franklin D. Roosevelt completed the linkage between Liberty and the immigrant. With the language that has become second nature for Democratic Party politicians, Roosevelt said the Liberty had become the symbol of American freedoms and beacon of liberty—freedom to worship, freedom of thought, and freedom of opportunity. It was the heritage of hope that brought the immigrants to the land of freedom.

But that was part of the official mythology of American life. "Liberty" speaks of welcome:

"Give me your tired, your poor,
Your huddled masses yearning to breathe free,
The wretched refuse of your teeming shore.
Send these, the homeless, tempest-tost to me,
I lift my lamp beside the golden door."

But when the Commissioner General of Immigration, Frank P. Sargent, visited Ellis Island in 1905, he talked to a reporter from the *New York Times* about the threats posed by "an enormous alien population." "Put me down as being fairly and unalterably opposed to what has been called the open door," he remarked:

> *for the time has come when every American citizen who is ambitious for the national future must regard with grave misgiving the mighty tide of immigration that, unless something is done, will soon poison or at least pollute the very fountainhood of American life and progress. Big as we are and blessed with an iron constitution, we cannot safely swallow such an endless-course dinner, so to say, without getting indigestion and perhaps national appendicitis.*

Immigration, which has done so much to shape New York City, was at heart a traumatic and explosive social problem. Sepia-tinted memories only confuse the picture.

Ellis Island

By the late nineteenth century, the immigrants arriving in New York were neither greeted by ticker-tape parades nor by a warmly extended hand, but by a government official demanding to see their papers. Each arrival was accompanied by precious forms and documents, each carrying a compulsory official stamp, obtainable only at certain places and from certain officials, and for most there was a fee to be paid. When Eva and Haim Weisman made their "Alien's Declaration oath" at the American Consular Service in Bucharest, a $1 fee was charged. The proud nation states of Europe, and those still hoping to achieve independence, sent their citizens off to America wrapped in bureaucratic forms and pompous language: "We James McNeill, Esquire, Governor General of the Irish Free State, request and require, in the name of his Britannic Majesty..." (provided for Michael J. Saults in Ireland, 1929). Alice De Capitani arrived in New York in 1915 bearing with her an equally insistent text: "In Nome di sua Maestà Vittorio Emanuelle III, per grazia di Dio e voluntà della nazione Re D'Italia..." Before a ship to America could be boarded, a certificate of vaccination and delousing had to be provided. The old isolationist slogan of "Fortress America" took on a new meaning to a nation protecting itself against foreigners, and their diseases, through bureaucratic forms and increasingly restrictive legislation.

Between 1875 and 1927, when the "national origins" system was enshrined in American law (allowing a total permitted immigration of 150,000 per year, via quotas based on the 1920 census), the American government, led by an increasingly hostile public opinion, struggled to find effective ways to limit immigration. An older anti-Catholicism fueled the attack on immigrants from Italy and Sicily. The American Protective Association demanded stricter naturalization requirements. Henry Ford's *Dearborn Independent* blamed Wall Street and the Jews for economic hard times. The Ku Klux Klan joined in the attack upon illiterate Catholics and Jews flooding into the cities. The American Federation of Labor demanded literacy tests to restrict the immigration of unskilled labor. *The Passing of the Great Race* by Madison Grant, published in 1916, warned that the pioneering Nordic peoples were in danger of being swamped by inferior racial stock. Grant called for the segregation of races to avert impending disaster. The enthusiasm of Tom Buchanan in F. Scott Fitzgerald's *The Great Gatsby* for the (fictional) book by Goddard, *The Rise of the Colored Empires,* neatly captured Madison Grant's form of American racial hysteria and racism. A Harvard-educated poet in 1919 labeled a singularly unattractive personage in one of his poems, as one might mark a creature in a zoo, "Chicago Semite Viennese." Across the nation prejudice against foreigners and racism were truly as American as apple pie.

The anti-immigrant campaigning achieved one success after another. Convicts, prostitutes, and coolies were barred in 1875. Lunatics and idiots were excluded in 1882, and Chinese immigration sharply curtailed. Contract laborers, paupers, polygamists, epileptics, beggars, anarchists, the tubercular, those with physical or mental defects, and unaccompanied children under sixteen were banned in the two decades before the First World War. A literary test was established in 1917. In the early 1920s, on top of the wide-ranging exclusions, even narrower quotas were imposed. The Johnson-Reed Act of 1924 served (among other effects) to reduce the quota for Italians from the 42,057 set by the 1921 act to 3,845. The new "national origins" quota system established by the Act, which came into effect in 1929, were strengthened by the McCarran-Walter Act of 1952 and remained in force until the passage of the Hart-Celler Act in 1965. Johnson-Reed had a sinister purpose to permanently fix the nation's ethnic and racial mix.

For a nation like the United States, quick today to celebrate its diversity and proud tolerance, the history of immigration legislation is sobering. Within living memory the legally enforced structure of racial segregation in the South, whose spirit pervaded hotels, apartment buildings, restaurants, nightclubs, golf clubs, and suburbs across the nation and persisted into the 1970s, might have bolstered an argument that the US contained many of the elements of a "race state" disturbingly akin to Nazi Germany or South Africa. Outside of the American left, such an argument would be scorned for its lack of balance, its tendentiousness. But as a visitor walks through the Ellis Island National Monument (take the Circle Line-Statue of Liberty Ferry—tickets are $8—from Battery Park, and plan to visit early in the day: by late morning the lines for the ferry are daunting, and when both attractions reopened for the public at Christmas, 2001, there were rigorous security checks involving the use of body scanners), maintained as "a symbol of America's immigrant heritage" by the National Parks Service of the US Department of the Interior, some less celebratory thoughts seem appropriate.

The Ellis Island Museum is worth visiting during school vacations. The hordes of children running between "graphic displays" and tearing through galleries filled with "artifacts, historic photos, posters, maps" allow adults no quiet contemplation, which is appropriate (if distracting), for this is a museum conceived uniquely as a tribute to the experience of ordinary people, with ordinary noisy children. The Ellis Island exhibits are a calculatedly poignant record of American immigration. Many of the objects on display have been donated to the museum by the immigrants themselves and their families. From display to display, the fragmentary records of a life may be traced. "This is evidence that Anthony Rando," begins a certificate issued by the Commonwealth of Massachusetts in 1927, "has attended regularly an Intermediate Course in English for American Citizenship." In the next room, amid the display of naturalization documents, is the confirmation that Anthony Rando was 24 years old, 5'8" tall, had dark hair, brown eyes and was living in Marlboro, Massachusetts, at the time of his naturalization. (Control of naturalization was assumed by the federal government in 1906. Requirement for naturalization was residence of five years, and a knowledge of the English language, American history, and civics.) The display of sheet music (from "Yes! We Have No Bananas" in the comic-Italian mode, to "Since Ma is Playing Mah Jong," Eddie Cantor's tribute to the vogue for the Chinese board game) is a reminder of the pervasiveness of the immigrant in American popular culture. It is a tribute to the integrity of the museum and its curators that the history of racist and ethnic hostility to immigrants, expressed in anti-immigrant cartoons, is not swept under the carpet.

In 2001 an interactive American Family Immigration History Center was established on Ellis Island to enable individuals interested in family history and genealogy to research a vast database of immigration records, passenger lists, ships' manifests and related archives of immigrants who arrived at Ellis Island from 1892 to 1924. The Center maintains a website (www.ellisisland.org), which is fully searchable.

From 1892 when it replaced Castle Garden, until 1924, when the National Origins Act transferred inspection of immigrants to their homeland, Ellis Island was the primary reception and inspection site for immigrants to the United States. Originally a three-acre mud sand-bank known as Gull Island, it has been re-named and expanded by landfill to 272 acres. Before 1924, more than 70 percent of all immigrants to America, some twelve million people, passed through Ellis Island. Steerage class passengers alone were ferried directly from ships anchored in the harbor and from Hudson River piers to Ellis Island for medical and legal processing. First- and second-class passengers were processed in the more comfortable conditions on board ship.

The present Ellis Island Museum occupies a large brick and stone building, opened in 1900, replacing a wooden structure that had burned down. The chief immigrant receiving facility of the United States served as hospital, hotel, prison, and transport station, and gave an interesting introduction to American values: Abraham Cahan, welcoming the new structure in the New York *Commercial Advertiser*, noted that it was designed

> *in the style of modern renaissance and looks like a huge railroad station or exposition building, built with a view to making it absolutely sanitary. There is plenty of room and air in every part of the structure, and it is amply equipped not only with ventilating and disinfecting contrivances, but also with bath accommodation for 500 persons... Among the innovations are dormitories, with regular beds and mattresses, and no immigrant is to be allowed to use Uncle Sam's bedding without first taking a bath.*
>
> *The first impression of the immigrant who must wait overnight for his friends' address or a railroad ticket, will be that this is a country of soap and hot water.*

Doctors employed by the United States Public Health Service examined the face, neck, hands and physical condition of each immigrant. Were there signs of heart trouble, or mental illness? Signs of moral degradation? Trachoma was the cause for more than half of all medical detentions on Ellis Island. Through a translator the immigrants were asked their name and age. Were they able to understand? Immigrants were asked 29 questions, and the "wrong" answer could provide grounds for denial of permission to enter.

> *Who paid for your fare?*
> *Do you have a job waiting for you?*
> *Is anyone meeting you?*
> *Where are you going?*
> *How much money do you have?*
> *Where did you get it?*

This was the harsh poetry of survival for immigrants on Ellis Island.

The questions confused and intimidated the immigrants, already deeply anxious at the noisy, crowded conditions in the main hall, and fearful that if they told the wrong story they would be returned to Europe. Answers were changed and retracted, elaborate explanations offered. Hands reached for purses containing a handful of silver and copper coins counted and re-counted on the long journey to Ellis Island. For most, after the ordeal, there was joy: a landing card, permission to enter the United States.

They might encounter on arrival an American photographer, Lewis Hine, who had come to New York in 1901 to teach botany at the Ethical Culture School. (Diane Arbus was a student at the same school in the late 1930s.) Hine began to take an interest in photography in 1903, when he organized a camera club for his students, one of whom was Paul Strand. Hine was drawn to the world of the tenement, sweatshop, Lower East Side, and the "cockroach" manufacturers and their employers. He had studied at the University of Chicago, home of the first sociology department in America and a leading center for the study of urban life, and felt a strong affinity with the workers in Social Settlements and researchers then scrutinizing the slums. Hine took pictures for the Charity Organization Society in New York, and became staff photographer for a magazine about charitable work in slums. From 1906 to 1918, he was investigator/cameraman for the National Child Labor Committee. He shared the reform aspirations of the progressive movement, but approached the question of how to take photographs of immigrants and tenement-dwellers with a cool, detached and objective eye. Working at the heyday of pictorialist "art" photography, when impressionistic lighting and effects copied directly from painting and sculpture were in vogue, Hine's aim was educational rather than aesthetic or propagandistic. He hoped to arouse and enhance sympathy, and was happy to call his photos "human documents." Hine's "Armenian Jew," taken on Ellis Island in 1924, is a simple photo of a well-dressed man, perhaps in his twenties or thirties. He is wearing a tie, an overcoat and a felt hat, and looks impassively at the photographer. You can catch a hint of the photographer reflected from the subject's cornea. The photo "works" because Hine has stripped away all the arguments that in the 1920s were swirling around the subject of immigration, and lets the (unnamed) subject, his dark

beard and handsome dark eyes, directly address the public. He had been taking photographs like that for more than a decade, allowing the immigrants' humanity to speak in a way that the public debate about American policy had obscured. His are among the most important photographic portraits of the twentieth century.

The island reverted to US army control in 1918–19, when it was used as a hospital ward. During the Second World War it served as a detention center for enemy aliens. Effectively abandoned after the war, the building was closed in 1954 and the deserted and derelict facility was placed under the care of the National Park Service, along with the Statue of Liberty. A Supreme Court decision ruled in 1998 that Ellis Island was mostly the territory of New Jersey. A proposal to preserve the decaying main building and convert the facility for use as a museum emerged in 1952.

Work has also begun on the 30 decaying structures on the south side of Ellis Island, abandoned since 1954. The 250,000 immigrants who needed medical care, or who had been declared insane, or in other ways were marked as unsuitable for entry, were housed in hospital wards and quarantine areas. The National Park Service, responsible for the restoration, will probably use the structures for a conference center for the study of immigration or public health. The main building of the museum has been brilliantly restored to its condition in 1918–24, with the spectacular 60-foot high Guastavino ceramic tile ceiling preserved in the Registry Room. Ellis Island today is one of the necessary stops on any visit to the city.

The Lower East Side

The Lower East Side—south of Houston Street, east of the Bowery, and bounded by the East River—has been for a century and a half a populous working-class district. The Lower East Side became a symbol of urban decay in the nineteenth century, an object of repeated study and investigation, and a target for evangelical crusades, reforming politicians and town planners. As a "problem" district, the inhabitants of the Lower East Side, whether Irish Catholics or Protestant working class, German or Eastern European, Jewish or *Latino*, came to the attention of urban crusaders, the police, journalists, novelists, settlement workers, and do-gooders beyond number. In sermons and editorials, the Lower East Side came to stand for everything that was wrong with urban life in New York. It also possessed a primary symbolic meaning as the site of the immigrant experience itself, where hundreds of thousands of immigrants first encountered American life.

When did the Lower East Side become the Lower East Side? Jacob Riis in *How the Other Half Lives* (1890), which is perhaps the most important single journalistic account of the district, suggests that in the early nineteenth century there were "decorous homes of the old Knickerbockers" lining these streets. The term "Knickerbocker" came into widespread use in New York in the early nineteenth century. Named after the fictional chronicler of Washington Irving's *History of New York*, published in 1809, the Knickerbockers were of Dutch ancestry and distinctly worldly temperaments. Their rivals were the "Yankees," recent arrivals from New England noted for their business acumen and Presbyterian sobriety. The fall from this Eden was precipitated not by sin or cosmic disobedience, but by the flood of immigrants who arrived in the city after the War of 1812. Population growth of New York strained every institution and every aspect of the fabric of the city as the numbers mounted:

1820	*123,706*
1830	*202,589*
1840	*312,710*
1850	*515,547*
1860	*813,669*

The "old residents" moved in increasing numbers to Bleecker Street, Washington Square, and Fifth Avenue, salubrious streets far from the immigrant population. "Their comfortable dwellings," wrote Riis, "in the once fashionable streets along the East River front fell into the hands of real-estate agents and boarding-house keepers." Residences, which before 1850 had housed a single family, were converted to multiple occupancy and called "tenant-houses." Where six or eight people had lived there might now be twelve or fifteen. And then twenty, as boarders were admitted. Private homes when converted into tenant-houses showed remarkably high levels of return upon invested capital. The owners of real estate and real estate agents saw an opportunity, and began constructing larger and larger structures—called tenements—to house the expanding population.

The worst of these was certainly a five-story structure called Gotham Court, containing 126 small two-room apartments at 36–38 Cherry Street. It is the location today of Gov. Alfred E. Smith Houses. Demolished in 1896, Gotham Court was notorious for its filthy and degraded state. Whenever social investigators wanted an example of everything that was wrong with tenements, they pointed to Gotham Court. In 1865 one resident out of three suffered from serious illnesses. One infant out of three died before the age of one. The appearance of the inhabitants was shocking. "To the unaccustomed eye," wrote a physician inspecting the sanitary condition of Gotham Court, "it is a sad and striking spectacle to witness the attenuated forms, the sunken eyes, the pinched and withered faces of the little patients, young in years but old in suffering, who are the prey of infantile marasmus. A glance is sufficient to designate this as one of the ghostly janitors, ever ready to open wide the gate which leads to early death."

Into the tenements of the Lower East Side came immigrants from Ireland, Germany and then from Eastern Europe. By 1890, there were 640,000 foreign-born residents in New York City. The population was composed of roughly equal slices: of Irish (30 percent), Germans (33 percent), and the remainder from the Austro-Hungarian Empire, Russia, Italy, England, and "other." Each wave of national immigration tended to settle in neighborhoods where the newcomers found their fellow-countrymen and the familiar churches, saloons, theaters, and stores.

Imagine the scene: it is Rivington Street in the Lower East Side, in 1905. Moscowitz's wine bar occupies a narrow basement lit with gas lamps. Mirrors line the walls on which an amateur artist has painted scenes from peasant life in Romania. Amidst the tied sheaves of wheat, and sunlit fields is a horse fair and a rural wedding. Strings of dried peppers hang in the traditional manner from nails in the walls. The Rivington Street wine bar, crowded at the end of the day with family parties seated at long tables covered in oilcloth, is highly popular with Romanian immigrants. The air is blue with cigar smoke, and everyone is talking in Yiddish, English, and Romanian with animation and laughter. The customers, bearded men wearing derby hats, enjoy themselves without the raised voices or the edge of drunkenness common (they are sure) to Irish bars in the city. At the end of the room two flags are displayed. An American flag is draped across a framed color chromolithograph of Teddy Roosevelt charging up San Juan Hill at the head of the Rough Riders. On a framed portrait of Dr. Theodore Herzl, leader of the Zionist movement, the flag (blue and white bars with a Star of David) of the Zionist movement neatly creates a dual symmetrical focus for the patriotic customers of Moscowitz's.

The scene at Moscowitz's appears in Michael Gold's autobiography *Jews Without Money* (1930). Gold's book is rich in the everyday details of New York immigrant life. Along with Abraham Cahan's *The Rise of David Levinsky* (1917) and Henry Roth's *Call It Sleep* (1934), Gold's book was among the first to make serious artistic claims on behalf of immigrants and ethnic minority groups. Among the customers at Moscowitz's was Mikey, the young hero of Gold's story, his father Herman, a house painter, and the vest maker Mottke, an old family friend. "Pop, I like this place," said Mikey. "Is he smart?" chuckles Herman Gold. "Is this boy smart, or no?" Mottke agrees: "He will be at least a millionaire." "No," father objects. The little boy must become a doctor. "Learning is more precious than wealth." Gold had joined the Communist Party in the 1920s, and had little patience with the Old World pieties of his father. In families where there is no wealth, there is no chance to study medicine either. Herman and Mottke at the wine bar on Rivington Street were performing roles in a sad, gentle comedy entitled Jews without money.

Rivington Street, running eastward from the Bowery to Pitt Street two blocks south of East Houston, was at the heart of the congested "Little Romania" on the Lower East Side. The Romanian presence was marked by kosher restaurants, a matzo baker (Streit's, precariously surviving at 150 Rivington), a kosher winery (Schapiro's, at 126 Rivington, has just closed, after a century in the wine-making business), *kazín* (coffee-houses), pastry-shops and, everywhere, Romanian immigrants crowding into the local tenements. Theirs was a world—lovingly re-imagined in Meredith Tax's historical novel *Rivington Street* (1982)—where a nickel went a long way:

> *"You call that thing a herring?" she said, poking it. "My daughter looks more like a herring than that. How much?"*
>
> *"Your daughter should only have such bright eyes! And look at all that roe—your daughter should only be so fertile. Five cents only and it's killing me, these prices, but I'm a generous man no matter how my family suffers for it."*
>
> *"Three cents," said Hannah* [Levy, the cigar maker's wife].
>
> *"You want me to starve my children? You want we should be thrown into the street?...*
>
> *"You don't want to sell, I don't have to buy." Hannah calmly wrapped her shawl around her as if to leave.*
>
> *"Four cents."*
>
> *"Two for six cents, the one with the roe and that little piece of nothing over there."*
>
> *"All right," he said, conceding defeat cheerfully enough now that the sport was over. "For you I'll make a sacrifice, two for six cents, only don't tell anybody..."*

Importance on Rivington Street was either religious or commercial, and the local stores were every bit as ethnically distinctive as the synagogues. The buildings sometimes carried memories of an earlier life on Rivington Street, and other religions. The Roumaniashe Shul, organized in 1885, occupied a former Methodist church at 89 Rivington. The building was in turn sold to Shaaray Shomayim, an orthodox synagogue famous on the Lower East Side for the outstanding musical quality of its cantors. At 58 Rivington the Congregation Adath Jeshurun of Jassy was opened in 1903. When

Adath Jeshurun moved out of the Lower East Side, the structure (whose "magnificent eclectic façade" was praised by White and Willensky in *The AIA Guide to New York City*) was occupied by the First Warsaw Congregation. When that small religious community disbanded, the building was purchased by an artist for use as a studio. Today on Rivington Street the Tasty Munchees Pizzeria stands next door to the Aliz Restaurant International Foods.

Across the city there were similar saloons, small restaurants, large "Gardens" and one-room tenement bars, each with a distinctive ethnic identity, each reflecting a component of the city's extraordinary ethnic, racial and cultural diversity. The paired flags of the United States and the Zionist movement, the patriotic "chromo" of the heroic Roosevelt and the intensely admired Herzl, were signs on Rivington Street of the hybrid nature of immigrant identity. Elsewhere, the flags of Italy, Germany, or Poland might decorate similar wine bars. Instead of a framed Herzl, there might be an engraving of Cardinal McCloskey, Garibaldi, or Bismarck. The Prussian victory over France in 1870 was wildly cheered in "Kleindeutschland," the German immigrant area in the Lower East Side. The Kishinev massacre in 1903 and the defeat of the 1905 revolution in Russia were mourned in the same area of the city by the hundreds of thousands of Jewish immigrants who fled the pogroms, discrimination, and cruel poverty of the Russian Empire. The Bund, a Jewish socialist party in Russia, was in effect funded by the donations of Jewish workers on the Lower East Side. Community leaders had to be adept at managing the dual loyalties of the immigrant community. A figure like the labor lawyer Meyer London, counsel to the International Ladies' Garment Workers' Union, was also a leading fund-raiser and campaigner on behalf of the Bund in Russia.

Hyphenated Americans, so familiar in politically correct usage today, pronounced their fervent loyalty to their new home in America while at the same time celebrating their Jewishness, Germanness, Polishness. Others, for whom the nation state was an abstraction, might identify more strongly with regional and provincial identities and festivals. In addition to the usual "American" holidays, Chinese New Year, St. Patrick's Day, Greek Independence Day, India Day, Mexican Day, Dominican Day, the Feast of San Gennaro and a dozen other national days are celebrated in New York with parades, street fairs and processions. New York is a city in which identities, patriotisms, and loyalties were always complex.

The Lower East Side is today more than a museum, or mausoleum, of that immigrant life. Successive inhabitants have left traces of their lives and social institutions. The German Winter Garden at 45 Bowery (demolished) and its near neighbor, the Atlantic Garden at 50 Bowery (demolished) were important institutions of Little Germany ("Kleindeutschland"), south of East 14th Street, and east of the Bowery, settled by German immigrants in the middle of the nineteenth century. The sheer Germanness of life in Little Germany startled contemporaries. "There is not a single business which is not run by Germans," noted a visitor from Germany in 1863.

> *Not only shoemakers, tailors, barbers, physicians, grocers, and innkeepers are German, but the pastors and priests as well. There is even a German lending library where one can get all kinds of German books. The resident of Kleindeutschland need not even know English in order to make a living, which is a considerable attraction to the immigrant.*

In 1880 there were over 500,000 German-Americans in New York. Nearly one New Yorker in three were either German-born, or the children of German immigrants. The social institutions of German New York set a pattern for successive waves of immigrants. The Germans were quick to establish the churches, foreign language newspapers, choral societies, political clubs and welfare associations that gave them an important social and economic presence in the city.

The industries located in the Lower East Side (from shipbuilding to cigar-rolling and slaughterhouses), and the rapid growth in population, made it an important commercial center. Merchants and bankers built handsome establishments, like the Italianate dry goods emporium opened by Lord & Taylor at 255–61 Grand Street, at the corner with Chrystie (demolished) for the booming trade on the east side. The most important surviving structure from the "old" commercial Lower East Side is the Home Savings of America at 130 Bowery, a stunning Classical Revival building designed by Stanford White for the Bowery Savings Bank in 1894. It was described by Robert A.M. Stern and his collaborators in *New York 1900* as "the first truly sumptuous bank in New York, [which] set a new standard of monumentality in bank design that was rarely equaled."

It is hard today to imagine the small street-corner *bodegas* and *carnicerias* as representing anything more than the marginal life of a declining neighborhood—a story that Bernard Malamud told in *The Assistant* (1957). But the rapidly expanding Asian population in Chinatown requires quite a different narrative than one of decline and demolition. (See the discussion of Chinatown in Chapter 6.) Yuppification has certainly begun, in the past decade, to attract younger white professionals who found themselves priced out of the West Village housing market. The Lower East Side is not today much of an attractive neighborhood, and access by public transportation from elsewhere in the city is restricted. There are few important cultural institutions to visit, but the resurrection of a discarded school building, P.S. 122 in the East Village, into Performance Space 122 suggests how creative the city has been in finding space for its arts community. Perhaps that is where the future of the Lower East Side is to be found.

Low rents, and a reputation for radicalism and bohemianism, made the East Village and Lower East Side attractive to the young writers who came to the city in the 1950s and 1960s. The "New York School" was built upon the relationships of a group of poets who had been friends at Harvard (Kenneth Koch, John Ashbery, and Frank O'Hara), and who found in New York the jobs (teaching at the New School), publishers (especially the Grove Press, publisher of O'Hara's *Meditations in an Emergency*, 1957, and Koch's *Ko: or, A Season on Earth*, 1959), periodicals (*Art News*), and art galleries sympathetic to the new writing. It seemed that everyone worked at the Museum of Modern Art. Tibor de Nagy published letterpress editions of work by O'Hara, James Schuyler, and Barbara Guest. The close links between modern art, at a particularly exciting time, and the emergence of a school of sharp, talented poets did much to create a distinctive New York tone.

The Lower East Side provided a home and a space for literary experiment in the 1960s of a kind that the Village had once provided. A second wave of poets, led by Ted Berrigan, who arrived in the city in 1960, and Ed Sanders, who came from Kansas in 1962, made the New York scene far more political and in tune with the radicalism that marked the second half of the decade. Little mimeographed poetry magazines like

Sanders' *Fuck You, a magazine of the arts* (1962) and Lorenz Gude's *"C"* (1963) were among the city's most iconoclastic voices. The Poetry Project at St. Mark's Church began in 1966, and *The Poetry Project Newsletter* followed in 1972. Berrigan, and his friends from Tulsa (who included Ron Padgett and Joe Brainerd), Clark Coolidge, Tom Clark, and Anne Waldman were followed in the 1970s by yet another generation of writers, small presses, and mimeographed magazines. Johnny Stanton's "newspaper," *Siamese Bananas,* with its ironic motto alluding to the *New York Times,* "If the Facts Don't Fit, Change Them," published Paul Auster's *A Little Anthology of Surrealist Poems* in 1972. The new poetry of New York was captured in defining anthologies like Allen DeLoach's *The East Side Scene: An Anthology of a Time and Place* (1968), John Bernard Myers' *The Poets of the New York School* (1969), Anne Waldman's *The World Anthology: Poems from the St. Mark's Poetry Project* (1969), and Ron Padgett's and David Shapiro's *An Anthology of New York Poets* (1970). They made writing in New York one of the great "scenes" in the nation.

Abraham Cahan and Isaac Bashevis Singer: Finding Voices for the Immigrant World

In a spirit of social exploring, take the F train downtown to East Broadway, the last stop before the train crosses the East River and begins the long run out to Coney Island. Coming out of the subway station, there is another New York to be encountered. It is poorer, more aggressively ethnic, in a sense more "foreign," and feels remote indeed from City Hall, St. Paul's Chapel, and Wall Street. It is also a place where an attentive eye can find many traces of the past, and of the changing present. Chinatown has reached here, too.

At the far end of East Broadway, where it intersects with Grand Street, is the East Side Mikveh. Tell-tale initials on 313 East Broadway reveal that the building, erected in 1904, once housed Arnold Toynbee Hall, a settlement house named in honor of an Oxford student who devoted himself to the cause of improving the lot of the immigrant masses in the East End of London. Volunteer and resident social workers at social settlements like Arnold Toynbee Hall provided educational facilities to the immigrant poor who a century ago made East Broadway a teeming commercial artery. The rise of state-provided social services, and the decline in population in the Lower East Side, accelerated by slum and tenement clearance, deprived settlement houses of much of their clientele. The settlement was closed, the building sold to a benevolent association and then put to use as a mikveh, a "ritualarium," a place of ritual bathing for orthodox Jewish women. Despite the provision of running water and in-door plumbing in tenements, cleanliness alone was not the point of the mikveh. It was a facility intended for acts of ritual cleansing, obligatory for women at the end of their menstruation and as a compulsory event in the preparations for an orthodox Jewish marriage.

Along the southern side of East Broadway are a sampling of the remaining communal institutions of the immigrant world of the Lower East Side. Except for the Bialystoker Home for the Aged at 228 East Broadway, virtually the whole of the northern side of the street has been razed to make room for the large apartment blocks of the Seward Park Co-Ops. "Shteeble Row" (small synagogues sharing rooms in a row of tenements) is at 225–283. The large home of the Educational Alliance occupies 197. Nearby, the Jewish Daily Forward Building is at 175 (currently being reconstructed); the site of the Garden Cafeteria, now a Chinese restaurant, is at 165 (where Leon Trotsky and Isaac Bashevis Singer were once customers); and Mesifta Tifereth Jerusalem, one of the last remaining orthodox religious schools or yeshivas is at 145. It was at a room above Garrett Berlyn's saloon at 46 East Broadway (long vanished) where Local 15 of the Cigar Makers' Union regularly met, and where Samuel Gompers began his long career in the American trade union movement. At its peak, the weekly attendance at the Alliance was 37,000.

The Forward (more properly in Yiddish, "Forverts"), edited for many years by its Russian-Jewish editor Abraham Cahan, was the largest and most popular of the vibrant Yiddish newspapers published on the Lower East Side. It once had a daily circulation of 250,000. Cahan—who can stand for many immigrant and ethnic leaders who rose to prominence on the Lower East Side—made a name for himself as a writer of mildly ironic tales of immigrant life. His stories attracted the attention of William Dean Howells, always on the prowl for signs of a new realistic spirit among younger American writers. Cahan's *Yekl*, published in 1896, was enthusiastically welcomed by Howells as the first novel in English about the immigrant city to have been written by an immigrant. Cahan's *The Rise of David Levinsky* (1917) was a larger-scale portrait of the ambiguities and human costs of assimilation. A sharp observer of the ironies of assimilation, the insights Cahan possessed into the inner life of the immigrant enabled him to speak with authority to American readers. When Lincoln Steffens was appointed city editor of the *New York Commercial Advertiser* in 1897, he hired Cahan to write articles about immigrant New York—about pious peddlers, strikes in the tailoring industries, marriage brokers, and the dilemmas facing immigrants as they take the first steps to enter American life. He also wrote about East Side political figures like Emma Goldman, and of contentious meetings of the Social Science Club. His vivid journalism was collected by Moses Rischin in *Grandma Never Lived in America* (1985).

While relishing the role of a cultural broker, of spokesman for the immigrant masses to the American public, Cahan was also a highly controversial and combative player within the immigrant world. (This duality, and the ability to play radically different roles inside and outside the Lower East Side, was one of the cultural legacies of the world the immigrants created.) In the pages of his Yiddish-language newspaper Cahan was a provocative figure, writing in a fluent, colloquial Yiddish that was assertively Americanized. There was nothing in Cahan of the preservationist's reverence toward Yiddish. Handy American phrases and words were imported into the Yiddish of the *Forward*, as needed, to the dismay of those who yearned for the transformation of Yiddish into a language of culture and refinement, instead of the argot of the kitchen, the peddler, and market trader, which it was throughout Eastern Europe.

Cahan was similarly irreverent toward Jewish religious life. As a socialist he freely abused Orthodox Jewish rabbis for their otherworldly lack of concern for the exploitation of Jewish workers. Jewish traditions and observances meant little to him, but the Jewish people meant everything. He was convinced that the future for the Jews in New York, in America, did not reside in wrapping themselves in the study of Torah, but in learning about baseball, about the popular dances of the day, about American music and dress. He turned the *Forward* into a thoroughly popular paper, with editorials on citizenship and good manners and encouraged contributions on topics of direct practical interest to his immigrant readers. The famous "Bintel Brief," the letters column in which readers poured out the dilemmas of their daily lives, and were answered by the editor, made for compulsive reading. There were letters from cantors who had lost their faith, and from "A Mother" whose daughter has fallen in love with a young man whose parents "never miss a Sunday at church and speak with reverence of President Coolidge." There was a self-deprecating, syntactically creative voice of the natural storytellers in these anonymous letters:

> *Dear Editor,*
>
> *Since I have been Forward reader from the early days, I hope you will allow me to unburden my heart in the "Bintel Brief".*
>
> *Nineteen years ago, when I was a child, I came to America. Later I was married here. I was never rich financially, but wealthy in love. I loved my husband more than anything in the world. We had seven children, the oldest is now thirteen. But God did not want us to be happy, and after years of hard work, my husband developed consumption…*

This was a voice from the kitchen table and the city's ghetto cafeterias, with "a glass tea" slowly cooling on the table as the story unfolds. It is also the voice of American-Jewish writing, from Cahan to Anzia Yezierska, Isaac Bashevis Singer, and Grace Paley.

Cahan made the *Forward* into a powerful instrument for Americanizing the Jewish masses. Hutchins Hapgood, whose *The Spirit of the Ghetto: Studies of the Jewish Quarter of New York*, published with drawings by Jacob Epstein in 1902, was one of the most sympathetic and best-informed accounts of Jewish life on the Lower East Side, called Cahan "the best type of the ethical agitator." High praise indeed.

The cultural life of the immigrant Lower East Side is strikingly reflected in the pages of the *Forward.* Cahan provided a diet of romantic soap operas, a regular column offering "Perl fun der yidisher poezye" ("Pearls from Yiddish Poetry"), and for many years a steady serialization of novels of a more literary character. Cahan published books by Scholem Asch, the realist novels of I.J. Singer (who had served as the *Forward*'s Warsaw correspondent before his immigration to America), and the work of Singer's younger brother, Isaac Bashevis. Singer's connection with the *Forward* lasted from his arrival in America in 1935, when he joined the staff of the paper, to well beyond the award of the Nobel Prize for Literature in 1978. *The Manor* and *The Estate*, Singer's panorama of Jewish life in Poland in the nineteenth century, which remorselessly underlines the perils of assimilation, appeared in the *Forward* in the 1950s. It was published in English translation in 1967 and 1969. His posthumous novel *Shadows on the Hudson*, published in 1998, was originally serialized twice weekly in the *Forward* in 1957–8. But Singer's relations with the paper, as with the Jewish world on the Lower East Side, were uneasy. He did not hesitate to communicate his scorn for the paper's journalists, who worked for a Yiddish paper but nevertheless brought their children up speaking English.

Unlike Cahan, Singer was devoted to the literary possibilities of Yiddish, and was dismayed to find in New York that there was no real Yiddish culture and no Yiddish readers to write for. He was stunned to find that most New York Jews in the 1930s spoke English, not Yiddish. "I mean, there was a Hadassah meeting, so I went and expected to hear Yiddish. But I came in and there were sitting about two hundred women, and I heard one word 'delicious, delicious, delicious.' I didn't know what it was, but it wasn't Yiddish. I don't know what they gave them there to eat, but two hundred women were sitting and saying 'delicious.' By the way, this was the first English word I learned." The effect of this insight on Singer was a paralysis, a loss. "For five or six or maybe seven years I couldn't write a word. Not only didn't I publish anything in those years, but writing became so difficult a chore that my grammar was affected. I couldn't write a single worthwhile sentence."

When in time he got over the initial shock of how *American* Jewish life was in New York and regained his ability to write, he became a prolific contributor to the *Forward* using a number of different voices. Cahan, too, was a different writer when addressing his American readers and when writing in Yiddish about immigrant life in the *Forward.* Singer felt it was necessary to adopt a series pseudonym, reserving to each a different aspect of his sensibility. "Yitskhok Bashevis" was restricted to his stories and most carefully wrought literary productions. Under the names "Y. Varshavsky" ("The man from Warsaw") and "D. Segal", he published more popular works, belles-lettres, autobiography, and polemical articles on contemporary politics and literature. A group of dedicated translators worked with Singer on the English versions of his novels and stories, but those who have read Singer in the original argue that the translations carry little of the idiomatic complexity and richness of his Yiddish, with its mixture of archaic usage and modern idiom that was an innovation in literary Yiddish. Singer also broke from the tradition of Yiddish writing in rejecting sentimentality. He objected to the idea that novelists should preach, write propaganda, or confuse the novel with a sociological treatise. Readers of Yiddish were disturbed by his interest in sex and absence of explicit moralism.

Singer had nothing of Cahan's radicalism (over time Cahan drifted rightward, as he became increasingly disenchanted with the Communist left), and Singer took every opportunity to attack leftists and "modern" Jews. Everything about Jewish life in New York offended his sensibilities: "the Anglicized Yiddish, the Yiddishized English," he wrote in the short story "A Wedding in Brownsville," "the ear-splitting music and unruly dances… [and] men who had no regard for Jewishness wore skullcaps; and the reverend rabbis and cantors aped the Christian ministers." Of this side of Singer's work his monoglot American readers knew nothing, other than the harsh edge of Singer's contempt for the dishonesties of the assimilated Jew in novels like *Enemies, A Love Story* (1972), *The Penitent* (1983), and *Meshugah* (1994). Most of Singer's readers preferred it when he wrote tales of the timeless world of the *shtetl*, and some felt there was an affinity with the art of Marc Chagall. But when the Russian-French artist was approached by Harper & Row to illustrate one of Singer's tales, the offer was never taken up. Cahan's readers, or at least the younger and more radical among them became increasingly hostile to his vehement anti-Communism. Other readers preferred such cultural figures to make them feel good about Jewish immigrant life. As they grew older, neither was prepared to oblige.

Social Settlements

On Henry Street, one block south of East Broadway, east of the intersection with Montgomery Street, stands the Henry Street Settlement. Founded in 1893, and occupying federal-style row houses purchased for the settlement by the Jewish philanthropist Jacob Schiff, it was once among the most famous benevolent institutions in America. A young nurse, Lillian Wald, was asked by charity workers in the Henry Street area to offer instruction in home nursing. A girl approached her after one of the classes and begged Wald to visit her sick mother. Led up the damp stairs of a tenement, Wald found a family of seven living in two rooms. The father was a cripple, who begged on the streets under the guise of selling goods. The mother had suffered a hemorrhage and lay in pain on an unclean bed. These were not degraded people, she felt, but they had been abandoned by society. Wald believed that such conditions were only allowed because the public remained ignorant of the truth. Along with Mary Brewster, a friend from nurses' training school, Wald formulated a venture: "We were to live in the neighborhood as nurses," she wrote in *The House on Henry Street* (1915), "identify ourselves with it socially, and, in brief, contribute to it our citizenship."

Wald was among the first generation of idealistic young Americans to seek in the Lower East Side a challenge commensurate with their social ideals. After visiting Toynbee Hall in London, Stanton Coit settled in the Lower East Side where he hoped to enhance the work of neighborhood regeneration. The Neighborhood Guild that Coit founded in 1886 was reorganized as the University Settlement. Opened in 1901 at 184 Eldridge Street, on the corner at Rivington, the University Settlement was a leading force in the larger movement. Vida Dutton Scudder and a group of college graduates formed the College Settlement in 1889. Located at 95 Rivington Street, the management board was drawn from graduates of elite colleges (Smith, Vassar, Wellesley, Bryn Mawr, and "the Harvard Annex," later Radcliffe). In 1892 the College Settlement received eighty applications by college women anxious to join its work.

Where there were six settlements in 1891, the number had grown to more than one hundred in 1900, and to four hundred by 1910, spanning the full range of secular and religious affiliation and sponsorship. Over 40 percent of the social settlements in 1910 were religious foundations, with Methodists, Jews, Episcopalians, Presbyterians, and Congregationalists among the most actively involved. The Catholic Church maintained its own substantial presence in the Lower East Side through parochial schools, charities, and parish-based organization. But it was a hard-earned wisdom that proselytizing settlements were regarded with suspicion by immigrants. Religious names were abandoned, and the settlements increasingly came to the view that a secular identity was more effective.

Settlements also found that too close an association with the idea of charity damaged their standing. Relations between the settlements and the established charities were sometimes uneasy. There was, as well, a certain element of class tension in the settlements, inhabited as they were by educated middle-class volunteers, more than willing to sympathize with the plight of the immigrants and ready to take up the cause of social reform. There were those in the settlement movement who were condescending, conservative, and powerfully convinced of the superiority of their social values. And there were others who chafed against such conventional attitudes and wanted to enhance the role of settlements in reform campaigns to improve sanitation, working conditions, and wages in the sweatshops. The wealthy and conservative philanthropists, who had long supported the efforts of charities in the Lower East Side, sometimes found their own shops or factories the target of strikers assisted by settlement workers.

In a story told by Jane Addams in *Twenty Years at Hull House* (1910), Addams and Ellen Gates Starr founded Hull House in Chicago in 1889. Hoping to bridge the gap between the immigrants and the native population, settlement workers were among the few groups with direct contact with immigrants and blacks. Hull House prepared a map of nationalities in 1895 (*Hull House Maps and Papers*), which was the first systematic attempt to describe immigrant communities in an American city. The settlement approach was to understand the customs and traditions of the immigrant population, and to seek opportunities for them.

The motivation of the settlement workers was widely discussed. What, after all, brought an educated young Protestant women of American lineage to share the life of poor foreigners? At a time when American opinion was turning increasingly against immigrants, the idealism of the settlement workers seemed to run against the grain of the national mood. Jane Addams addressed that question in a lecture she gave in 1892 on "The Subjective Necessity for Social Settlements." Americans of social standing generally wished to have nothing to do with the tenement-dwellers. But the young, strongly feeling the weight of American ideals, were moved by a need to express their social idealism. "I had been beating my wings against the bars," wrote Vida Dutton Scudder in her memoir *On Journey* (1937) "—the customs, the assumptions, of my own class. I moved in a garden enclosed, if not in a hothouse, an enclosure of gracious manners, regular meals, comfort, security, good taste. I liked the balmy air. Yet sometimes it suffocated me. I wanted to escape, where winds buffeted, blowing free." People like Coit and Scudder on Rivington Street and Lillian Wald on Henry Street needed the Lower East Side as much as the tenement-dwellers had need of the resources and support of the social settlements. In that reciprocal relationship between settlement worker and immigrant, which crossed the divides of gender, class, and religion, the Lower East Side acquired a meaning in modern American life that went beyond the many social problems that flourished so mightily east of the Bowery.

The Tenement

In 1899 a Tenement House Exhibition sponsored by the Charity Organization Society of New York was held at Sherry's Hotel on Fifth Avenue. The choice of Sherry's Hotel was significant: a luxurious and socially-prominent social venue chosen as the location of an exhibition about tenements was an attempt by reformers to reach out to "Fifth Avenue" with news of a dire social problem that the elite had largely been happy to ignore. Out of frustration at the failure of the city's politicians and public to take seriously the need for new laws governing the construction of tenements, the Exhibition was intended to present before the public full evidence of the scale of the tenement problem, and the nature of the "terrible evils" of what came to be called the Old Law or dumbbell tenements. "Being convinced," wrote Lawrence Veiller, secretary of the Tenement House Committee of the Charity Organization Society, "that no real progress was to be made unless the whole community was aroused to a knowledge of existing conditions, the committee then set itself at work…" Lillian Wald had concluded in 1893 that public ignorance of conditions in the tenements was the single greatest obstacle to reform; Veiller came to the same conclusion several years later.

There were 40,000 tenements in Manhattan and the Bronx in 1899, built on lots generally 25 feet wide by 100 feet deep. The tenements were planned to house four families on each floor, and were between six and seven stories high. Built in most cases to the lowest costs by real estate speculators, the tenement was a vastly profitable investment. The Superintendent of Buildings of New York put the meaning of the term succinctly in 1862: a tenement was the building where "the greatest amount of profit is sought to be realized from the least possible amount of space, with little or no regard for the health, comfort, or protection of the lives of the tenants." Tenants knew that they would have to sublet space to boarders, who would help them meet the high rental costs. Overcrowding, which was denounced by contemporaries as one of the worst of the many evils of tenement life, was arguably a sensible strategy for poor immigrants in a city where living costs were high. And the benefits of being a boarder loomed largest among the "greenhorns," newly arrived immigrants who desperately needed a place to stay and someone to show them the ropes. The "greenie" was a comic figure, the butt of music hall jokes. There is a wonderful greenhorn moment in Yuri Suhl's autobiography, *One Foot in America* (1951). After arriving at Ellis Island, he traveled by subway to the Myrtle Avenue home of his Uncle Feivish. Suhl was introduced to six first cousins, five second cousins, three aunts from his father's side of the family, four aunts from his mother's side, and "about a half dozen neighbors"—all perfect strangers:

> *"Here's your greenhorn," Uncle Feivish announced to a houseful of people.*
>
> *I took this to be a title that America bestowed upon every new arrival, a title to be worn with dignity, and I smiled.*

But the greenhorn could also be a figure of bewildered dignity and pathos, struggling against the mayhem of everyday life in the tenement world. Bernstein, the scholarly sweatshop worker who boards with Jake and Gitl in Cahan's *Yekl* (1896), was good company for the uneasy couple, as well as someone who helped with the rent. Joan Micklin Silver's *Hester Street* (1974), a film adaptation of Cahan's novella, adds a scene in which Bernstein lovingly teaches Jake and Gitl's son Joey the letters of the Hebrew alphabet.

Reformers were shocked and angered by the architecture of the dumbbell tenements (there is a striking example at 19 Eldridge Street, erected in 1879). Only those rooms facing the front and rear of the building had direct light and air. Some of the other "dark" rooms had no windows at all. Others had windows that opened upon a narrow air shaft between adjacent buildings. Inadequate for the circulation of air, and beyond the reach of sunlight, the tenement air shaft acted as a flue, rapidly carrying smoke and flames throughout the building when there was a fire. It was also a convenient receptacle for garbage, a source of foul odors, and an echo chamber for noise. Privacy was the rarest commodity of all on the Lower East Side. Veiller argued that such environments were breeding grounds for disease, vice, and crime. And there were few who thought otherwise.

Large maps on display at Veiller's exhibition showed each block in the tenement districts (the Lower East Side had the greatest density of tenements in the city). Every building was represented in scale, with an indication of the type of structure and its use. Drawn to the same scale was a poverty map, with a black dot representing each family who had applied for charity, and a disease map indicating cases of tuberculosis, typhoid, and diphtheria recorded at the Board of Health over the past five years. Along with scale models of tenements, floor plans, and maps, the exhibition presented diagrams revealing the need for parks, playgrounds, and public baths in the Lower East Side. One thousand photographs were on display, some showing the fruits of successful urban improvements, others—the vast majority—forcefully portraying conditions in the tenements. There was a series of photographs showing the worst workingmen's housing in every US city with a population above 25,000. Only in Boston and Chicago were there buildings that rivaled the overcrowded and degraded condition of New York's tenements. Jacob Riis had used photographs in the form of lantern slides in his famous 1889 lectures on "How the Other Half Lives" and in his book with that same memorable title. The alliance of photography and social reform was formally sealed by Veiller's Tenement House Exhibition in 1899.

As the population grew, housing conditions sharply deteriorated. There had been repeated complaints about housing conditions in New York as early as the 1840s. But complaints and governmental inaction went hand-in-hand in the nineteenth-century city. Sanitary reformers and charity workers investigated conditions in the tenements, but their calls for reform, even when strongly supported by an enlightened public opinion, were opposed by real estate interests, the building trade, and owners of unreformed tenement houses. There were self-interested defenses of the right of contract between tenant and landlord. What authority, after all, did the city have to interfere with property rights? Landlords were often wealthy, powerful men, with political influence. Immigrants were transient, voteless, and often entirely powerless. Humanitarian reformers, led by physicians who regarded the slums as a breeding ground for disease, successfully persuaded the state legislature to create a Board of Health in the 1860s, which addressed some of the worst problems.

Concerns about tenements went beyond their physical condition. They were also seen as dens of crime and immorality. Children growing up in such an environment were often physically stunted, poorly educated or not educated at all, and entered adulthood with a terrifying absence of moral restraint. Jimmie Johnson in Stephen Crane's *Maggie* (1893), a lurid exercise in literary naturalism, was a type of the aggressive urban male who filled contemporaries with dread:

> *After a time his sneer grew so that it turned its glare upon all things. He became so sharp that he believed in nothing. To him the police were always actuated by malignant impulses and the rest of the world was composed, for the most part, of despicable creatures who were all trying to take advantage of him and with whom, in defense, he was obliged to quarrel on all possible occasions.*

Charles Loring Brace, founder of the Children's Aid Society, published *The Dangerous Classes of New York* in 1872. The children of the tenements were the "dangerous classes" for Brace, who feared that if society did nothing about the vagrant children living in the streets, it would reap a terrible harvest of crime. Brace's solution was to teach the street children a skill at Industrial Schools, and to place orphans with good farm families in the Midwest. Every threatening aspect of urban life was readily traced back to the tenement, in sermons, public lectures, newspaper editorials, and magazine articles.

There was another story to be told about immigrant life, and one not exclusively lived out in tenements or in the Lower East Side. Joseph Heller, celebrated author of *Catch-22* (the most widely-read of all American novels of the Second World War), told the story of his childhood in *Now and Then*, a memoir published in 1998. He was born in 1923 in Coney Island, at the far reaches of Brooklyn. Life in an immigrant family had little in common with the smart world celebrated by Rodgers and Hart in "Manhattan" or Cole Porter's "You're the Top." His was a family story of poverty, the struggle of Jewish immigrant parents, and the loneliness of a bristling, intelligent young boy, whose truck driver father died of a bungled operation when Heller was five. This was also a world largely without the stereotype of warm, family-centered sentimentality that still clings to immigrant life. "About my father," Heller recalled, "I simply lost interest in him after he was gone… I didn't have that tender admiration for a large and generous nature that Nabokov expresses for his father. I hardly knew mine at all. If anything, the passing away of Mr. Isaac Daniel Heller was for me more a matter of embarrassment than anything else." His mother took in boarders and sewing to survive in the Depression. At sixteen, Heller delivered telegrams for Western Union. Between Joey and his older brother and sister, there was deep affection. He discovered only as an adult that they were, in fact, half-siblings. In unexpected ways immigrant life could be like the plot of a Victorian novel, with bizarre twists, changed names, previously unknown relations and sudden catastrophic misfortunes. For the immigrant in Coney Island life itself was a roller-coaster ride.

Veiller's Tenement House Exhibition had a dramatic impact upon public attitudes toward the tenements and led to the passing of the New York Tenement House Law of 1901, which created the Tenement House Department with responsibility for sanitary welfare for the 2,372,079 occupants of tenements in New York City. Veiller was appointed deputy commissioner of the department and went on to exercise important influence upon national housing reform policy. Tenements built under the 1901 law (thus New Law Tenements) differed in important ways from the Old Law structures. Newly built tenements were limited to five stories, which reduced some of the worst overcrowding. Bathrooms were made compulsory, replacing the communal water closets located in the halls. There were strict safety precautions, requiring public halls and stairs to be fireproofed. Every room was meant to be "light" and the air shaft was banned from future buildings.

Everywhere on the Lower East Side today the fruits of Veiller's Exhibition and the 1901 law are visible. Owners of Old Law tenements found unimproved buildings at a disadvantage in the property market, and grudgingly made improvements. The law did not retroactively mandate improvements, but the real estate market did. There are still many telltale signs of the older structures. When a tenement is torn down, one can sometimes see the surviving half of an air shaft.

The wholesale clearing of inner-city slums began in earnest in the 1930s. Public housing projects, funded in large part by the Federal Housing Agency and named after local heroes (from Samuel Gompers and Mayor LaGuardia to Lillian Wald), and private developments (Peter Cooper Village and Stuyvesant Town) replaced the run-down tenements in large swathes of the Lower East Side. New parks were built upon the cleared sites of Old Law tenements. Those in better condition survived, and when rents in the city rose sufficiently in the 1980s to make renovation financially viable, tenements became once again attractive propositions. For some time now, there have been signs that gentrification has been going on in earnest in the Lower East Side: copies of the *Wall Street Journal* on doorsteps, a Gap store, and private art galleries tell part of the story. The conversion of former tenements into high-priced condominiums inevitably reduces the stock of affordable housing. That process has taken place in dozens of neighborhoods in Manhattan, and the Lower East Side is no exception.

There are other indications of changing attitudes toward the Lower East Side. In 1966 the New York City Landmarks Preservation Commission listed the Bialystoker Synagogue on Willett Street. It was the first of an important series of landmarkings: Beth Hamedrash Hagodol Synagogue on Norfolk Street (1967), Eldridge Street Synagogue (1980), the Forward Building (1986), and Congregation Anshe Slonim on Norfolk Street (1987). A Lower East Side Historic District covering an L-shaped tract of the Lower East Side was added to the National Register of Historic Places in 2001.

An even more striking sign that the Lower East Side and the East Village, and other areas across the city, were changing was the emergence in the 1980s of an ecologically-minded community garden movement. Today there are 750 or so community gardens in New York. With so few parks, and so many vacant lots where tenements once stood, and with a population variously perceived as poor, demoralized, transient, and (most likely) to be on drugs, the decision of Normand Vallee and Reinaldo Arana to begin clearing by hand vacant lots that had been used

as a dumping ground for local refuse attracted little attention. When cleared, planted and intensely loved as a neighborhood community garden, the idea caught on. The city eventually established a "Greenthumb" program to facilitate temporary uses of city-owned property. In neighborhoods marked by little community feeling, the gardens became a focus for social reconstruction. Impromptu networks of social activism crossed ethnic lines. In what is a classic example of grassroots activism, grape arbors, trees, and attractive gravel paths have replaced barren, demoralizing wasteland.

When Mayor Giuliani realized that there was so much empty land

off the tax rolls, he ordered that community gardens be auctioned off to private developers. "We are trying to privatize as many city-owned properties as we can," remarked the first deputy commissioner at the city's Department of Housing Preservation and Development. Among the targeted gardens in the first scheduled sale in 1999 were the Parque de Tranquilidad and the All People's Garden in the Lower East Side. The dollars that the mayor planned to raise came with quite a cost in terms of community demonstrations, lawsuits, and letters denouncing Giuliani in the *New York Times.* A compromise was eventually found, theoretically preserving most of the gardens. The city now plans to build on 131 of the original 711 Greenthumb site. There is an online Lower East Side Garden Map at:
www.earthcelebrations.com/gardens/gardenmap.html.
The gardens are worth the visit.

The Tenement Museum

Visitors to the Lower East Side will of course miss out on the real tenements, with their stale, damp air, overflowing toilets, cockroaches, infestations of lice, contented rats, peeling wallpaper, cracked paint, and the smells of dozens of families cooking. Above all, we can have no sense of the sheer crowdedness of the classic tenement, with its ebb and flow of boarders, and noisy sewing machines crowded into sweatshops. But the Lower East Side Tenement Museum, at 97 Orchard Street, between Broome and Delancey, has provided something that novels, reportage, and photographs cannot quite provide: the feel of the real thing. (There is a virtual online tour at www.wnet.org/tenement).

The museum consists of three apartments, once occupied by the Baldizzis, Rogarshevskys, and the Gumpertzes, returned now to the condition they would have been in when occupied. The building is "pre-Law," that is, it was built before passage of the first of the tenement laws in 1867. Erected by Lucas Glockner, an immigrant tailor, in 1863–4, 97 Orchard Street was designed to house 20 families in three-room apartments, each consisting of 325 square feet. In line with the prevailing standards of the 1860s, there was no running water in the building. A water spigot and a row of privies were located in the backyard of the building, overlooked by tenements on Allen Street, which were later demolished when that street was widened. Two water closets were constructed on each floor in 1905, and the structure was wired for electricity some time after 1918. Other than some other small structural changes, it remains as an example of the first wave of tenements erected in New York City.

In the 1860s it probably seemed neither a barracks nor a slum. The builder and his family moved into the building when it was completed and lived in it for a number of years. The last of the tenants of 97 Orchard Street were evicted in 1935 when it was condemned as a residence. For half a century the building was used only for commercial purposes. Abandoned, it has proved to be a gold mine of urban artifacts: toys, cosmetics, bottles, fabric, printed ephemera, and a well-worn ouija board.

Discovered by Anita Jacobson and Ruth Abram, who wanted to create a museum to help people today understand what happened to the immigrants after they left Ellis Island, they found that the upper floors had been left untouched. Researchers were able to identify the names of some of those who had lived in the building. Josephine Baldizzi, whose family moved from the building when she was a child, has donated some personal memorabilia, and recorded her recollections of life at 97 Orchard. You can hear a recording of her voice in the apartment in which she lived as a child. Furnishings were found that closely matched the period and class of the inhabitants. The Tenement Museum was made a National Trust Historical Site and landmarked by the city. Along with the Statue of Liberty and Ellis Island, it has become a tourist attraction and an important site of collective memory.

At 5 Ludlow Street, near the intersection of Canal and Ludlow Streets in the Lower East Side, stands the Morace-Mascagna Funeral Home, sharing space with Hong Kong Funerals, Inc. The striking building that these undertakers occupy was erected in 1892 by the Independent Kletzker Brotherly Aid Society, a "Landsmanschaftn" or mutual aid society established by immigrants from the Polish village of Kletzk—one of hundreds of such bodies (the Independent Wilner Association, the First Odessa Benevolent Association, United Brethren of Pomevisch, Kurlander Benevolent Society, Independent Grodno Sick Support Society, and so on) created in the Lower East Side after the 1880s. The present occupants of the building, and the ethnic succession they imply, are living reminders of the enduringly complex life of ethnic New York.

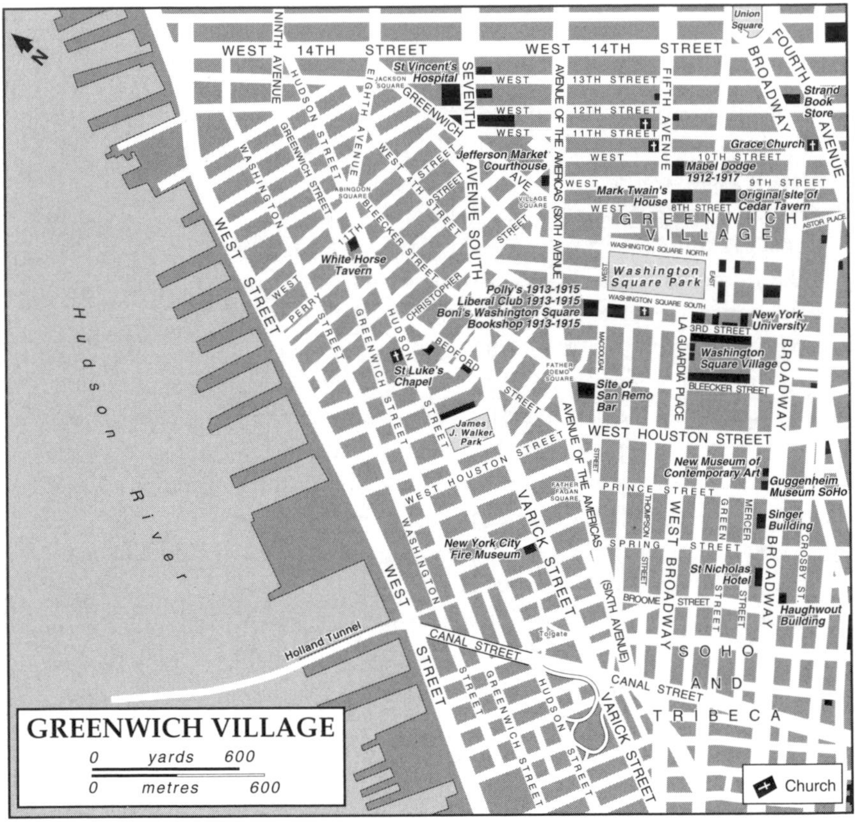
N
Hudson River
WEST 14TH STREET
WEST 14TH STREET
NINTH AVENUE
HUDSON STREET
EIGHTH AVENUE
JACKSON SQUARE
GREENWICH
SEVENTH AVENUE SOUTH
AVENUE OF THE AMERICAS (SIXTH AVENUE)
FIFTH AVENUE
BROADWAY
FOURTH AVENUE
Union Square
WEST 13TH STREET
WEST 12TH STREET
WEST 11TH STREET
WEST 10TH STREET
WEST 9TH STREET
WEST 8TH STREET
St Vincent's Hospital
Strand Book Store
Grace Church
Mabel Dodge 1912-1917
Mark Twain's House
Original site of Cedar Tavern
Jefferson Market Courthouse
GREENWICH AVE
VILLAGE SQUARE
GREENWICH VILLAGE
ASTOR PLACE
WASHINGTON STREET
GREENWICH STREET
WEST 4TH STREET
ABINGDON SQUARE
BLEECKER STREET
WEST 11TH
White Horse Tavern
WEST STREET
WEST PERRY STREET
CHRISTOPHER STREET
WASHINGTON SQUARE NORTH
Washington Square Park
WASHINGTON SQUARE SOUTH
Polly's 1913-1915
Liberal Club 1913-1915
Boni's Washington Square Bookshop 1913-1915
New York University
3RD STREET
Washington Square Village
LA GUARDIA PLACE
MACDOUGAL
BEDFORD
St Luke's Chapel
FATHER DEMO SQUARE
Site of San Remo Bar
BLEECKER STREET
James J. Walker Park
WEST HOUSTON STREET
WEST HOUSTON STREET
New Museum of Contemporary Art
Guggenheim Museum SoHo
FATHER FAGAN SQUARE
PRINCE STREET
THOMPSON STREET
WEST BROADWAY
GREENE STREET
MERCER STREET
Singer Building
CROSBY ST.
VARICK STREET
New York City Fire Museum
SPRING STREET
St Nicholas Hotel
BROOME STREET
Haughwout Building
Holland Tunnel
CANAL STREET
Tollgate
SOHO AND TRIBECA
CANAL STREET
0 yards 600
0 metres 600
Church

GREENWICH VILLAGE

CHAPTER FOUR

Greenwich Village

Greenwich Village was indeed once a village—or, more precisely, a rural hamlet surrounded by farmland and open fields—an easy morning's carriage ride from Manhattan. Originally the site of the native settlement of Sapokanikan (brave etymologists suggest that the name derives from the Delaware term for "wet field or plantation") it was purchased by the Dutch West India Company and developed as a tobacco farm, the "Bossen Bouwerie." Part of the farm was given to Trinity Church (see Chapter 2), which remained an important landlord in the Village. The name "Greenwich" appeared on maps as early as 1713, when wealthy sea captains and merchants began to build handsome country estates along the shore of the Hudson River. The grandest of these estates was that of Sir Peter Warren, later buried in Westminster Abbey as Vice-Admiral of the Royal Navy, whose large mansion was erected at the present intersection of Charles and Bleecker Streets. After his return to London in 1747, the Warren estate passed to his daughters and was eventually partitioned into twelve- and fifteen-acre estates, ideal country homes for city merchants and businessmen. Warren's home and the remaining land, over fifty acres, survived intact until the Civil War.

A similar story might be told about the Richmond Hill estate (see pp.44–45) erected at what is today the intersection of Varick and Charlton Streets. The mansion, with its wide verandah and a portico supported by Ionic columns, was built in the 1760s by Abraham Mortier and sold to Aaron Burr and then John Jacob Astor. It greatly suffered from the financial rapacity of successive lease-holders: the hill that gave the mansion its view across the Hudson was cut away, and the mansion was turned into a tavern in 1822. It was used briefly as an opera house before being razed in 1849. The character of Greenwich Village in its early days was largely shaped by large country properties like the Warren estate and Richmond Hill. The wealthy men who owned such properties made the Hudson shore of New York a place of elegance and considerable charm. In comparison with the great estates of the Livingstons on the Hudson River and the immense land holdings of the Van Rensselaers, Warren and Mortier were merely country gentry, but the Village began its curious history as a terrain of country parks and large wood frame mansions, set in a landscape of venerable old oaks and marked by stunning views across the Hudson to New Jersey.

Symbols and Yellow Fever

The grid set out in the Commissioner's 1811 plan bypassed the Village, a decision reflecting its isolation from the larger city to the south. It was a quiet backwater. The odd orientation of the streets of the Village, set at oblique angles to the grid, made it unsuitable for northbound traffic. Accessible only by the Greenwich Road, the Village retained something of its autonomy into the nineteenth century. By 1811 the Greenwich stage ran from Federal Hall five times daily, for a fare of 25¢.

The character of the Village was conveyed in a curious mix of symbolism. Its patrician mansions and much-admired position as a country village gave New Yorkers the sense that the Village retained the way of life of an earlier age. Yet at the foot of Christopher Street, behind 14-foot stone walls, stood a state prison (named Newgate after

the London prison), which was the cause of frequent alarm in the Village at the prospect of riots and escapees. Newgate was closed in the late 1820s when a larger prison was opened in the Hudson River village of Ossining (the Ossining Correctional Facility was vernacularly referred to as Sing-Sing prison). The eastern edge of the Village was the site of the city's Potter's Field, its pauper's burying ground, established in 1794 at the junction of Post Road and Bloomingdale Road. The burial ground was moved to what later became Washington Square in 1797, where it remained for three decades. When needed for public hangings, a gallows was erected in Washington Square. In 1890, when the foundations of the Washington Arch (which stands at the foot of Fifth Avenue) were excavated, tombstones were uncovered, showing that the area was not solely reserved for paupers.

Above all, the growth of the Village was shaped by the annual summer outbreaks of yellow fever, smallpox, and then the great scourge of cholera in 1832. At first, such plagues were seen as inevitable illnesses of the sinners, immigrants, and the poor. Despite public days of prayer and a National Fast, the illness spread and there was a panicky flight from the city. William Cullen Bryant, alarmed at the silent streets and deserted dwellings in 1832, wrote reassuringly in the *Evening Post* that the victims of cholera were mainly drawn from "the intemperate, the dissolute, and the poor creatures who are too ignorant to know what to do." "Our safety [he wrote] is in ourselves, not in our place… Fear but assists the action of those malign influences which exist in the air we breathe." Despite Bryant's calming advice, half of the city's population of 100,000 fled. Even the New York Board of Health recommended evacuation from the infected areas.

Seeking a place of refuge from the outbreaks, New Yorkers fled the crowded downtown streets and settled in the Village. Wood frame buildings, scarcely more than modest farmhouses, were demolished by wealthy New Yorkers and replaced by brick houses. Life in the main commercial district was simply too dangerous for their families. (Throughout the Village there are surviving simple, carpenter-built federal row houses—see 4–10 Grove Street, 59 Morton Street, 127–31 Macdougal Street and 131 Charles Street—which give a vivid sense of the Village in the 1820s and 1830s. These are all very, very valuable properties in today's real estate market.) Businesses became skilled at relocating to the Village at the first rumor of an outbreak of disease. The new buildings, houses, and incoming businesses transformed the Village and made it for the first time an integral part of the city.

Washington Square

After the Civil War, the streets of Greenwich Village were lined with small two-and three-story brick dwellings where shoemakers, blacksmiths, tailors, and tobacconists did business. Christopher Street, one of the most commercial streets in the Village, was the home of carpenters, masons, stonecutters, turners and sawyers, along with stables, shops, and saloons. Left behind as the great procession of fashionable life moved uptown, the narrow streets of the Village had little appeal to the wealthy who were building their grand brownstone homes on Bond Street, Lafayette Place, and Gramercy Park or their large mansions on Fifth Avenue. Without factories or warehouses to employ large numbers of workers, the economic pressures that transformed family residences on the Lower East Side into tenant-houses, and that made tenements so good an investment, passed the Village by. The absence of broad avenues for north-south traffic (Varick Street was not cut through to join Seventh Avenue, and Sixth Street was not extended to the junction with Prince Street until the 1920s) meant that the Village was bypassed by fashionable society, by the working class, and by industry.

The Village remained a community apart from the city in other ways. A pier at the foot of Christopher Street was used for the unloading of timber and construction materials from upstate, and in 1841 became the station for the Hoboken Ferry. These were among the few signs in Greenwich Village that the opening of the Erie Canal had made New York a major seaport. In the middle of the nineteenth century the Village had a reputation as a sober and attractive residential neighborhood. "The Knickerbocker element is widely diffused," noted a visiting physician in 1865, "and exercises no small influence in maintaining the high reputation for salubrity which the Ninth Ward has always enjoyed. There are very few wealthy families, and *comparatively* few of the very poor or vicious. The great bulk of the inhabitants consists of what may be called the middle-class of people, composed mainly of trades-people, clerks, mechanics of the better class, cartmen, etc."

As the flood of immigration increased, altering the ethnic and religious mix of the population, and thus transforming the city's politics, the Village was largely unaffected. The Ninth Ward was known (perhaps ironically) as the "American ward." In 1875, the Village had the lowest proportion of foreign-born inhabitants of any ward in the city. The first significant number of immigrants only arrived in the Village in the late nineteenth century. The Irish settled in the northwestern section, and were followed by the arrival of a significant African-American population (not immigrants, of course, but newcomers to this part of the city) in the southern Village. Italian immigrants began to make the Village an extension of Little Italy.

The largely residential character of the Village was reinforced when the city acquired the Potter's Field and had the site cleared and laid out as a parade ground (the Washington Military Parade Ground, or Washington Square) and public park. It was officially opened on the Fourth of July, 1826, to celebrate the 50th anniversary of the signing of the Declaration of Independence. Additional land was purchased by the Common Council, enlarging the park to its present area of 132 acres. The first homes were built facing the northern side of Washington Square in the 1830s. Memories of the disheveled Potter's Field and the crowds who flocked to witness hangings were soon enough forgotten. It was an early example of the rapidity with which a neighborhood in New York might take on a new social identity.

The first development was known as "The Row," at 1–13 Washington Square North, an impressive group of Greek Revival row houses. They were built on a scale and finish aimed explicitly at wealthy New Yorkers—leading merchants, bankers, lawyers, and military men. Purchasers resembled Henry James' Dr. Sloper, in *Washington Square* (1881), a comfortably settled physician who moved to Washington Square North, and with steely determination was prepared to defend his daughter against any and every "adventurer." James was born nearby, at 21 (later 27) Washington Place East, but was taken to Europe when he was six months old, and only came to know Washington Square after his family returned to New York in 1847 and rented a house at 48 West 14th Street. His grandmother still lived at 19 Washington Square North. Even without childhood recollections,

James' visits to his grandmother gave the novelist a rich sense of the distinctive atmosphere of the square. From his recollection of conversations in his grandmother's parlor, and visits from her neighbors, James was able to reinvent the domestic world of Dr. Sloper.

The appeal of Washington Square was intimately connected with its location in the city. It was not too far from the bustle of Broadway, and not too far from the cultural attractions of the opera on Astor Place. The park itself, with its ailanthus trees and leafy walks, was much the largest in the city in the 1840s. The well-dressed crowds watching the handsome troopers of the Seventh Regiment of the state militia made an attractive subject for popular lithographic prints. Daguerreotypes from the Broadway studios were used to ensure that the officers in the lithographs were faithful to real life. Like the enclave around St. John's Chapel and Gramercy Square, a park was regarded as a necessary ingredient for the making of an aristocratic neighborhood. Bond Street and Lafayette Place, just on the eastern side of Broadway, had no park as a focus and succumbed to commercial pressures long before Washington Square.

The eastern side of the park was the location of two institutions that did much to define the spirit of the square. The University of the City of New York and the Reformed Dutch Church, both opened in the late 1830s, gazed in Gothic benevolence across the broad gravel paths of the square. The university began life in 1831 under the leadership of Albert Gallatin, who lived in nearby Bond Street. From the start, divisions about the purposes of higher education were clearly visible within the institution. The Dutch Reformed and Presbyterian ministers demanded that the religious content of education should be strongly stressed. Another group of trustees, led by merchants and bankers, wanted the emphasis to fall upon practical and scientific education. Although the university was formally a secular institution with a non-denominational curriculum, the ministers seized control of the board of trustees, and tilted it toward evangelicalism. Columbia University (see Chapter 2) was an Episcopalian institution, dominated by the Anglican community in New York. Higher education in New York was caught up in conflicts within the city's Protestant communities.

When the city began to discuss plans for a festival to commemorate the centenary of the inauguration of George

Washington in 1889, a Washington Square worthy proposed the construction of a triumphal arch as the focus of the celebrations. The society architect Stanford White came up with a design and a painted wood, plaster, and papier-mâché structure was erected facing Fifth Avenue on the north side of the park. The popular success of the arch led to the formation of a committee to raise funds for a permanent structure. Unlike the uphill struggle to build the Statue of Liberty, the memorial arch fund soon raised the $134,000 needed to turn Stanford White's plaster into white stone. When the arch was dedicated in 1895, it was greeted with near-universal approval. (Henry James regarded the arch as "lamentable" because of its "poor and lonely and unsupported and unaffiliated state.") It provided a gateway to fashionable Fifth Avenue in accord with the ideals of the City Beautiful Movement.

From the first, painters, photographers, illustrators, and watercolorists were drawn to the arch, which provided an urban scene resembling something in Paris or London. The painter Childe Hassam's 1893 "Washington Arch, Spring," in the Phillips Collection in Washington, uses the arch as a setting for a park scene dominated by a line of trees, elegant private horse-drawn carriages, and fashionable women strolling in the park. Painters and illustrators of the "Ashcan School," like Everett Shinn and William Glackens, found the park an inexhaustible subject. Instead of a setting for the city's elite, Glackens painted the nannies and nursemaids with their charges and immigrant Italian women wearing shawls who filled the park when the weather was good. John Sloan, a friend of Shinn and Glackens, lived on or near the Square for two decades, executing etchings of boys playing in the park.

Photographers like Jessie Tarbox Beals took photographs of Washington Square on picturesque snowy evenings, misty nights, and in the rain. André Kertész, who lived in an apartment building at 2 Fifth Avenue, compiled a portfolio of photographs taken from the balcony of his 12th-floor apartment overlooking the park. The first Washington Square Outdoor Art Show was held in 1932, to provide a boost to artists in the hard times of the Depression. By the 1950s, the semi-annual exhibit had long outgrown Washington Square. The quality may no longer quite be what it was, but the outdoor show has become a fixture in the (amateur) artistic life of the city. Like the Flatiron Building, artists and photographers made the Washington arch a key visual icon for the city.

Traffic was permitted to cross the park through the memorial arch, and in the 1950s city planners led by Robert Moses proposed to extend Fifth Avenue south. Then he came up with the idea for a sunken highway to carry traffic to Washington Square South. It was only when a political uproar followed, in which Jane Jacobs played an important part, that the Board of Estimate agreed in 1958 to close the park permanently to traffic.

The final closure of the park to traffic in 1963 made Washington Square, with its large student population, even more attractive as a setting for informal folk music and the "beatnik scene" that attracted crowds of tourists. But the park soon began its long decline when it became a drug supermarket, as recalled by Richard Sennett: "[T]he swings of the children's north sandlot serve as a stand-up boutique for heroin, the benches under the statue of a Polish patriot serve to display counters for various pills, while all four corners of the square deal wholesale in cocaine. No young people sleep in the park now, and though the various dealers and their outriders are familiar figures to the mothers watching infants on the swings or to students at the university next to the square, these criminals seem all but invisible to the police." "Weegee" and Diane Arbus recorded a Washington Square that had become a setting for drunks, the mentally disturbed, and derelicts. By the 1970s, when the city was descending into an apocalyptic financial crisis and seemed to be overcome by graffiti, squalor, and social decay, Washington Square became one of its many symbols of decline. Conditions have sharply improved since then, but the park remains a place with edge. There are few strollers nowadays carrying parasols.

The university demolished its Gothic building in 1894 and renamed itself New York University two years later. Like St. Vincent's Hospital in the West Village, in the past two or three decades NYU has become one of the most rapacious players in the Village real estate market. The development of NYU into its present size, together with its distinguished standing as a research institution with a strong emphasis on professional training, have led to repeated conflicts with the surrounding community caused by the university's seemingly unquenchable demand for classrooms, laboratories, and student dormitories. NYU today owns or leases much of the real estate around Washington Square, and owns 60 buildings across the city with more than 6.3 million square feet. That figure has doubled since 1970. When in 2000 a classroom and office facility for the law school was proposed for West Third Street, obliterating a town house where Edgar Allan Poe once lived, and when a State Supreme Court justice could find no reason in law to prevent the demolition of the Poe home, the tensions between a large university and the surrounding community were abundantly revealed. A spokesperson for the university blandly issued reassurances, as the Poe demolition was scheduled: 'The university and the law school will continue to work… to design and construct the best possible building for this site and the neighborhood."

The New Village, 1912–1917

With the coming of the subway and the automobile, livery stables and small carriage-repair shops in the Village closed, creating a glut of unoccupied low-rent real estate space—ideal for artists' studios. The remodeling of older buildings created the small, inexpensive apartments that writers needed. (The same process occurred in SoHo in the 1960s, when artists moved into industrial lofts. See Chapter 6).) A floating bohemian population of artists, writers, and social radicals were drawn to the Village by low rents and its rapidly developing reputation for being somehow different from the rest of the city. It was no longer simply a neighborhood, or the Ninth Ward, but an attitude, a state of mind and style of rebellious self-assertion. Hippolyte Havel, anarchist militant and chef, made the point succinctly: "Greenwich Village is a state of mind—it has no boundaries." The proud assertion of the distinctiveness of the Villagers was nicely put by Martin Green, no rebellious Villager himself but one of the Village's most perceptive social historians: "The Village lived in perpetual secession from the rest of the country." The flowering of the Village was not simply a matter of a changing property market and cheap rents. The Village offered diverse, intangible things, like a human scale, unmodernized saloons, and a flourishing cultural life. The Village was an ongoing rebuke to censors, bluenoses, the "booboisie," and the provincialism of American culture.

Since the heyday in the 1840s of the struggle between "Young America" and the Anglophile *Knickerbocker Review*, New York has had a culture of cliques and "crowds," of partisan cafés, ideological saloons, and tendentious neighborhoods. Artists and writers found fellowship in unlikely places, and among the most significant has been Greenwich Village.

There were countless groups, crowds, and circles in the Village, sometimes defined by employment or politics, sometimes by a magazine or journal, a saloon or restaurant. The midtown journalism crowd, fond of slumming, found its center at Lincoln Steffens' apartment on Washington Square. The artistic life in the Village was dominated by the friends and disciples of Robert Henri, and of John and Dolly Sloan, who had all moved to New York from Philadelphia and who created in "The Eight" America's first great artistic grouping in the twentieth century. "The Eight" painted Greenwich Village scenes, exhibited their work in the Village, and contributed drawings and political cartoons to *The Masses*, which was the Village's radical voice. William Glackens and Everett Shinn lived on Waverly Place. The anarchists were to be found at the offices of Emma Goldman's *Mother Earth* at 210 East 13th Street and at the Modern School of the anarchist Ferrer Center on 104 East 12th Street (where Robert Henri and George Bellows taught art classes). Lewis Mumford's first public lecture, on the Russian anarchist Prince Kropotkin and the philosophy of regionalism, was delivered to a Ferrer Society meeting in New York in 1917.

There was a university crowd at New York University on Washington Square; and a somewhat snootier "uptown" intellectual life centered around Columbia University to which Rudolph Bourne and Max Eastman belonged (Eastman studied philosophy at Columbia under John Dewey before coming downtown to be editor of *The Masses* in 1912). The social settlement crowd, which included Hutchins Hapgood and Neith Boyce, came in from the University Settlement, Lillian Wald's Henry Street Settlement, and from Mary Simkhovitch's Greenwich House on nearby Barrow Street, but were never truly comfortable with the irreverence of the Village. At the apartment at 12 Charles Street of Crystal Eastman, the suffragists and feminists who were defining the "New Woman" (Madeleine Doty, Inez Milholland, Ida Ruah) met in an ongoing seminar on emancipation.

There was a small socialist crowd in the Village, led by William English Walling, whose brilliant political essays were published in the *New Review*. And then there was *The Masses*, published from 91 Greenwich Avenue. The central figures around *The Masses* were the editor, Max Eastman, who lived with Ida Ruah on Waverly Place, and John Reed and Floyd Dell, neighbors at 42 and 45 Washington Square South. By temperament they were all on the left wing of every cause, every issue. They sided with the left of the Socialist Party against the leadership group around Eugene Debs; with the IWW against Samuel Gompers and the American Federation of Labor; and took the side of the Communist Party against Wall Street. The freewheeling radicalism of *The Masses* was great fun, and was an important precursor of the counter-culture of the 1960s, but it lacked a certain sobriety and credibility. It is also true that sobriety, in the eyes of the Village, was a much over-rated virtue. Credibility inevitably raised the question: to whom and for what? To be a Villager meant that you never had to be credible to anyone, ever. The prominent Wobblies (Big Bill Haywood) and later the commissars of the Communist Party were hostile to anything that smacked of "Villagism." Miscellaneous advocates of free love, disciples of Freud, and hangers-on of doubtful talent who were interested in the new ideas found their natural home in the Village and its radical publications.

Alfred Stieglitz's circle of artists, photographers, and younger writers, who were appearing in *Camera Notes* and *Camera Work* and who were often to be found at Stieglitz's 291 Gallery on Fifth Avenue, included Benjamin De Casseres and Sadakichi Hartman, among the most perceptive and original critics of the new movements in art. De Casseres' essay on "The Unconscious in Art" and Hartman's essay on "The Esthetic Significance of the Motion Picture," both in *Camera Work* in 1911–12, were important contributions to the emerging cultural avant-garde in America. These were men who brought to New York word of the most striking artists in Paris—Matisse, Picasso, Rodin. Novelists in the Village were generally of the realist persuasion (Ernest Poole, Theodore Dreiser, Sherwood Anderson); as were the playwrights (Eugene O'Neill). Younger poets were appearing in Alfred Kreymborg's little magazines, *The Glebe* and *Others*, whose motto was "The old expressions are with us always, and there are always others." At its peak *Others* had 200 subscribers. That was, in the Village, an indication of its credibility. There was another group of young writers around Guido Bruno, publisher of *Bruno's Chapbooks*. Bruno rented a garret at 58 Washington Square and hung a poster proclaiming it to be Bruno's

Garret, headquarters of art and genius. He accepted fees from wannabe poets and promised to publish their work in *Bruno's Bohemia* or *Bruno's Weekly*, and sometimes actually did so. At the Minetta Tavern (Minetta Lane and Macdougal Street), Joe Gould, all of 5'1" tall and 90 pounds, could usually be found, cadging drinks and talking up his endless *Oral History of the World.* Gould's panhandling rap was justly celebrated:

> *It took me four years at Harvard to make me what I am today. People sometimes ask me how I live. Air, ketchup, self-esteem, cowboy coffee, fried-egg sandwiches, cigarette butts—what else is new? What's my religion? I'm from New England. In the winter I'm a Buddhist, in the summer I'm a Nudist. And now you can make a contribution to the Joseph Ferdinand Gould fund, if you care to. You can find me at a table later.*

There were, in other words, many different forms of Village bohemianism, and endless polemics on matters of sex, gender, race, politics, and aesthetics.

None of the crowds or sets was made up of native inhabitants of Greenwich Village. (The Beat poet Gregory Corso was an exception to this rule, having been born above a funeral parlor at 190 Bleecker Street, across the street from the San Remo bar.) Village culture was created by newcomers, by immigrants from Europe, or from the equally remote American Midwest. Proud of its diversity and tolerance, the Village created no typical New York "bohemian" type or Greenwich Villager. Nonetheless, the Village was an idea, and served as a powerful cultural magnet. It was also characterized by an extreme fluidity of cultural activity, and of social relations. The sharply differentiated crowds have a disconcerting reluctance to stand still for the cultural photographer. Relations (erotic, political, artistic) were unstable, alliances short-lived; latent tensions flared up and then were forgotten. The fissiparous quality that gave life to the Village and strengthened its extreme individualism makes the tidying up operations of social history a thankless task.

Perhaps the best example of Greenwich Village complexity is at 137 Macdougal Street, near Washington Square, where a bookstore was opened in 1913. The proprietors, Albert and Charles Boni, had taken money that one of the brothers had been given by his parents to pay for an education at Harvard and then law school, and committed something akin to class treason by opening a book shop. The Boni brothers hoped their shop would become a cultural nexus for the younger generation of writers. They also wanted to publish books that could find no outlet in a New York publishing world, dominated as it was by Scribner's Sons and Harper's—high-minded, conservative, and largely controlled by New England Brahmins.

After an unexpected success with a book about the sociology of crime by the English socialist Robert Blatchford, the Boni brothers welcomed Alfred Kreymborg, when he brought examples of the new poetry that had begun to appear in London periodicals. Kreymborg had been in correspondence with the American poet Ezra Pound, and had received from Pound the manuscript of the Imagist anthology that Pound had assembled as a riposte to the considerable success of Edward Marsh's *Georgian Poetry 1911–1912*. Kreymborg wanted to found a magazine in New York for the new poetry. Harriet Monroe's Poetry in Chicago (founded 1912), *The Poetry Journal* in Boston and Pound's ventures in London left New York without a "poetry scene" or periodical sympathetic to the younger spirit. With Pound's manuscript in hand, Kreymborg persuaded the Boni brothers to publish *The Glebe*, which survived for ten issues in 1913–14. (While encouraging Kreymborg's efforts, Pound was also cultivating John Quinn, a wealthy New York lawyer, whose feelings about the Village were forthrightly expressed: "I don't know whether you know the pseudo-Bohemianism of Washington Square. It is nauseating to a decent man who doesn't need artificial sexual stimulation. It is a vulgar, disgusting conglomerate of second and third-rate artists and would-be artists, of I.W.W. agitators, of sluts kept or casual, clean and unclean..."). Boni also employed Kreymborg as a reader of manuscripts, and general talent scout for "youthful novels." There was in Kreymborg, according to a contemporary, "some powerful insinuation of novelty, of fresh discoveries, of new ideas and imaginative adventures." Kreymborg brought manuscripts by Carl Sandburg, Edgar Lee Masters and Vachel Lindsay to Macdougal Street. Younger women writers (such as Marianne Moore and Lola Ridge) found in Kreymborg a sympathetic reader.

Next door to the Washington Square Book Shop was the Liberal Club, founded in 1913 by Henrietta Rodman as a place where writers and artists, living in small rented rooms nearby, might enjoy the pleasures of "creative gossip." According to Floyd Dell, Rodman was a believer in "beauty and goodness, a Candide in petticoats and sandals." "Long hair and corsets," she once explained, "were less comfortable than short hair and loose clothing." She had worked for 25 years as a public school teacher in New York and was an activist in building the Teachers' Union. Rodman led opposition to the School Board policy of dismissing married women teachers after childbirth. The policy was overturned in a court ruling in 1915, and attempts to penalize Rodman for mocking the School Board in the local press similarly failed. She was a radical who had a real impact in the city, one of the few who connected the Village to feminist campaigns and trades union issues. Rodman brought together the diverse components of a counter-culture that had begun to form in the Village, making the Liberal Club a unique institution in the city. It was a crossroads for social workers, idealists, and reformers, and an ongoing challenge to the values of respectable New York.

At 23 Fifth Avenue, Mabel Dodge, the wife of a well-heeled architect, had begun to see herself performing a similar role. Where Rodman presided over an informal, *gemütlich* world at the Liberal Club, where ideas and politics did not have to dress for dinner, Dodge's exquisitely decorated apartment and midnight suppers brought the Village into contact with "Society." The radical journalist John Reed was Mabel Dodge's lover, and (when he was in town) a regular at the Liberal Club: lines crossed and re-crossed in the Village. A play entitled *St. George in Greenwich Village*, by Floyd Dell, which featured Sherwood Anderson in a small part, set the satirical tone for the club. Nothing was sacred in the freewheeling republic of the Liberal Club. "Pagan Routs" held at the club, with intellectuals and artists dressed as bacchi and bacchantes, satyrs and nymphs, attracted city-wide publicity, not all of which was positive. (H.L. Mencken regarded the Liberal Club as the home of "Washington Square mountebanks.")

Polly Holladay's restaurant was located in the basement of the Liberal Club. The banter of Polly's lover, chef, headwaiter, and anarchist ideologue, Hippolyte Havel, rivaled the goulash as an attraction. Havel had once been Emma Goldman's lover when they both lived in London, and after settling in New York in about 1909, he became a regular fixture at anarchist events in the city. Described by Ben Reitman as someone who "thought in German, spoke in English, and drank in all languages," Havel's jousts with the socialists of *The*

Masses enlivened the political life of the Village.

The passion of Villagers was for improvisation, not the building of institutions. When *Mother Earth* or *The Masses* needed additional funds, a costume ball was held, or a distinguished European writer cajoled into delivering a lecture. (It was an enduring tradition: *Partisan Review* was launched in 1934 on the proceeds of a lecture in New York by the English Marxist, John Strachey.) Yet the aspirations of the Villagers for a liberal feminism, racial and class justice, and sexual liberation, which placed their publications and artistic work at the remote margins of culture in the Progressive era, in time came to set the agenda of liberal and libertarian values in America. But Villagers did not seem to make particularly effective political advocates. *The Masses* was too irreverent for the Socialists, too bohemian for the Communists, too depraved for the respectable, and too intellectual to win a broad popular readership. The term "Greenwich Villagism," when used by radicals in the 1920s and 1930s, carried with it a scornful dismissal. Later inhabitants of the Village, such as e.e. cummings, regarded the political passions of the pre-war Village with amused disdain. Those who broke with its ethos, like Floyd Dell, were no less critical of the Villagers' hypocrisies and faddishness.

Eastman, editor of *The Masses*, urged in 1913: "Tie up to no dogma whatever." The injunction of Ezra Pound to "make it new" was true to the cultural ethos of Greenwich Village. But how deprived would American culture have been without the cultural radicalism and advocacy of Freudianism in *The Masses*, and the contribution of the Provincetown Players, who began life in the Washington Square Book Store? When they returned for the winter season in New York, a converted stables building at 139 Macdougal Street was rented and rebuilt as an intimate theater. Two years later, the Players moved into number 133, where Eugene O'Neill's *The Hairy Ape* and *The Emperor Jones* were given their first performances. American culture had, on Macdougal Street, one of its great moments of energy.

Caroline Ware's Village

When Allen Ginsberg arrived in Greenwich Village in the 1940s, there were a few old timers around who remembered the Pagan Routs of *The Masses* and who could point out where John Reed lived—a rented room above Polly Holladay's second restaurant, at 147 West 4th Street—when he wrote *Ten Days That Shook the World.* Joe Gould was still cadging drinks at McSorley's or the Minetta Tavern, boasting about his *Oral History of the World.* "It took me four years at Harvard to make me what I am today," he ironically remarked, holding up his glass. But the Village of *The Masses* was gone.

It was destroyed by the changes that swept across the western world during and after the First World War. The decision of President Wilson to enter the war in 1917 deeply split the anti-war radicals from those who, out of conviction or pragmatism, supported Wilson. The Russian revolution and the formation of the Communist Party in America irrecoverably split the Village left. The savage partisanship of the Communist Party ended the disputatious seminar of all brands of radicalism that had been such a distinctive feature of the Liberal Club, Polly's restaurant, and their customers. The wartime onslaught against the IWW and opponents of the war forced the closure of periodicals like *The Masses,* and led to the imprisonment or deportation of leading radicals. Emma Goldman and Alexander Berkman were deported to Russia, and, after a closer look at what was happening in the Soviet Union, became the revolution's most implacable enemies. Reed went to Russia as a journalist in 1917 and became a star-struck cheerleader for the revolution. When he died in 1920, word of his disillusionment at the course of Soviet tyranny filtered back to New York and was largely discounted as anti-Communist propaganda. The post-war Palmer raids against radicals finished off what remained of the left. Rodman died of a tumor in 1923. Floyd Dell entered psychoanalysis, got married, and left New York. And Eastman, the silver-haired and eloquent editor of *The Masses* and *The Liberator,* became a leading anti-Communist and a popular contributor to Republican periodicals. Prohibition ended the Village's tavern life. Speakeasies, bathtub gin, and gangsters with Tommy-guns belonged to another mentality than the Village. The election of Harding on a conservative Republican ticket in 1920 confirmed the sense that the party was indeed over.

The reaction of the Village bohemians to this rapid and violent change of cultural climate was disillusionment and a turn inward. Some moved to the suburbs. Betrayals, resignations, closures, political excommunications, and a strong feeling of the need to escape led to the post-war flight to Europe. Paris, not Greenwich Village, was the home of the American avant-garde in the 1920s.

The Village, too, had changed. Progressive era social theorists were alarmed at the signs of social disintegration in America and sought to find some way to re-establish social order. One strand of Progressive thinking focused on the city and saw great promise in the struggle to make local urban neighborhoods once again into communities. There were leading figures like Jane Addams whose work at Hull House in Chicago served as a model of community-based social reform. In the late 1920s the Rockefeller Foundation supported further research into the potentialities of settlement houses for social renewal. It soon became clear that deeper study of the neighborhood, its structures and forms, was needed. With the support of Columbia University, Caroline Ware, a professor of sociology at Vassar College, was invited to become director of research for a study of Greenwich Village.

Ware hoped to throw some light onto the nature of the changes in urban life affecting the Village. Ware's *Greenwich Village 1920–1930* (1935) is something of a classic in urban social research. The portrait she offers of Village life was far from the vivid memoirs of figures like Floyd Dell, Max Eastman, or Alfred Kreymborg. Ware found in the 1930s that the inhabitants of the Village had little sense of solidarity or feeling that they were part of a community. They were drawn from three groups, with little contact between them: the remaining bohemians of the 1912 era, who had escaped from their families and detached themselves from hometown communities; Italian immigrants, who found that American life offered models of adjustment that were contradicted by everyday realities; and the Irish, who had made their own adaptation to New York, with the Catholic Church, the police, and politics at its center. The Irish migration into the Village had taken place in the 1890s, and had created a one-party Democratic stronghold dominated by the ward-level political clubs whose allegiance was owed to the political machine of Tammany Hall. Once a center of sociability, with the changes in the neighborhood and the departure of the old families the small-town atmosphere of widespread participation in public life was lost. By the time Ware did her research in the early 1930s, the "real Americans" of the old Ninth Ward were playing little or no role in Village life.

Ware found that the traditional sources of social cohesion—family, church, school, work—had lost much of their old power. Even after the tragedy of the fire in 1911 at the Triangle shirtwaist company at 22 Washington Place East, in which 146 women died because the proprietors of the firm kept the fire exits locked to stop the seamstresses from taking time away from their sewing machines, class consciousness was almost completely absent among industrial workers in the Village. Changes in the population had made the Village seem less of a neighborhood or meaningful social unit for all of its inhabitants. Only those at the lowest income level seemed to feel there was much "neighborliness." For an increasing number of Villagers, even the family played no role in their lives.

> *Many Villagers* [she wrote] *repudiated family relationships altogether. The district abounded in single people living alone or in groups... There were others of all ages, both men and women, who repudiated everything which had to do with home and family and made no attempt to turn whatever living arrangements they might make into any substitute for the family and home life which they had discarded... For many of the Villagers, no institution, not even the family, retained significance in their lives.*

What Villagers liked best was the freedom to be left alone, and "the chance to live unhampered by what one's neighbor thought." It was a negative tolerance that the Village afforded. For Ware, this freedom was the "negation of neighborliness." In the absence of recognized community leaders, or social institutions that brought coherence and commitment, the Village was no longer a community; it had become a district in the city, much like others in its anonymity.

Village Scenes: Folk Singers, Beats, Hipsters

By the end of the Second World War, the cultural dominance of New York was a fact of American life. In theater, television, publishing, magazines, popular music, the art world—in everything except movies—New York was the arbiter of America's cultural marketplace. The Village was at a remove from these commercial pressures, but not immune to them. With the foundation of the *Village Voice* in 1955, the Village again found a voice—fractious, self-absorbed, partisan—that was largely missing elsewhere in American life during the "tranquilized Fifties."

The Village was once again being reshaped by the real estate market. Rising rents drove out some of the remaining small craft workers, bookstores, and artisans. Cold-water flats, which particularly appealed to young artists and writers because the rents were so low, were disappearing. But the famed social tolerance of the Village enabled shifts in taste to find expression more readily than elsewhere in the city. Young folk singers, recalling the tradition of Woody Guthrie and Pete Seeger, who had appeared frequently in New York in the previous decade, made Washington Square a venue for impromptu performances. By the mid-1950s, hundreds of young people were turning up in the park every weekend with stringed instruments of any and every variety. The city press was scornful of such enthusiasms, as it was of hipsters, beatniks, "hopheads," and jazz-fiends. Politicians were equally prompt to see electoral benefit in hostility to radicalism and deviance, and were visibly antagonistic to the New York of cultural experiment and "scenes."

The police made occasional efforts to expel the crowds of amateur performers. Police detectives covertly taped the scabrous comedian Lenny Bruce as he performed at the Village Vanguard, hoping to arrest Bruce, raid the club, and check the growth of subversion in the Village. It was standard police fare to shake down jazz clubs, and an occasional narcotics bust that placed liquor licenses in jeopardy did much to keep the kickbacks coming. Police regularly rousted folk singers in Washington Square. The imaginative lengths to which the police were prepared to go cannot but look like they, too, were part of the city's entertainment scene. Dressed in tight pantsuits, wearing wigs, they paraded up and down Times Square as decoys to trap rapists and pimps. Mostly, they busted johns. There was an NYPD squad that grew goatees, dressed in beatnik garb, and joined in the jazz and poetry scene in clubs and coffee houses by reading poems of their own devising, to give them cover for narcotics raids.

Since the Depression, owners of cabarets and performers had to have mug shots and fingerprints taken by the New York police before a "cabaret card" could be issued. Artists with prior arrests had to figure out how to bribe someone in the license office to get a cabaret card. It gave the police many opportunities to hassle black performers and those known or suspected to be drug users. The folk singers' riot and the "cabaret card scandal" of 1960 was a prelude to the much more brutal confrontation between the police and the gay community at the Stonewall Bar on Christopher Street later in the decade.

Jazz clubs like the Village Vanguard, and coffeehouses (the Figaro, Rienzi, Caricature, Café Wha?, Bizarre) latched on to the folk singing enthusiasm, allowing folk singers to perform for peer approval and any change they might collect. They were known as "basket houses." The folk scene was soon professionalized when the growing audience ("folkniks") for a new kind of music was discovered by clubs like the Village Gate and the Blue Angel, where jazz had previously been the major attraction. At the Village Gate leading folk singers were booked, and paid for their appearance, and their audiences charged admission. Max Gordon booked The Weavers for the Village Vanguard, and high-profile groups like the Kingston Trio, Peter, Paul, and Mary, Harry Belafonte, and Miriam Makeba, as well as stand-up comics like Woody Allen, Mort Sahl, and Lenny Bruce.

When a nineteen-year-old Bobby Zimmerman, a college dropout who had been performing at coffeehouses in Minneapolis, arrived in New York in January 1961, he found a folk "scene" already well established. There was a meeting place for folk culture at Allan Block's Sandal Shop on West 4th Street. Izzy Young's Folklore Center opened at 110 Macdougal Street in 1957. Gerde's Folk City on West 4th Street opened in May 1960. Every night of the week Zimmerman performed as "Bob Dylan" at one coffeehouse or another for "basket change," and was able to rent a flat on West 4th Street for $80 a month. In April 1961 he met Joan Baez, who had driven down to New York to protest restrictions being proposed on folk singing in Washington Square Park. Baez' first record had been released in November 1960 by Vanguard Records, whose office at West 14th Street off Eighth Avenue was on the northern edge of the Village. Its phenomenal success (140 weeks on the *Billboard* chart) alerted every recording label in town, who scrambled to find their own Baez, and soon enough their own Bob Dylan. The folk scene neatly indicates the links between cultural innovation in the Village and its commercial exploitation.

From the late 1940s there were three bars that between them divided the cultural world of the Village. The San Remo, at the corner of Bleecker and Macdougal Streets, and the White Horse Tavern, still at Hudson and West 11th Street, had a clientele drawn not from established sets or groups in New York, but composed of individuals, often strangers in the city, who were detached by choice from their social background. The third was the Cedar Street Tavern at 24 University Place, between 8th and 9th Streets (it was later relocated to 82 University Place), the bar of choice of the younger abstract artists who occupied studios and lofts in the East Village and the Lower East Side. Jackson Pollock, Franz Kline, and Willem de Kooning were regulars. There was little connection between the writers at the San Remo and the artists at the Cedar. The "New York Poets" (Frank O'Hara, John Ashbery, Kenneth Koch, and Barbara Guest) were among the few who moved easily between the two scenes. "In the San Remo," O'Hara remarked, "we argued and gossiped; in the Cedar we often wrote poems while listening to the painters argue and gossip."

The San Remo was a favorite hangout of New York writers. Maxwell Bodenheim, whose posthumous *My Life and Loves in Greenwich Village* appeared in 1954, was one of the few surviving writers of the Old Village to haunt the San Remo. Newly arrived writers like James Agee, James Baldwin, Michael Harrington, William Styron, and Edward Albee made the San Remo a regular port of call, establishing it as the center of Village literary life in the late 1940s. It was known as a favorite haunt of existentialists and a meeting place for musicians playing in nearby jazz clubs. It was also the home away from home of the "Three Graces," three young women who would turn up at the bar wearing flamboyant costume jewelry, wire-framed glasses and old fashioned dresses. They were, thought Barry Miles, pioneers of the hippie look of the next decade, and were mentioned in Allen Ginsberg's "Howl."

Ginsberg, who rented a room on 15th Street in 1952, became one of the regulars at the San Remo. In a letter to Neal Cassady he referred to the San Remo crowd as "the subterraneans." It was a phrase Jack Kerouac later used as the title of a novel that he relocated in San Francisco, but was a very New York story of his relationship with a black woman and the circle of friends who were in and out of Kerouac's apartment on East 7th Street. Ginsberg had known Kerouac since 1943, when he met Edie Parker and her then boyfriend (and later husband) Kerouac at a favorite hang-out, the West End Bar on

Broadway, across from the Columbia campus. With a friend, Lucien Carr, Ginsberg visited a mutual friend, David Kammerer, who had an apartment at 48 Morton Street, just off Seventh Avenue in the Village, and where they met another friend from St. Louis, William Burroughs, who was working as a bartender in the Village. The leading lights of the Beat Generation found the San Remo a useful place to meet, and it was on Macdougal Street that Ginsberg, Kerouac, Corso, Lamantia, and Burroughs spent useful time with each other.

Greenwich Village was a place for experimenting with drugs and sexual encounters for Ginsberg and his friends, and a place for unexpected bar-room chats. "I was in the San Remo sitting relaxed toward closing time," Ginsberg wrote in his journals in 1952, when Dylan Thomas and a friend walked into the bar. What followed was high literary bar-talk:

> *"Do you know—ever study English literature[?]" said* [Thomas'] *companion.*
> *"Of course, I'm a poet myself" I said.*
> *"Do you know who this is" he said.*
> *"Of course man it is obvious."*
> *"Oh another," said Thomas.*
> *"Well don't look at me," I said, stiffening up.*
> *Thomas, "I was just in another pub—drinking place—whatever you call them—and a girl said to me—would you like somewhere to go to see a girl and me do a trick?"*
> *"Is it a question of interpretation of 'trick'" I said.*
> *"No, I'm a professional," Thomas said "I'm a professional."*
> *"Well, I just thought it was a question of language," I said.*
> *"But she wanted $50.00—which I didn't have."*
> *"Oh well."*
> *"Do you know any amateurs?" he asked.*

Ginsberg, Kerouac, and friends breezed across Manhattan, carrying away little more than memories of their parties, meetings, couplings, moments of dazzling illumination. When they appeared in San Francisco in 1955, the encounter with an existing "poetry scene" was uneasy and became more strained over time. Ginsberg carried a polite letter of introduction to Kenneth Rexroth from William Carlos Williams. (Rexroth read Ginsberg's poems, and was not impressed: "You went to Columbia University too long. You're too old to be going on with all this formal stuff like that. What's the matter with you?") It was a rebuke Ginsberg listened to. After enrolling in an MA program at Berkeley, in July 1955 he moved to a little cottage at 1624 Milvia Street, near the Berkeley campus. In August he wrote "Howl," dedicating his first great poem to Carl Solomon, a fellow denizen of the San Remo and friend from New York who was then in an insane asylum.

Through Rexroth Ginsberg was introduced to Robert Duncan and Jack Spicer, and on Rexroth's suggestion he looked up a 25-year-old graduate student of Chinese and Japanese at Berkeley, Gary Snyder. He met Kenneth Patchen and Michael McClure in San Francisco. The famous poetry reading at the Six Gallery on October 13, 1955, at which Ginsberg read the first part of "Howl," was the first public reading for Ginsberg as well as for McClure, Whalen, Snyder, and Philip Lamantia. (Michael McClure thought that the 1960s really began with the reading at the Six Gallery.) It was followed by a similar reading, to a wildly enthusiastic audience, at Berkeley. Within days there was an explosion of poetry readings across the Bay Area. Word soon reached New York of the birth of a new scene.

Kerouac, who had just arrived from Mexico City, was in the audience, as was Lawrence Ferlinghetti, poet and co-founder of the City Lights Bookstore on the corner of Broadway and Columbus in North Beach. It was the first bookstore in America solely devoted to quality paperback books. "One of the original ideas of the store," remarked Ferlinghetti, "was for it not to be an uptight place but a center for the intellectual community." For the Beats, being "uptight" was a particularly distasteful emotional state of being hung up, repressed. The Beats had an idea that there was a true "community" of artists, of those who were not uptight, and which was not restricted to the poets and poetry-readers in the Bay Area or Greenwich Village. It was a free-floating international fellowship of bards and live spirits tied to no neighborhood and owing allegiance to no community other than to their own vision. For Ginsberg the Beats were committed to an idea of themselves as creative geniuses.

A media myth of the "Beat Generation" was born in September 1957, accompanying the publication of Kerouac's second novel, *On the*

Road. The origin and derivation of the term "Beat Generation" was hotly debated. John Clellon Holmes claimed to have first used it in his jazz novel *Go* (1952; reissued in 1959 as *The Beat Boys*). For Kerouac the term alluded to "beatitude" and the states of blessedness and happiness of the truly free spirit. *Time* and *Life* carried articles on the "Beats" and lexicons of the new jargon. The teenage followers of the Beats were labeled "beatniks" when, several weeks after the publication of Kerouac's novel, the first Russian satellite "Sputnik" was launched. The Beats made good copy in Eisenhower's second term, and the brooding, handsome Kerouac was everywhere in the media; *Playboy* and *Esquire* wanted think pieces by him on the "meaning" of the Beat Generation. There were centerfold photos of Beatnik "chicks."

"Beat Generation," "Beats," and "Beatnik" offered an addition to the modest nomenclature of American cultural dissidence. What set the Beats apart from previous American avant-gardes was the sudden, overwhelming glare of publicity. Overnight, writers who had been unpublishable were being hounded, interviewed, lionized, seduced; they found themselves able to make a living at writing. But the expectations greeting their subsequent publications were destructive of their development as writers. Success killed off the Beat Generation virtually at birth. A modest acclaim, one to encourage experiment and artistic development, was denied them; at the moment when they triumphed, it all went stale. By 1959 you could buy sweatshirts proclaiming "The Beat Generation" (with an imitation university insignia). Jokes about Beatniks were told by Jack Benny. Jack Paar conducted highbrow discussions of the Beat and the zeitgeist. High schools held "Beatnik" parties. Maps and city guides identified the main attractions of the beat "scene" in San Francisco and Greenwich Village. No literary movement had ever gone so swiftly from obscurity to marketing strategy. But the Beats had skedaddled—to Morocco, Japan, Mexico, anywhere but the cafés, galleries and poetry readings where the idea of the Beat was being watered down. Ginsberg did not return to New York until 1959, when he gave a reading at the Gaslight coffee shop on Macdougal Street.

Ginsberg liked a sense of aggression, an "anti-police ethos," in the San Remo bar and its customers. Having had repeated trouble with the police, it made him feel at home. But when bartenders at the San Remo started

talking tough and pushing the customers around, they provoked a customer walkout. Trade shifted to Louis' Bar in nearby Sheridan Square. The San Remo never quite regained the customers it lost in the early 1950s, and it was the White Horse Tavern on Hudson Street that was the primary beneficiary of the change in customer sentiment.

In the early 1950s Dylan Thomas made the White Horse Tavern something of a shrine for aspiring writers. The novelist James Jones was a White Horse regular when he was in town. Delmore Schwartz, by the 1950s living in cheap hotels and boarding houses and struggling against his inner demons, spent long hours in the White Horse, surrounded by writers, Village boozers, and a ready supply of young women. With two glasses of beer before him, recalled his biographer James Atlas, "Delmore would hold forth on politics, baseball, the *Partisan Review* days, or pull out one of his tattered, annotated copies of *Finnegans Wake* and read a few pages aloud." But it was Norman Mailer, who joined the hard-drinking macho crew at the White Horse, who made "hip" a New York response to the inflated beat world that emerged in San Francisco in 1955. Mailer's "The White Negro," published in *Dissent* in 1957, did not set out a doctrine that naturally lent itself to high school consumption. "Hip" was a special language, one that could not readily be taught. Mailer's essay called attention to a new vocabulary that the hipster had made his own: "The words [Mailer wrote] are man, go, put down, make, beat, cool, swing, with it, crazy, dig, flip, creep, hip, square." Mailer attempted to define a "hip morality" ("to do what one feels whenever and wherever it is possible, and… to be engaged in one primal battle: to open the limits of the possible for oneself, for oneself alone, because that is one's need"), which opened the writer to "murder, suicide, orgy, orgasm, incest." It sounded suspiciously like the old-time American individualism wedded to a vein of European existentialism and anarchism.

Mailer was suggesting in his essay a deeper resonance between white hipsters and black America. He has been accused of expressing a wild romanticism, which inevitably exploited the African American in the service of the guilt of white American liberals. "You have to be black to understand them," James Baldwin warned Mailer. In another way, Mailer had touched upon one of the most striking significances of the Village: in the 1950s and 1960s it was among the few places in New York (and indeed America) where white and black performers mingled easily before audiences who were themselves just as likely to be drawn from every nationality, race, and every ethnicity.

Mailer's careful distinction between the hipster and the beatnik inevitably fell apart. (The reaction of the Beats to Mailer's essay was at first one of amused contempt: they felt he missed the point, and the significance of mysticism for the Beats, and that he had allowed himself to be seduced by images of Dostoevskian violence.) There really was no way that Mailer could disguise the shared terrain of individualism that the "hip" and the "beat" shared. The terminology had changed in the 1950s, but the Village remained the Village, and it is hard to imagine that the members of the Liberal Club in 1912 would have been the least bit uncomfortable at either the San Remo or the White Horse in 1959.

It was at the White Horse where an oddly meaningful scene of civic reconciliation took place after 9/11. Wearing ash-caked boots, helmets, and their grimy coats, four firemen entered the White Horse. The brokers and "bearded intellectuals" who made up the usual White Horse crowd fell silent, and then cheers broke out across the bar. "USA! USA!" The scarred wooden tables were pounded. Waitresses danced with the firemen and took pictures together. A fireman remarked, "You can't walk a block in uniform without people saying thank you."

Warhol and the Factory

There was a pop art scene or scenes in New York in which the hard-drinking types at the White Horse, the Cedar, or the San Remo were unwelcome. It was explicitly a gay scene, with a distinctive sadomasochistic subculture; the shifting personnel were heavily into drugs; and the major figures shared the Catholic sensibility of the church in which they had been raised and which they then abandoned. Focused on the icons and imagery of popular culture, Andy Warhol and the photographer Robert Mapplethorpe became stellar presences connecting the "downtown" world of writers and painters living in the Village and the Lower East Side, and the 57th Street galleries, the wealthy collectors on Park Avenue, and the social world of the Upper East Side. After a decade working in commercial art (he decorated windows for Bonwit Teller, designed Christmas cards for Tiffany, and illustrated the advertisements for I. Miller shoes), Warhol made a commitment to bring the techniques of commercial art into the New York "high art" world. His "Factory," occupying a floor at 231 East 47th Street, was opened in 1963, where it remained until 1968, when he relocated it to 33 Union Square West. The third Factory was located at 860 Broadway. These were combined spaces where Warhol and his assistants worked, and where he shot his films.

Pop Art, in Warhol's hands, turned sharply away from the swirling paint surfaces of the Abstract Expressionists, with their violent brushwork, drips, and smudges. In 1960 Warhol experimented with several paintings of a Coca-Cola bottle, each in a different style. He greatly preferred the third version, which had the look of something from an advertisement, with all hints of the painter (his personality, his drama) suppressed. "Real art" could use the impersonal, techniques of the commercial artist. The use of silk-screen printing and photographically manipulated images gave him the anonymity of finish that became Warhol's mature style.

The Factory became the great "happening" of 1960s New York culture. It was one of the places where a new style of gay life, self-confidently displayed, was being created. In a society that was aggressively homophobic, Warhol surrounded himself with a "bodyguard" of good-looking gay young men. His movies were designedly scandalous and erotic, at least in theory. Viewers hoping for something explicitly pornographic left Warhol's films in puzzlement. Nicknamed "Drella" by the Factory hands, half-Dracula, half-

Cinderella, Warhol attracted punk celebrities, socialite wannabes, and a bevy of good-looking, snooty female English aristocrats. He took up Baby Jane Holzer, a young Park Avenue socialite, and briefly made her into a gossip column superstar. Writers and photographers soon found Warhol a fickle, grasping, and unpredictable manager of the greatest art-circus New York had ever known. Warhol's silk-screened soup cans, Marilyn Monroes, Elvises, and Jackie Kennedys made him famous.

Having your portrait done by Warhol conveyed a certain status in New York culture. Warhol's collectors appreciated the social advantages of commissioning a portrait. Like Ethel Scull, "done" in large-scale silk-screened image, they, too, became mini-celebrities. Expecting to be treated like a person of some distinction, the way Richard Avedon handled his socialites or with the decorous politeness encountered by the subjects of Yousuf Karsh's famous portrait photographs, Ethel Scull dressed accordingly. She was taken by Warhol to a photomat machine on 42nd Street, where Warhol pulled out $100 in coins and told her to get inside and look for the little red light. "We were running from one booth to another," she wrote. "Pictures were drying all over the place. At the end he said, 'Now do you want to see them?' They were sensational."

Warhol kept alive his ties to the downtown world, filming *Kiss* in late 1963 at the Lower East Side apartment of Naomi Levine, and arranging for the first screening of *Blow Job* at Ruth Kligman's Washington Square Gallery. *Flesh* opened for its sensational seven-month run at the Garrick Theater on Bleecker Street in October 1968. He created an apartment on the Lower East Side in which everything was either painted silver, or covered in silver tinfoil.

Robert Mapplethorpe, who worked in a studio in Bond Street, shared Warhol's Catholic upbringing. But where Warhol was in some respects curiously asexual, for Mapplethorpe the sexual appetite was utterly dominant. Seven nights a week prowling the gay bars in the West Village, Mapplethorpe was at the crest of the S&M wave that had begun to reach American culture in the 1970s. In the Village there was a greater variety of rubber and leather gear for sale, more studded leather collars and bondage masks, than copies of the books of the Beat poets. While taking thousands of photographs of his friends, lovers, tricks, and assorted drop-ins, Mapplethorpe pursued another career as a photographer of (highly erotic) flowers, and portraits (Truman

Capote, Susan Sontag, the artist Alice Neel), and subjects like the bodybuilder Lisa Lyon, who appealed to his sense of the sexually exotic. By 1980 he had lost interest in white S&M and had turned with avidity to the subculture of black gays. Like Warhol, he preferred a cool, classical detachment in his images, and there was a sharp tension between the sexually provocative nature of his subjects and the calm elegance of his images. Also like Warhol, Mapplethorpe employed skilled printers to make his pictures. He boasted sometimes about being a photographer who had never made a print. The AIDS epidemic of the 1980s killed Mapplethorpe, and many of the writers, socialites, artists, and friends who had made Warhol's Factory the defining art scene of the age.

CHAPTER FIVE

Parks

Urban Space and Romantic Landscapes

Cities are places where the uses of space are highly complex. Central Park illustrates the point: what was once a created open space, democratically free and open to all, has been regulated, fenced in, and subdivided. The park's defenders have often objected, sometimes effectively, against mindless vandalism, inappropriate "vanity" gifts, and politically motivated improvements. But to speak of the purists versus the despoilers, the good guys versus bad guys, misrepresents the processes at work. It obscures the way Central Park, as it is today, represents a process of accommodation over a century and a half by an extraordinarily pure and strong conception to the fact that the park is situated in the midst of a vibrant democracy. Pressures, whether from politicians, benefactors, or reformers, can, sometimes, be resisted by high-minded defenders of ancient virtue. But the real world, with its budget cutbacks and institutional indifference, and its sensitivity to changing public ideas about space, recreation and access, turns out over time to have been the most powerful influence upon the shape of the park and its state today.

There are quite a lot of "Keep Off the Grass" signs in Central Park, and a lot of fences to reinforce the message. There are also a startling number of facilities for organized play. In 1972 Henry Hope Reed, appointed the first Curator of Parks by Mayor Lindsay in 1967, drew up a list of sporting activities available in the park: baseball and softball, bicycling, boating, bowls, croquet, fishing, handball, hockey, horseback riding, horseshoe pitching, ice skating, model yachting, paddleball, roller skating, shuffleboard, skiing, soccer, swimming, and tennis. The provision of so many specialist facilities represents only a part of the way the park is used. There are gaggles of joggers, began an account of the park in 1992,

> *(some guiding high-speed baby buggies, some with trotting dogs on long leashes), race walkers and casual strollers. There are swarms of bicyclists that hum like hornets while less driven cyclists coast by with the ease of a paddle wheeler on the Mississippi. The inner-park roads are also crammed with carriages, skate boarders, skaters and more recently hundreds, perhaps thousands, of people indulging in the latest fad—Rollerblades and other in-line skates.*

There are zoos, museums, nightclubs, theaters, and band shells for music in Central Park. The park is the people.

Central Park today, nonetheless, has to be protected from the public. We can understand now, perhaps more clearly than a generation ago, that the park is a fragile organism that desperately needs to be allowed to recover from the polluting city itself and the many-footed assault of its visitors. As a result, in certain areas of Central Park there are fences and barriers, designed to keep people off the grass and away from threatened plants, as well as defining organized use of the park's facilities. For Frederick Law Olmsted, superintendent of the park and co-author of its 1857 design, it was New Yorkers who were the threatened ones (by pollution, over-crowding, unsanitary housing, the sheer pressure of urban life) for whom a park with open green fields was a cure, an antidote.

The city's abundant provision of public parks came in the second quarter of the nineteenth century out of a change in the way American people thought about cities and about nature. Romantic and Transcendental attitudes toward nature preferred to think of the natural world as a repository of civic and spiritual values. Nature provided a touchstone, a frame of reference against which to understand, and judge, the rapidly growing city. The expansion of trade, industry, and commerce was accompanied by the social problems that pollution, overcrowding, great wealth, dire poverty, and sharpened social inequality brought with them.

Americans loved nature, but many felt that the unadorned, wild landscape of the West cried out for "improvement." The drudgery of hard-scrabble farming and life in a remote log cabin, or the plainness of Thoreau's life at Walden Pond, was not what most Americans had in mind, however fondly they admired the idea of the "simple life." Rather, as the books and articles on landscape and houses by Andrew

Jackson Downing made clear, the new rural ideals were to be articulated by a new profession, the landscape gardener, and were to be expressed in attractive Gothic cottages set in picturesque rural locations. Downing was twenty-six years old and the proprietor of a commercial nursery in Newburgh on the Hudson when his *Treatise on the Theory and Practice of Landscape Gardening* appeared in 1841. His mixture of patriotic homilies ("The love of country is inseparably connected with the *love of home*"), botanical advice (the oak is "the most varied in expression, the most beautiful, grand, majestic, and picturesque of all deciduous trees"), hints on practical gardening, and advocacy of "natural" or English landscaping, made him the most influential of the first generation of American landscape gardeners.

Downing believed that country houses in the rural Gothic design, with high gables, tracery, bay windows, and bold overhanging cornices, were the most appropriate for American conditions, and would best serve as an instrument of moral elevation and social order. Country houses, he argued, should avoid excessive ornamental display. "The simple and more chaste forms," he wrote in *The Architecture of Country Houses* (1850), "are in better keeping with the more simple habits which prevail in country life." He was a persuasive voice against the "Greek mania," the enthusiasm for Classical Revival architecture that had been embraced with such avidity for the United States Custom House on Wall Street in 1842 (see Chapter 2). But when domestic architecture began to sprout porticos and columns in whitewashed formality, Downing urged the superiority and the appropriateness of wood and stone cottages in the English or Gothic design; these, he felt, would become an organic part of the American landscape.

Downing's ideal villas stood in a "picturesque" landscape characterized, he wrote,

> *by irregular and broken lines—lines expressive of violence, abrupt action, and partial disobedience… The Beautiful is an idea of beauty calmly and harmoniously expressed; the Picturesque an idea of beauty or power strongly and irregularly expressed… We find the beautiful in the most symmetrical edifices, built in the finest proportions, and of the purest materials. It is, on the other hand, in some irregular castle formed for defense, some rude mill nearly as wild as the glen where it is placed,*

some thatched cottage, weather stained and moss covered, that we find the Picturesque.

As a result of Downing's influence, American parks were self-consciously rustic and natural, with a minimum of formal design features. When Americans visited the urban parks conceived under the sway of Downing's ideas, they entered an idealized pastoral landscape, intended in every respect to be unlike the surrounding urban world. Naturalness and simplicity guided the designs of urban cemeteries and parks in New York.

The first American attempt to embody the new thinking about the uses of naturalness in romantic landscapes came in 1831 when Mount Auburn Cemetery in Cambridge, Massachusetts, was developed as a "cemetery-arboretum" in conjunction with the Massachusetts Horticultural Society. It was soon followed in New York by Green-Wood Cemetery in Brooklyn, laid out in 1839 on a site of nearly 500 acres on Gowanus Heights. The main entrance and gate house, a stunning Gothic confection designed by Richard Upjohn in the 1860s, is on 5th Avenue opposite 25th Street (take the M, N, or R subway to 25th Street in Brooklyn). It contained six artificial lakes in a carefully graded and planted landscape, and has subsequently become the site of over half a million burials. Green-Wood is a treasure-trove of Victorian architecture and design.

The public's response to Mount Auburn and Green-Wood reflected a growing appreciation of parks and the ideals of picturesque landscape. Green-Wood became something of a pleasure-ground, where the Brooklyn gentry could take fashionable carriage rides. So popular did it become that there were traffic jams on Sunday afternoons. The picturesque effect of headstones, urns, and memorial statuary sited in a striking landscape of irregular surfaces, winding carriage paths, open meadows, and leafy glades was a vindication of the new ideals of the "controlled wildness" of natural landscape design. And with the popular success came an unexpected problem. People who came to the cemetery to be amused, and who behaved as though they were on a pleasure jaunt, disturbed those who wished quiet contemplation. There was too much wildness and the social controls were too weak. The bustle and ostentation of carriages changed the atmosphere of burial grounds, and before long strict regulations were imposed to control behavior and limit casual access to visitors. Entrance to Green-Wood today is restricted, a legacy of that struggle to regain control of the public's pleasure. Nonetheless, advocates of parks and rural cemeteries argued that they were "marble pulpits," where good influences predominated.

Woodlawn Cemetery

The American preference for rural cemeteries and growing interest in urban parks led to the creation of Woodlawn Cemetery in the Bronx River Valley in 1863. Located ten miles north of midtown Manhattan, along the line of the New York and Harlem Railroad (Woodlawn is at the northern end of the number 4 subway), it occupies an historically important site. In 1776 General George Washington ordered a redoubt to be erected to block British troops advancing north along the Post Road in the Bronx, while the main body of the Continental Army retreated to White Plains. The Gunhill Redoubt stands along Heliotrope Avenue on the southern edge of the cemetery.

Three-quarters of the 400 acres purchased for Woodlawn had survived into the nineteenth century as farmland and the remainder was wooded. Like Green-Wood and Central Park, its "naturalness" was created. James C. Sidney, a Philadelphia architect, laid out the site in a complex pattern of curving drives, walkways, and oval plots of land. There are twenty miles of tree-lined walks in Woodlawn, offering one of the nicest and quietest landscapes in the city. Unlike Green-Wood, it is open to the public.

There have been 300,000 burials at Woodlawn since the first interment in 1863, and it has occasionally been compared to Père Lachaise cemetery in Paris. Opened in 1804 on the eastern side of Paris, and on land once owned by the confessor of Louis XIV, Père Lachaise became the burial site of choice for writers, artists, politicians, musicians (from Chopin to Jim Morrison), philosophers, photographers, generals, and scientists. The idea that Woodlawn might become an American Père Lachaise was not far-fetched. Six mayors of New York are buried at Woodlawn (including Fiorello La Guardia), three US Senators, a Supreme Court Justice, and Ralph Bunche, winner of the Nobel Peace Prize in 1950. The graves of four of the nation's most influential and wealthiest retailers are at Woodlawn: R.H. Macy, F.W.

Woolworth, J.C. Penney, and Samuel Kress, founder of the Kresge retailing business, which metamorphosed into K-Mart. The entertainers buried at Woodlawn constitute a who's who of American popular culture: Irving Berlin, George M. Cohan, W.C. Handy (father of the blues), Victor Herbert, "Fatty" Arbuckle, the famous dancing partners Vernon and Irene Castle, and the violinist Fritz Kreisler. Duke Ellington, Miles Davis, and Coleman Hawkins are among the jazzmen at Woodlawn. There is a sprinkling of great press barons (Joseph Pulitzer); capitalists (Jay Gould, William C. Whitney, and Collis P. Huntington); feminists (Elizabeth Cady Stanton, Carrie Chapman Catt, and Alva Vanderbilt Belmont); literary critics (F.O. Matthiessen); fabled law men ("Bat" Masterson); cartoonists (Thomas Nast); and cultural benefactors (Robert Lehman, the financier who left his spectacular collection of paintings to the Metropolitan Museum, and Augustus D. Juilliard, whose will established the famous Juilliard School of Music). Along Oak Hill Avenue in Woodlawn are the burial sites of the "400." Their handsome mausoleums remind us that these were people, the leading socialites in late nineteenth-century New York, who lived in high style on Fifth Avenue, had "cottages" at Newport, and were buried with similar prominence at Woodlawn. In the Catalpa section are the very modest graves of the writer Herman Melville and his family.

Cemeteries seldom appear in the standard guidebooks of New York City. Nonetheless, they are spaces of real historical and cultural interest, and are among the least touched by the city's restless pace of change. The historical interest of the burying ground around Trinity Church (see pp.47–48) is obvious, but the large Trinity cemetery uptown, between 153rd and 155th Street, west of Amsterdam Avenue, offers a unique feel for the ruggedness of the original landscape of Manhattan. The First Shearith Israel Graveyard, on St. James Place, between Oliver and James Street, is believed to be the oldest Jewish graveyard in New York. It has almost entirely been swallowed up by the housing on three sides of the small plot. The gravestones marking Jews who took part in the Revolutionary War are reconstructed monuments, but seem sufficiently eroded and decayed to be original. The Green-Wood Cemetery shares with Woodlawn an important place in the romantic nineteenth-century ideal of the "natural." Like Woodlawn, it has an abundant register of the famous and formerly famous among the interred.

Parks and the City

The city had a scattering of parks in 1850, each of modest size, amounting in total only to 170 acres for a population that exceeded half a million people. New Yorkers who had seen the spacious parks of Vienna, London, and Paris knew how poorly their hometown compared to the great European capitals. There was much that could be done to persuade a community of the social advantages of parks. It was an occasion for elite leadership. The city elites feared that democracy, left to its own devices, would never create a truly civilized and cultured urban environment. Everyone on Fifth Avenue could see that parks were an expression of civic pride, a measure of urban aspiration, and regretted how indifferent were the city's efforts at improvement in the decades before the Civil War.

The oldest public spaces in the city were relics of the Dutch colony of New Amsterdam. The park where City Hall stood was on the common ground set aside by the Dutch West India Company. The low density of occupancy of New Amsterdam meant that some inhabitants—the proportion is hard to fix—enjoyed large and handsomely laid-out gardens and walkways lined with trees and shrubs. There was perhaps less need to think about creating green open space in a colony where private gardens were plentiful and where there was easy access to the surrounding countryside.

So it was that Bowling Green, a small oval enclosure at the foot of Broadway, became the city's first public park. Located at the heart of the English colony, the land where Bowling Green was laid out, formerly a parade ground, was leased by the Common Council in 1732 to a group of residents who petitioned to enclose the space and lay out a bowling-green "for the recreation and delight of the inhabitants of the city." The Governor, wrote Abigail Franks in 1734, "has made a Very Pretty bowlling greens with a handsome Walk of trees Raild Just before the fort in t[ha]t Large Durty Place it Reaches three doers beyond..." The streets around remained unpaved until cobblestones were laid in the 1760s. The land in the vicinity of Bowling Green fetched a premium in the colonial real estate market and was favored by wealthy merchants. Artisans found the rents beyond their means—part of a process that created residential districts marked by strong cleavages of wealth and class. Cricket teams from Brooklyn and Greenwich played at Bowling Green during the British military occupation. But there were several dramatic moments of revolutionary tumult around Bowling Green. Protesting the Stamp Act, a mob of New Yorkers stoned the British garrison in the Fort in 1765, hanging the governor in effigy and burning his carriage at Bowling Green. On July 10, 1776, the day when word of the Declaration of Independence reached New York, an equestrian statue of King George III at Bowling Green was torn down by a mob celebrating the break with Britain. It was said the lead statue was melted down to make bullets and cannon balls to fire against the redcoats.

After the arrival of peace in 1783, Bowling Green resumed its former colonial identity as a highly desirable residential enclave, close to the commercial and social center of New York life in the late 1790s. It was called "Nobs' Row" and perhaps other, less polite, names. (The small park was most recently reconstructed in 1978.) Nearby streets—Greenwich, Whitehall, Beaver, Broad, Water, State, and Pearl—were lined with handsome brick and stone buildings. The colonnaded James Watson House at 7 State Street, erected 1794–1806, is the lone survivor of the mansions that once dominated this area.

The Battery

The land where Battery Park was created, at the southern tip of Manhattan, was known to the Dutch as "Capske Hook," or rocky ledge. Today's Battery, with its carefully laid-out paths and popular walk along the bulkhead with its unsurpassed view of the New York harbor, acquired that handsome identity in the nineteenth century. Due to repeated extensions of the waterline by landfill, Battery Park became an amenity the island had never possessed. Until 1788, when the site of the fort was razed, the Battery was mainly used to land small vessels that did not need to be sailed into the East River to reach the larger docks and slips.

On a small outcropping of stone, some hundred yards off the tip of the Battery, Castle Clinton (the "West Battery") was erected in 1807–9. Today, tickets for the Statue of Liberty and Ellis Island boats are sold from a kiosk in the center of Castle Clinton, now thoroughly incorporated within the Battery. It was designed by John McComb, Jr. (See Chapter 6 for his role in the construction of City Hall). Considering the fact that the English had previously invaded New York in 1664 and 1776, it was perhaps not totally irrational to assume that the most likely attacker would once again be the Royal Navy. In the event, no invasion took place (instead, a British army burned the White House in Washington), and in 1823 Castle Clinton was ceded by the United States government to the city corporation. Converted into Castle Garden, it was leased to promoters for use as a place of public amusement and theatrical events. The triumphant appearances of Jenny Lind (the "Swedish Nightingale") at Castle Garden in 1850 before an audience of 6,000 brought the city to an ecstasy of admiration for the Swedish soprano. Gradually encompassed by landfill extensions of the park, Castle Garden served as the primary immigrant receiving station from 1855 to 1890. Between 1880–4, almost two million immigrants arrived at New York. The vessels would drop anchor in the harbor, anywhere up to six miles from Castle Garden, in quarantine, awaiting the arrival of an inspection officer to approve the passenger list and lead the vessel to the depot. Upon release from quarantine, any passengers regarded as falling within the requirements would be ferried to Castle Garden, where customs officers would examine baggage and health officers conduct cursory examinations before the newly-arrived passengers were allowed to proceed to their destinations in the city or across the nation. It was altogether a big, largely efficient operation, with only a small minority of immigrants spending more than one day being processed for entry. The opening of Ellis Island improved the ability of the government to handle large numbers of newcomers.

The fierce armament of Castle Clinton (28 32-pound cannons) made the Battery a site of public curiosity. The firing of blank cartridges attracted crowds lining the wooden fence along the waterside. Where there were soldiers and a flagpole, and regular performances of military marches, the brave men of New York paraded, enjoying cool drinks. (The tradition of curbside carts carrying large blocks of ice, ready for the vendor to shave a cupful and add flavored syrup—called a SnoCone—goes back a long way in the history of the city.) Lower Broadway, Bowling Green, and the Battery offered ladies an opportunity to show themselves, an opportunity not so attractively available elsewhere in the bustling city.

As the city's commercial district at the southern tip of Manhattan expanded, the political and commercial grandees of the city, who had once occupied fine mansions on lower Broadway, moved uptown. The Battery lost some of its social standing. "Battery a very pleasant place to walk on a Sunday evening," noted Jeremy Cockloft in Washington Irving's *Salmagundi* in 1807, "—not quite genteel though—every body walks there, and a pleasure, however genuine, is spoiled by general participation—the fashionable ladies of New-York turn up their noses if you ask them to walk on the Battery on Sunday." The view of the harbor was (and is) spectacular, but by the 1850s those who could enjoy Washington Square or promenade along the fashionable part of Broadway around Grace Church at 10th Street, were not inclined to bother with the long walk downtown to the Battery.

The Battery was an important staging ground for troops passing through New York during the Civil War and retains its military associations, with the erection in 1963 of a memorial to the American servicemen who lost their lives in the Atlantic during the Second World War. During the rescue and recovery work at the World Trade Center in September and October 2001, hundreds of Marines and National Guardsmen camped in tents in the park. The very ambitious Battery

Park City—so shatteringly affected by the destruction of the World Trade Center—was, like the Battery itself, the creation of a vast program of landfill. Ninety-two acres of new land were created, in large measure from the excavation of the massive WTC, in an extraordinarily ambitious development by the Battery Park City Authority, formed in 1968 by the New York State legislature. Funded by the sale of state bonds, construction began in 1974 and by the mid-1990s the City was housing more than 5,000 residents, with an infrastructure of schools, shops and retail space, as well as a greatly-admired bulkhead walkway with spectacular views across the Hudson to New Jersey and the Statue of Liberty. The closure of the 1/9 subway line, and the massive dislocation caused by the events of September 11, 2001, has severely shaken the program to revivify downtown for residential occupation.

Private Property and Radicalism

There was one public space planned for New York that might have rivaled Central Park. In fact, if it had ever been opened, it is likely that there would never have been a Central Park in its present location and size. In 1807 the commissioners charged with laying out the grid plan for the city reserved a substantial open space (between Third and Seventh Avenues, from 23rd to 34th Streets) for a "Parade." As development proceeded uptown, the "Parade" was reduced in size and then was abandoned as a public space altogether in 1829.

Of the smaller public spaces, Washington Square, laid out as a park in 1828, probably exerted the greatest benevolent influence upon the surrounding neighborhood (see Chapter 4). The smallest, Gramercy Park, laid out in 1831 by Samuel G. Ruggles, was a private pleasure ground barely an acre in size and kept under locked restricted access. The Italianate brownstones that surrounded the park looked out upon willow, maple, and chestnut trees, which gave the park a charming aspect—mostly for the benefit of the key-holders. The question of access to the park has been fiercely disputed in the past, and the Gramercy Park Trust, whose members are elected for life, has taken a strong line against widening access. This in turn led to a lawsuit filed in federal district court in 2001 by O. Aldon James, Jr., president of the National Arts Club at 15 Gramercy Park South, which claimed that the park's administrative body had excluded invited children on racial grounds. The suit asks the court to declare the governing structure illegal and replace it with an elected body. In turn, detectives from the New York City Department of Finance raided the National Arts Club as part of an investigation into possible grand larceny and tax fraud. Tongues are wagging on Gramercy Square.

Tompkins Square, a ten-acre site between Avenues A and B from 7th to 10th Street, was laid out as a park in 1833. As late as 1851, Tompkins Square was mainly used as a parade ground, and the surrounding streets were occupied by small factories, workingmen, artisans, and Irish immigrants. With the arrival of the large-scale German immigration in the mid-nineteenth century, the character of the square changed. The Germans who called the East Side "Little Germany" unofficially re-named Tompkins Square *der Weisse Garten*, the white garden. Surrounded by beer halls, restaurants, cigar factories, music societies, athletic associations, and breweries, Tompkins Square was overwhelmingly German.

It was also at the center of the German trade union movement. *Der Weisse Garten* was a frequent location for demonstrations in support of the eight-hour day, and police attacks upon the demonstrators. The most notorious of such conflicts occurred on January 13, 1874, at a time of deep depression in the city's economy, when a permit to demonstrate in Tompkins Square against the growing unemployment in the city was canceled the night before a planned meeting. News of the cancellation had not been fully circulated, and when 10,000 people assembled in the park the next day they were suddenly attacked by police carrying clubs. A young activist in the International Cigar Makers' Union, and future leader of the American Federation of Labor, Samuel Gompers, recalled the events of that day in his autobiography:

> *Shortly afterwards the mounted police charged the crowd on Eighth Street, riding them down and attacking men, women and children without discrimination. It was an orgy of brutality. I was caught in the crowd on the street and barely saved my head from being cracked by jumping down a cellarway...A reign of terror gripped that section of the city.*

By the later nineteenth century, the center of the German population in New York had begun to move uptown along Third Avenue to Yorkville, north of 86th Street and east of Central Park.

Tompkins Square remained at the heart of radical agitation, the natural starting off point for marches against American entry into the First World War in 1917, and a host of left-wing causes and anti-fascist protests. The great "Red Scare" in New York of 1919–20, when city and state governments tried to smash radical political groups and protesters, saw the passage of a law against criminal anarchy (maximum penalty of five to ten years in prison) and a Red Flag law, which made it a misdemeanor to display a red flag. Socialists were expelled from the New York State legislature in 1920, and there was an anti-red state investigative committee, under the chairmanship of Clayton R. Lusk, which brought forward anti-radical measures aimed at the suppression of the Socialist Party and other left groups.

The battle that was being waged in the streets around Tompkins Square was decided in the city's law courts and in the legislature in Albany. Despite the city's reputation for freewheeling radicalism, the truth is that anti-radicalism played pretty well in New York politics. It was a style, and a program, that persisted in the city. In the 1960s, by which time there had been an influx of African Americans and Puerto Ricans into the Tompkins Square area, the atmosphere was livelier and more diverse. In the dark days of the Vietnam War, there was a confrontation between police, anti-war protesters, and the floating community of beatniks, hippies, poets, and artists, who had made Tompkins Square the home of an ongoing demo against the war, police brutality, and the State. Three protesters were hospitalized on May 30, 1967, and 30 were arrested. In 1991, when the area had begun to be gentrified, there was a riot when squatters were forcibly evicted from the park. For over a century Tompkins Square has had a reputation for immigrant radicalism, rioting and social dissidence.

Olmsted and Central Park

Before Central Park, the city had small, tame green spaces, laid out with obvious pedestrian routes and too little to spur the imagination. No one would have ever talked about the "benefits of nature" in such parks or regarded them as places of retreat and renewal. The 840 acres of Central Park established a new and previously unimaginable scale for urban parks, which the 3,000 acres of Fairmount Park in Philadelphia, planned in 1859, vindicated.

Editors, poets, preachers, and journalists picked up the idea of parks and launched a barrage of publicity, claiming that not only would parks be an adornment of the city, but that they would improve civic life, strengthen social discipline, and mark the ascent of New York to the rank of the world's great cities. In the 1850s, thoughts about the parks in Europe sharpened New Yorkers' dissatisfaction with their own city. "There was no place within the city limits in which it was pleasant to walk, or ride, or drive, or stroll," wrote Clarence Cook in *A Description of the New York Central Park* in 1869. The city provided few places for public amusement. There was "no place for skating, no water in which it was safe to row; no field for base-ball or cricket; no pleasant garden where one could chat with a friend, or watch his children play, or, over a cup of tea or coffee, listen to the music of a good band." In the mayoral election in 1850 both the Democratic and the Whig candidates supported the idea of a park, and it fell to the winner, a sperm-oil importer and Whig named Ambrose Kingsland, to formally propose that the city create a large public park.

The commercial interests of the city doubted the need or the value of a park, and attacked the first proposed location, a strip of land along the East River owned by John Jones. There were complaints that the proposed park at Jones Wood was too large, too expensive, and too remote from the rest of the city. Tribunes of the workingman thought the whole thing was a plot to steal the honest dollars of workers to provide a place of amusement for the carriage class. Fears that rowdies would dominate the park were expressed by the refined. Downing mocked those who expressed alarm about the proposal and repeated his argument that the parks of Europe demonstrated how the people together can enjoy "the same music, breathe the same atmosphere of art, enjoy the same scenery, and grow into social freedom by the very influences of easy intercourse, space and beauty that surround them." The park, so its defenders argued, would strengthen American democracy. Nothing less.

A large central site, north of 59th Street, between Fifth and Eighth Avenues, was accepted in 1852. By the time the land had been acquired (including the summary removal of the occupants of Seneca Village—see Chapter 2) and topographically surveyed, political control of the city had passed from Whigs to Democrats. There was a new charter for the city's government, and in 1857 the nation sank into a financial depression that threw men out of work across the city. An eleven-man Board of Commissioners was appointed by the state legislature in an attempt to remove control of the large project from the notoriously corrupt city government, and work began on draining the bogs of what was already called Central Park. In 1857 Frederick Law Olmsted, a farmer, journalist, and sometimes publisher, was appointed superintendent of Central Park. It was this appointment which gave the park its shape and identity.

There is a tendency in recent thinking about Olmsted, led by Witold Rybczynski of the University of Pennsylvania (*A Clearing in the Distance: Frederick Law Olmsted,* 1999), to see him as a modern figure, advocating an open-ended, tolerant, and pragmatic approach to town planning, largely content to let parks hold their own. There was another Olmsted, one immersed up to his eyeballs in the politics of New York, for whom the struggle against urban corruption was among the defining experiences of his adult life. It was in the attempt to overturn the notorious "Ring" of "Boss" Tweed, which controlled New York after the Civil War, that men of honesty came to formulate a program for the political future of the city. Keeping the hands of the "Ring" off the lucrative funding that was being lavished on the park gave Olmsted his opportunity, and the moment of one of his most important contributions to nineteenth-century New York.

Not only did Olmsted design the park; he established and defended its independence from the politicians who had made New York a byword across the nation for urban corruption. His contemporaries regarded Olmsted's achievement as nothing less than heroic, and there was talk about what a good candidate he would make for president. He was happy just to design parks—though it is important to see that for Olmsted the design was a weapon in the larger struggles his contemporaries were waging to reform the city and make it habitable. A laid-back pragmatist could never have resisted Boss Tweed.

Olmsted had tried his hand at farming and authorship, but he had little practical experience of architecture or urban design. His collaborator Calvert Vaux, a London-trained architect, worked as Downing's assistant in 1850. Within two years he became Downing's partner, and inherited his mantle in 1852 when Downing drowned in

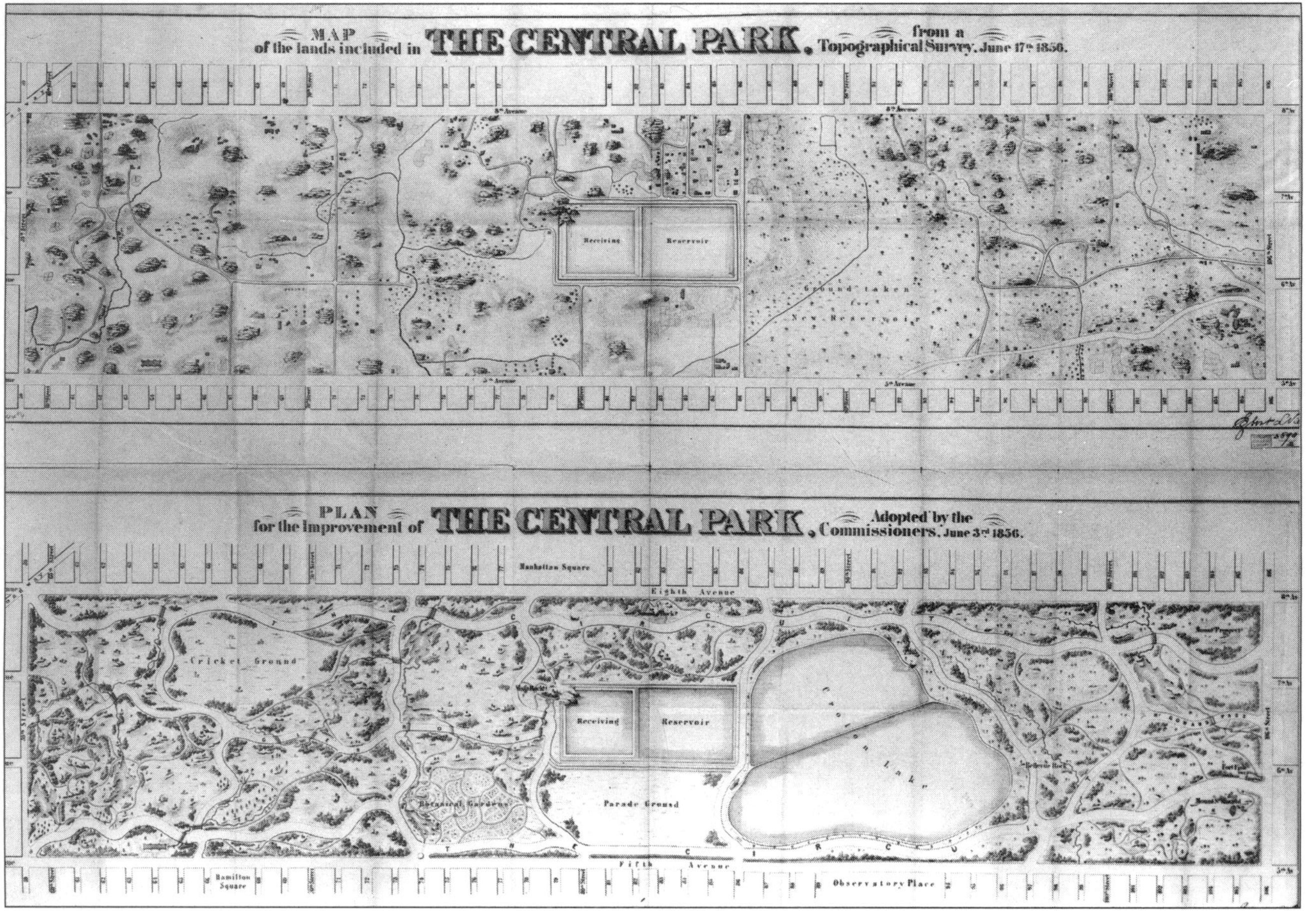
MAP of the lands included in THE CENTRAL PARK, from a Topographical Survey, June 17th 1856.
Receiving
Reservoir
Ground taken for New Reservoir
5th Avenue
PLAN for the improvement of THE CENTRAL PARK, Adopted by the Commissioners, June 3rd 1856.
Manhattan Square
Eighth Avenue
Cricket Ground
Receiving
Reservoir
Botanical Gardens
Parade Ground
Fifth Avenue
Hamilton Square
Observatory Place

a riverboat accident. When Olmsted and Vaux put together a submission for the Central Park design competition in 1857, Olmsted had already been hired as superintendent of construction for the park. He was personable, well-liked, and widely supported by the political elite of the city. Vaux was the one with substantial experience of design, but Olmsted was an admirable front man, best able to articulate the ideas of the project. He has by far the larger public reputation, but the contribution of Calvert Vaux and the ornamental designs of Jacob Wrey Mould made the individually designed bridges, the belvedere, and the terrace a perfect complement to the landscaping conception.

Underlying the plan for Central Park, which Olmsted and Vaux titled "Greensward," was a conception of the park as "a single work of art," created to embody a "single, noble motive, to which the design of all its parts, in some more or less subtle way, shall be confluent and helpful." In an oft-quoted remark, Olmsted stated the purist conception: that "the idea of the park itself should always be uppermost in the mind of the beholder." The park should, in other words, be a vehicle for the virtue of nature,

and ideally should be allowed to remain uncluttered by monuments, statues, and other expression of cultural values. Nonetheless, for Olmsted the park idea had about it a large component of social engineering and reform. He wanted Central Park to offer to citizens of every class an elevating vision of nourishment and civility, which incorporated and went beyond the virtues of simplicity so interconnected with the American idea of nature.

Olmsted hoped that the park would encourage and strengthen higher standards of behavior and social order. He firmly believed that design could do much to avert social evils: "It will effect a marked change in the habits of our people—bringing out every pleasant day hundreds and thousands of carriages and creating a kind of delightful recreation which thus far has no existence in this City."

In the 1850s, when Olmsted drew up his plan, only ten percent of the inhabitants of New York lived above 40th Street. It was, in other words, a suburban park located in an undeveloped semi-rural, semi-urban environment. It was far from the tenements of the city's poor, who would have had the greatest benefit from "Greensward." Olmsted hoped the park would maintain the feel of the countryside, however much work and expense it took to create the semblance of naturalness. Before the building of the Brooklyn Bridge in the 1880s, the scale of the construction and the money spent on Central Park were unique. (Between 1859 and 1862, nearly 150,000 trees were planted.) But the integrity of Olmsted's design was interfered with almost at once: the state legislature set aside land within the borders of the park for the Metropolitan Museum of Art. The design was constrained by the presence of two important reservoirs that effectively divided the upper from the lower park. (The lower reservoir was declared redundant in the 1920s, when landfill was trucked in and grass planted to create what became the Great Lawn. The larger receiving or distributing reservoir bounded by 86th and 96th Streets, which was excavated like so much else in Central Park by a small army of immigrant Irish laborers, was dropped from the city's water system in 1993.) But the design that Olmsted and Vaux created, and which was opened to the public in 1858, gave the city something to set New York apart.

Yet it would be a mistake to assume that the park, or its design, was regarded with absolute sanctity in the city. Progressive reformers in the early twentieth century, pioneering the movement to build playgrounds in the city's poorest neighborhoods and to provide organized facilities and supervised play, took their campaign into Central Park. The first of nineteen such playgrounds to be built in the park, and the first "named" gift by a private benefactor, was the Heckscher Playground at 61st Street and Seventh Avenue, erected in

1925. (The grandson of the benefactor, also named August Heckscher, later became Parks Commissioner, and wrote a feisty account of the park and city politics in the era of Mayor Lindsay in *Alive in the City: Memoir of an Ex-Commissioner*, 1974.)

Central Park was a natural target for any and every civic improvement, and at various times a home for the National Academy of Design, a new Opera House, an outdoor theater seating 50,000, a football stadium, housing projects, and a host of other wonderful ideas have been proposed and successfully resisted. Others proved impossible to derail or were enthusiastically supported by Robert Moses, Parks Commissioner from 1934 to 1960. When the sheep were banned from Sheep Meadow in 1934 and exiled to Prospect Park in Brooklyn, Moses pushed the conversion of Jacob Wrey Mould's Sheepfold into a restaurant, the Tavern on the Green. The Wollman Skating Rink (1950–1) and the Delacorte Theater (1963) enjoyed similar high-level support.

Paying for the City's Parks

Olmsted and many of those who most enthusiastically supported the park conceived it as a place for placid, contemplative pleasures. There was more than a token of democratic instinct about the design of "Greensward." It was, after all, meant to be free, paid for by general taxation, the sale of bonds, and specific levies upon adjacent property owners. Olmsted's park possessed its own force of police to maintain order.

The vicissitudes of New York politics and public finance have had a traumatic impact on the park. It was all too easy, when budgets were tightened and hiring freezes declared, for proper upkeep to be ignored. The lakes in the upper park were allowed to silt up. The staff of gardeners was pared and pared again. When flowering shrubs were planted in parks, they were linked together by chains around their roots. It was assumed that otherwise they would be stolen. The chain gangs of flowers were a powerful symbol of the city's social crisis. The historical pattern of neglect was deeply entrenched in New York's mentality. Expenditure on Manhattan's parks dropped by 50 percent between 1913 and 1919. Although expenditure levels gradually rose in the 1920s, the damage caused by neglect was done. Vaux's Marble Bridge was allowed to fall into decay and was finally demolished in 1934. The office of Landscape Architect was omitted (one sees the hand of Robert Moses in this) from the 1936 city charter. The Department of Parks has been a municipal Cinderella, the stepchild no one quite loved enough.

The fiscal crisis of New York City in the 1970s left a disastrous legacy of neglect to the park system. In the 1960s the New York economy had ceased to grow, but the city's budgets rose by over eight percent a year. It was a period of great social tension (the war in Vietnam, violent crime, the growing drugs crisis, and aggravated racial tension) when politicians frantically tried to address the needs of the community and the demands of powerful constituencies within the city's unionized workforce by one temporary expedient after another. Welfare for the poor and the unemployed claimed a larger and larger share of resources, while basic services (police, fire, sanitation, and education) declined as a proportion of the total budget. In real terms, school buildings were not maintained, textbooks were not replaced, streets were not cleaned to the old standards, and potholes spread like a cash crop on roads across the city. The cost of a ride on the graffiti-scarred subway went through the roof. The budget for parks was slashed, and Senator Daniel Patrick Moynihan argued that since the city could not look after its own parks, they should be turned over to the National Park Service. The city looked shabby and threatening. New York's total revenues in 1975 brought in $10.9 billion. Expenditures amounted to $12.8 billion. The annual operating deficit was just under $2 billion. With repeated tax rises, New York became one of the most expensive places in America to live in and gained a reputation as an unfriendly place to do business. Drawing an obvious conclusion, New Yorkers moved out of the city in increasing numbers. Factories fled to Sunbelt states. The tax base was weakened, and the city debt sharply increased. In March and April 1975 the city's 104th mayor, Abe Beame, a politician not noted for imaginative approaches to urban problems, found himself way out of his depth. Following its exclusion from the credit markets (Beame complained of a "conspiracy" of bankers and Republican newspapers), the city lost control of its financial affairs. To avoid an unthinkable default, the state advanced the city $800 million, and imposed the Municipal Assistance Corporation. A partner from the investment bank Lazard Frères, Felix G. Rohatyn, was appointed chairman of MAC, where he exercised great influence over the financial fortunes of the city during his term of office. (He retired from MAC in 1993.) Further measures were needed, and New York limped from crisis to crisis for the rest of the decade. Taxes remorselessly went up, and services declined. A decade later, with the 1980s building boom in midtown, employment rising, and new skyscrapers planned, the financial picture looked much brighter. And things got much, much better in the 1990s. But the legacy of neglect of the physical fabric and a reputation for financial mismanagement will take a long time to repair. Meanwhile, the real power brokers in New York (the unions and the banks) have lost none of their ancestral hunger for power.

"The increasing crowds," wrote Henry Hope Reed, Curator of Parks in the 1960s, "have been welcomed by a melancholy spectacle of downtrodden shrubbery, dust bowl lawns, erosion, trash, and bridges—especially Bow Bridge on the Lake—neglected to the point of endangering the public." The creation in 1980 of the Central Park Conservancy by Elizabeth Barlow Rogers brought to this large, rundown and venerable public space an innovative notion. Mrs. Rogers (called by the Parks Commissioner Henry J. Stern "the woman who saved Central Park in the 20th century") treated the park as though it was a cultural institution, comparable to the Metropolitan Museum. She raised $150 million from leading families, socialites, and companies with high visibility in the city (think Exxon and the Rockefellers). With her substantial success at fundraising, the city steadily withdrew funding.

The commission chaired by Robert F. Wagner, Jr., which published its findings with the upbeat title *New York Ascendant* (1987), had some pertinent reminders of the importance of parks for the city, linking the responsibility of the city and the responsibility of citizens:

> *The city government must... strive to develop a more beautiful and humane city, not just a commercial city. The quality of public spaces (parks, streets, subway stations) should be preeminent in the planning and rebuilding of New York—and respect for public spaces should be preeminent in the behavior of New Yorkers. Such respect, which must become a dominant part of New York's public culture, should be the individual New Yorker's contribution to the life of the city.*

It is a reflection of the changes in the city's finances and the success of the first public-private partnership in Central Park that widespread privatization of maintenance was attempted in the 1990s. Small groups began to take initiatives, staging clean-ups and planting gardens on their own. When park administrators discovered these projects (closely parallel to the community garden movement in the East Village) a first instinct was to send them packing. But the experience of repeated budget cuts persuaded Charles McKinney, administrator of Riverside Park on the Upper West Side, to accept and organize the role of volunteer groups. They were granted control over particular areas in parks, but with many appropriate limitations about rights of access and ultimate control over changes. The trick was to welcome volunteers and make use of their energy, while ensuring that the Parks Department's control remained intact.

Mayor Giuliani used recipients of Home Relief, a state welfare program for unemployed adults without children, for large-scale clean-ups. The mayor's office has also allowed the Parks Department to keep concession revenues above an established baseline. Giuliani repeatedly pushed to make the parks more commercial, to stage larger and more lucrative public events, and to reduce their burden upon the public purse. It is hard to imagine a strategy better calculated to change the "feel" and character of public space in the city than this invitation to each park to transform itself into a place where consuming and being entertained replace whatever vestigial sense of custodianship remained toward the parks themselves. When the highest official in the city treats them like Disneyland, we can hardly expect the public to think otherwise. Improvements to the city's parks today will only be funded to 50 percent of the projected costs, the remainder having to be raised by donations from the public and commercial revenues. There is a very important catch to the permission the mayor has given the park system: the neighbors who support improvements must also pay for maintenance. When neighborhood groups asked the Parks Department to lock up McCarren Park in Brooklyn, to prevent a new sprinkler from being vandalized at night, the department said it did not have the staff to lock the park. The race between increased commercialization and vandalism is being won, handily, by the vandals.

It is scarcely surprising that the level of maintenance of parks across the city further deteriorated in the 1990s. Despite the highly favorable city finances through most of the decade, most parks show few signs of improving. The budget of the Parks and Recreation Department has languished. In 2001 the city employed a total of 27 gardeners to look after its 27,000 acres of parkland. In 1997 the Central Park Conservancy was given a ten-year contract to maintain the park. Able to draw upon private sources for three-quarters of its expenditure, the Conservancy employs 73 gardeners for the park's 843 acres.

Privatization, with its unavoidable hints of entry charges and restricted access, is a troubling and in truth unacceptable strategy. So the question squarely remains: how can the parks be defended? If we go back to the original debates swirling around the proposal to create Central Park in the 1850s, we can find a clearly articulated statement of why parks are not only desirable adornments of a city, but a necessity for what they add to the quality of life in a heavily populated urban environment. We can discount one strand of that debate, that parks would serve to inculcate habits and forms of behavior that would reinforce social order. If that was ever true (it may well have been), it is not an argument likely to sway attitudes today. Beyond the notion that parks are an adornment and attraction that give any city a competitive advantage for tourist dollars (or pounds or euros), and the proposition that parks contribute substantially to the improvement of the surrounding residential areas, there is another argument, stated by Lynden Miller, garden designer of Bryant Park and Wagner Park, in the *New York Times* in the aftermath of the attack on the World Trade Center: "City life is not just about Midtown excitement; it is also about neighborhoods, green spaces, swings, a baseball diamond and the chance to sit on a bench."

Parks, and what they offer to the community, express something fundamental to the democratic city. Memberships of private gyms and health clubs are expensive and open only to a fraction of the population; summer holidays in the first-class resorts and mid-winter breaks in the Caribbean, even a brisk jog in the park early in the morning, may not, we might hypothesize, be available to most of the families of the hundreds of thousands of children in the city's schools. The parks are for *those* children, and their parents, though it's a hard sell for politicians to say so. When the parks are left under-funded and poorly maintained and the city largely washes its hands of the problem, some of the fragile social glue of the community is weakened.

Yet "realistic" alternatives are hard to find to deal with the ongoing financial crisis of the park system. In the light of the enormous budget shortfall the city expects as a result of the attack on the World Trade Center, and the decline of tax revenues caused by the national recession, the amount of private support required to keep the parks going will surely grow. For decades the city has been walking away from its responsibility for maintenance of public parks. The parks' current condition is a tribute to the devotion and tenacity of the Parks and Recreation Department leadership and workers and to the public advocacy of well-meaning private individuals and the city's press. It would hardly be credible to expect that private funding will take on the support for the system as a whole. Only the largest parks can summon the glitzy publicity and professional support of bodies like the Central Park Conservatory and the Prospect Park Alliance—and no one knows that better than the Conservatory and the Alliance itself. On the consolidation of the city's park system in the 1930s, Robert Moses stipulated that playgrounds needed six attendants. A brief visit by one Parks Department worker for an hour a day has become the norm. The imbalance in capital spending also stores up problems for the future. The $200,000 per acre that was available for the reconstruction of Bryant Park on 42nd Street in the mid-1990s, compared to a citywide figure of $5,700, is not available for parks in less prominent neighborhoods or which are normally patronized by less well-heeled New Yorkers. But when other needs are so pressing, and at a time when the city's financial position looks so shockingly perilous, perhaps some combination of bodies like the Conservancy, and Senator Moynihan's proposal about the National Park Service, may be the only way, at present, to preserve the system. This might be an appropriate moment for visitors, entranced by the parks, to get their checkbook out.

It is a striking indication of the meaning of the city's parks for New Yorkers that after the September 11 attack there was a sharp increase in the number of visitors to parks, botanical gardens, and zoos. The major cultural institutions, meanwhile, led by the Metropolitan Museum of Art and the Brooklyn Museum, suffered sharp falls in attendance. Down by as much as a third, the decline was attributed to the collapse of the tourist industry in the months following the attack. Cultural institutions in the vicinity of the World Trade Center, such as the Museum of Jewish Heritage in Battery Park City, were hardest hit of all. Smaller museums and those with strong links to the communities where they were based came through the crisis in better shape. But it was the parks, and perhaps the unusually mild autumnal weather of late 2001, that continued to attract growing numbers of visitors.

NEW YORK
in
Slices.

CHAPTER SIX

Broadway

"You do not go for a walk in New York," wrote Jean-Paul Sartre of his visit to the city in the winter of 1945, "you either loiter at a drugstore or travel by express subway." It is time, surely, to reassert that walkers get the best of New York. If one can observe Wall Street and the Stock Exchange sitting, coffee in hand, on the steps of the Federal Hall National Memorial, then Broadway is made for walking.

With good shoes and some determination it is possible to walk the seventeen miles from Bowling Green to the northern tip of Manhattan in a day. For *flâneurs*, strollers, and coffee-sipping window-shoppers, it can take two or three days, even a week, of pleasurable afternoons. There is no street anywhere like it in America. "Broadway is a very noble street," wrote George Foster in *New York in Slices* (1849), "altogether the most showy, the most crowded, and the richest fashionable thoroughfare on the continent." Walks suited to an abundance of interests are there for the taking: sampling foods along the way, viewing the city's spectacular architecture, calling in on churches, synagogues, or historical monuments, pausing to take photos of an interesting and unexpected architectural detail, shopping, and, inevitably (and what makes Broadway such a feature of the life of New York) its rich opportunities for people watching.

Making Broadway

The Dutch "Heere Straat"—High Street or Broadway—was a wide, unpaved road running north on the western side of the city from Fort Amsterdam to "Het Cingle," which the British renamed Wall Street. Veering to the northeast at the beginning of the Common (City Hall Park today), Park Row carried farm carts and the occasional traveler to the High Road leading toward Boston. Following the line of the city's natural north-south ridge, colonial Broadway was well drained and because it skirted marshy ground was well suited for horseback and coach travel. Looking east toward Brooklyn and west across the Hudson to New Jersey, Broadway afforded unique views of the city and its surroundings. It was a less obviously a commercial street in the colonial city than "Heere Gracht" (Broad Street), with its "canal," a narrow ill-smelling ditch, which at high tide was used to haul goods by small barges to the breweries and warehouses lying at the center of New Amsterdam. On the west side of Heere Straat lay the finest residential area of the Dutch city, lined with the pleasant homes of clerics, merchants, and officials of the Dutch West India Company. Each of the houses had gardens and orchards leading down to the banks of the Hudson River. The country estates and farms (*bouweries*) of Jan Jansen Damen and Everardus Bogardus lay along the shore of the Hudson. On the east side stood smaller buildings, the modest houses and workshops of the city's artisans. The social distinction enjoyed by the residents on the western side of the street, strengthened by the construction of the first Trinity Church and an emerging prejudice against the socially and economically inferior east side, persisted well into the nineteenth century.

In the 1690s, when a host of other improvements were undertaken in New York, the intersection of Broadway and Wall Street became the center of the English colony. The old Stadt Huys was replaced by the new City Hall. A wharf was constructed where Wall Street reached the East River. And Trinity Church was erected. The first of the three structures that have stood on the west side of Broadway, Trinity looked down Wall Street toward the site where the slave market was later built. Broadway was more a country path than a road, crossed by footpaths and the well-worn routes of cows, but civic improvements were in hand. Cobblestones were laid in 1709, and a sewer ditch was formed in the middle of the street. Residents along Broadway were allowed to plant trees and in time the street began to take on a more elegant appearance. It was the English in the early eighteenth century who began to think of Broadway as an urban showcase. When the movement uptown of the city's population gathered pace, it was Broadway that became the "genteel lounge." Neither the Park nor the Battery, wrote a visiting Englishman about New York in 1808,

> *is very much resorted to by the fashionable citizens of New York, as they have become too common. The genteel lounge is in the Broadway, from eleven to three o'clock, during which time it is as much crowded as the Bond-street of London: and the carriages, though not so numerous, are driven to and fro with as much velocity. The foot paths are planted with poplars, and afford an agreeable shade from the sun in summer.*

It is only through an effort of bold imagination that we can connect Broadway today with that rutted dirt road lined with small provincial structures that the Dutch and English colonists knew. On the site of Fort Amsterdam, erected by the Dutch West India Company to protect the settlement from the native tribes and their occasionally unfriendly ways, stands Cass Gilbert's lavish Alexander Hamilton Custom House of 1907. Gilbert's Beaux-Arts design for the Custom House incorporates 48 Ionic columns, an imposing marble rotunda with WPA-era murals by Reginald Marsh, an ornate frieze, and Daniel Chester French's sculptures on an heroic scale representing the four continents. The symbolic figures are women seated in a contemplative pose, at first glance looking as though they are in mourning. War memorials and civic and military cemeteries erected across Europe after the end of the First World War feature sculptures created as expressions of communal mourning uncannily like French's. It is an unexpectedly somber group of figures for such an exuberant building.

Taking over the tax-collecting functions formerly located on Wall Street (see Chapter 2), the Custom House is now jointly occupied by the Federal Bankruptcy Court and the Museum of the American Indian. (Housing has always been a problem in New York.) Abandoned by the Custom Service when the World Trade Center was opened in 1973, Gilbert's extravaganza became the home of the George Gustav Heye Center of the National Museum of the American Indian in 1994. The Heye Center, a branch of the vast Smithsonian Institution, houses over million artifacts (only a tiny proportion are on display at any given time), as well as possessing a rich archive collection of photographs and other visual materials recording the native cultures of Central and South America as well as the many tribal cultures of North America.

Starting Out at Number 1

One Broadway, a large office building overlooking Bowling Green, is the latest in a long line of structures to have occupied this important site. The proximity to the fort and its thirsty garrison makes Mrs. Kocks, proprietor of a Dutch tavern at 1 Broadway, an early exponent of the mantra of the city's real estate brokers: location, location, location. The land on which the tavern stood passed through the hands of assorted Dutch and English owners until the 1740s when it was purchased by Archibald Kennedy, the colony's Receiver-General (that is, collector of customs), who later became the Earl of Cassilis. The tavern was torn down and Kennedy erected an elegant mansion on the site. The Kennedy mansion served as the headquarters of the British forces in 1776 when they occupied the city. When the British left New York in 1783, Isaac Sears, who had been a prominent figure in the ranks of the Patriots during the revolutionary struggle, returned to New York and rented 1 Broadway ("one of the finest houses in the city") for the unprecedented sum of £500 a month.

The Kennedy mansion retained its reputation as one of the most imposing residences in the city, and was occupied at various times in the antebellum period by prominent bankers and a Democratic mayor (Andrew Mickle). Its downward course began when the city's residential life moved uptown. After the Civil War, new tenants of social distinction could not be found to live on Bowling Green, and the Kennedy mansion was briefly run as a hotel, a boarding school for girls, and before being demolished in 1882, a boardinghouse. The Washington Building was then erected on 1 Broadway, home of the United States Line, the main American challenger for supremacy on the North Atlantic passenger run. Its rivals were the mighty Cunard line (whose offices were a half-block north, at 25 Broadway), and the French and German shipping lines. The Washington Building was refaced in limestone after the First World War, and again in the 1980s, and today it is the International Merchant Marine Company Building.

At the head of Bowling Green is the "Charging Bull," a menacingly virile statue by Arturo diModica, erected in 1988. Children give the beast a friendly pat on the nose and clown around, posing for a picture, while parents try to explain why there is a life-size statue of a bull on Broadway. Instead of taking the time to talk about metaphors and market movements on Wall Street, it might be a better bet to walk five blocks up Broadway to Liberty Street, to enjoy Isamu Noguchi's upended "Red Cube" at the Marine Midland Bank at 140 Broadway. Then, getting into the swing of contemporary sculpture, turn east on Liberty and proceed past the Federal Reserve and its great gold vaults buried 80 feet below street level, before resuming art lessons at Louise Nevelson Plaza before her "Shadows and Flags" (1977), seven imposingly large steel sculptures, and then move on to Jean Dubuffet's "Group of Four Trees" (1972) at the plaza of the Chase Manhattan Bank Tower, which occupies the entire block between Liberty and Pine Streets. Noguchi's former studio on Vernon Boulevard in Queens has been transformed into a Garden Museum. In addition to carved stone pieces in the garden, there are twelve indoor galleries containing more than 250 works of art. The Garden Museum is linked to the Museum of Modern Art, P.S. 1 Contemporary Art Center, and other Queens museums by the free weekend Queens Artlink bus service. There is also a Noguchi sculpture at the Associated Press Building at Rockefeller Center. Another work by Nevelson, "Night Presence IV," is sited in the center island on Park Avenue at 92nd Street. "Bent Propeller," Alexander Calder's bright red 25-foot-tall steel sculpture in 7 World Trade Center (1970), was smashed within the collapsing building. But half of the 15-ton sculpture has been found and there is a hunt for the remaining part. The Calder Foundation believes that the sculpture can be rebuilt if another 30 percent of the original can be found. (Among the important art irretrievably lost on September 11 were the Rodin sculptures in the Cantor Fitzgerald private museum on the 105th Floor of 1 World Trade Center; Juan Miro's "World Trade Center Tapestry" from 1974, crushed in the 2 World Trade Center mezzanine; and a 1975 painting from Roy Lichtenstein's "Entablature" series, vaporized in the lobby of 7 World Trade Center.)

There is a convenient "Heritage Trail" plotting a route among the dozens of works of public art on display in lower Manhattan. Free maps are available in many commercial locations.

Lower Broadway, from the Battery to City Hall Park, is principally a commercial canyon, a wind tunnel created by tall buildings. People walk purposefully here. There is no loitering, nothing interesting to see, other than two small museums on Lower Broadway: the Police

Museum at the intersection of Broadway with Morris Street, and the Museum of American Financial History on the east side of Broadway next to the former Standard Oil building at number 26. At least some of the commercial buildings on Lower Broadway have mildly interesting stories attached to them. From 1884, 26 Broadway, an intimidating 480-foot structure at the corner of Beaver Street, was the home of John D. Rockefeller's Standard Oil company. When the Standard Oil Trust was broken up in 1911, one of the successor companies created out of Rockefeller's colossus remained at 26 Broadway until the 1950s. The real legacy for New York from the Rockefellers came in midtown, with the building of Rockefeller Center in the early 1930s. The original Rockefeller building on Broadway has been heavily altered and expanded. Its neighbor at 25 Broadway, the former Cunard Building, stands on the site occupied by Delmonico's hotel and restaurant in 1846. The faux-Renaissance façade overlooking Bowling Green and the richly decorated booking hall, currently occupied by the United States Post Office, are reminders of how elegant and imposing New York commercial architecture once was.

North of Wall Street, Broadway is all banks and insurance companies. The Equitable Building at 120 Broadway, between Pine and Cedar Streets, has a story better than most. This vast edifice stands on a plot of just under one acre. On to that site 1.2 million square feet of floor area was erected. The Equitable was a very large statement of the gigantic possibilities of modern architecture, but to contemporaries it was erected without any consideration of the consequences of such a huge structure on Broadway, over which it cast a shadow in the mornings, or the impact of such a large number of office workers on the already over-congested traffic and public transportation system. In a panicky response to the Equitable, and with a looming sense of the great social problems it threatened to cause, the Board of Estimate adopted a zoning resolution in July 1916, which divided the city into three permissible forms of land use: commercial, residential, and unrestricted. About 40 percent of Manhattan was set aside for exclusively residential use, and new factories were forbidden in Manhattan above 23rd Street. There were "districts" created by the 1916 zoning law within which the height of new buildings was limited in proportion to the width of the adjoining street. The combination of "use" and "bulk" restrictions proved exceedingly complex to administer and resulted in a striking architectural form, drawn from the Babylonian Ziggurat, in which the upper stories of high buildings were set back to allow sunlight to penetrate to street level. The zoning laws were not retroactive, and so they left all existing buildings as they stood. And since the planning laws were written with perhaps an excess of concern for property rights as such and with a tight interpretation of the "public welfare," they successfully withstood judicial challenge. It was the first American attempt to control development across an entire city. The 1916 law permitted housing density to remain high, and it was estimated that under that legislation the entire population of the United States in 1900 could be housed in the permitted tenements of New York City. The mixed zoning legacy of the Equitable has shaped in incalculable ways the built environment of New York.

St. Paul's Chapel

From Trinity Church it is a short walk to St. Paul's Chapel on the east side of Broadway between Fulton and Vesey Street. Designed by the Scottish architect Thomas McBean, the cornerstone of St. Paul's was laid on May 14, 1774, on farmland sloping down toward the Hudson River. (The view of the nearby World Trade Center twin towers was particularly dramatic.) Uniquely, the chapel faces away from Broadway, though a carriage portico supported by Ionic columns extends nearly to the Broadway sidewalk. When it was built, recalled an early historian of the chapel, *the western end commanded an uninterrupted view of the river and the Jersey shores; for the waters of the Hudson then flowed up to the line of Greenwich Street; all beyond is "made land." The prospect must have been a pleasant one, and charming to the eye; we can imagine our forefathers, in those old days, grouped in the porch, before or after service, and standing still awhile to look down the slope of the green fields, and through the trees, towards the beautiful stream which rolled its waters to the bay.*

St. Paul's was the second of three chapels built by the Vestry of Trinity Church to accommodate the rapidly growing Anglican community in the city. The planned building program was interrupted by the fire that destroyed the "first" Trinity Church in the aftermath of the British military occupation on September 22, 1776. Until the "second" Trinity was built in 1787, St. Paul's was the city's principal Anglican house of worship. Opened for prayers in the year the revolution broke out (James Crommelin Lawrence's rough stone tower and steeple were erected in the next decade), virtually the first act of the newly consecrated chapel was the sale of pews to raise funds for the support of the chapel.

There are older buildings on Manhattan, but St. Paul's is unique in having survived continuous use in the city center for over two centuries. Its proximity to the World Trade Center made its burial ground a favorite place for a lunch time pause in the sun. After the attack it became one of the most important of the unofficial shrines which New Yorkers created across the city in remembrance of the dead. And it was in St. Paul's where Mayor Giuliani gave his moving farewell address on December 27, 2001, at the end of his term of office:

...being in this chapel is very, very appropriate... The reason I chose this chapel is because this chapel is thrice-hallowed ground. This is a place of really special importance to people who have a feeling and a sense and an emotion and an understanding of patriotism. This is hallowed by the fact that it was consecrated as a house of God in 1766. That's a long time ago. And in 1789, in April of 1789, George Washington came and after he was inaugurated as the first president of our republic he prayed right here in this church, which makes it very sacred ground to people who feel what America is all about.

But then it was consecrated one more time, in 2001 on Sept. 11. When I walked in here from the back I looked up because every time I've walked in this church when I looked up I saw the twin towers just way, way above. This church existed for many years in the shadow of the twin towers. And on Sept. 11 when the twin towers were viciously attacked and came crashing to the ground in the worst attack on America, destroyed buildings all around, did damage as far away as City Hall all the way south in the southern part of Battery Park City and covered this whole area with debris, body parts and in many, many ways damaged buildings, this chapel remained not only not destroyed, not a single window was broken, not a single thing hurt. And I think there's some very, very special significance in that. The place where George Washington prayed when he first became president of the United States stood strong, powerful, untouched, undaunted, by the attacks of these people who hate what we stand for. Because what we stand for is so much stronger than they are.

So this chapel stands for our values. And it's a very important place. And I hope you return here often to reflect on what it means to be an American and a New Yorker.

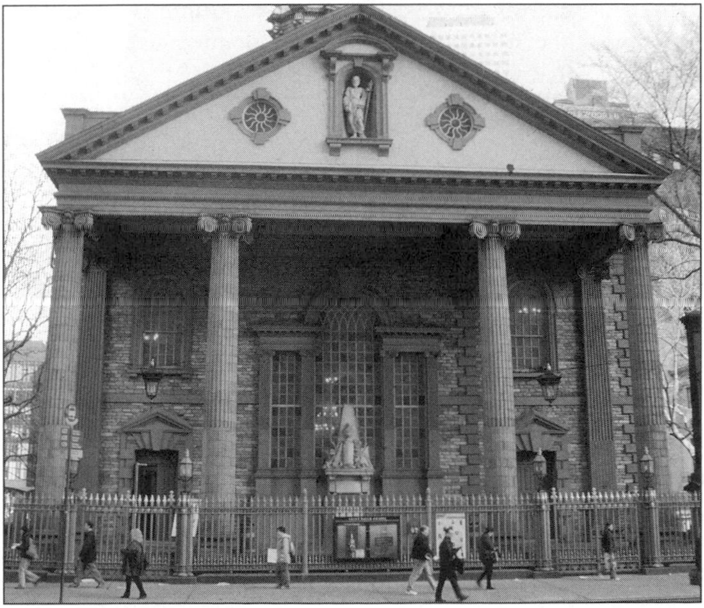

The design for St. Paul's was modeled upon St. Martin's-in-the-Fields in London, and it was built in a stone (Manhattan schist) quarried from the field where the chapel stands. Remodeled in the 1790s, the altar is attributed to Pierre Charles L'Enfant, the Frenchman who served as Major of Engineers in the Continental Army, rebuilt City Hall on Wall Street (see Chapter 2), and drew up the plan for the national capital at Washington, D.C. The interior of St. Paul's is light and spacious. On a sunny day, when the sunlight streams through the Palladian window onto the polished black and white tiled floor and the reflected glow of the delicate pink and light blue of the interior, the structure seems to possess a light unlike any other church in the city. From the gallery there is a good view of the chapel's fourteen hand-cut Waterford crystal chandeliers. One may also look respectfully down upon the pew reserved for President George Washington and, across the central aisle, the pew reserved for the revolutionary era Governor of New York State, George Clinton. The same pews were used by the royal governor of the Province of New York, and during the British military occupation of the city were sat upon by Lords Howe and Cornwallis, commanding officers of the British forces.

In 1848 the artist John William Hill was commissioned to climb to the top of the steeple of St. Paul's and undertake a panoramic drawing of the city displayed before him. Engraved by Henry Paprill and published by Henry Megarry, one can see in the details of Hill's drawing that St. Paul's stood at the center of mid-century New York.

Around St. Paul's were major institutions of the city's cultural life in the nineteenth century. Matthew Brady's Daguerrean Miniature Gallery, where the prospect of seeing the latest images of politicians and entertainers drew a crowd, stood on the corner of Broadway and Vesey Street. Peale's Museum and Gallery of the Fine Arts was at 252 Broadway, where there were displays of "scientific" interest, specimens of natural history, a collection of paintings and portraits of 150 "celebrated citizens and foreigners," and a Grand Cosmorama painted by Italian artists offering a "magnificence of views" of exotic places and wonders. In a lecture theater Peale staged learned demonstrations of the new science of mesmerism. In nearby Clinton Hall, located on the corner of Beekman and Nassau Streets, were to be found Orson and Lorenzo Fowler's Phrenological Rooms. Walt Whitman was a frequent

Courtesy of the Metropolitan Museum of Art, The Edward W.C. Arnold Collection of New York Prints, Maps, and Pictures, Bequest of Edward W.C. Arnold, 1954. (54.90.587)

Henry Papprill, 1849. After John William Hill; New York from the Steeple of St. Paul's Church; hand colored aquatint.

visitor, and one of the Fowler brothers drew up a phrenological chart, after making a close study of the poet's cranium. "I have it yet," he proudly remarked.

Nearby, at the corner of Broadway and Park Row, stood P.T. Barnum's American Museum, founded in 1842. Barnum staged cleverly faked mesmerism exhibitions until he drove Peale out of business. At which point he bought the contents of Peale's Museum, and offered "Two Museums in One" without extra charges. The loud advertising of the American Museum set a new pattern, not for the city's "high cultural" institutions (which remained provincial, respectable, and staid), but for American show business. In 1842 Barnum secured the services of Charles S. Stratton, a child weighing sixteen pounds and standing at less than two feet tall who went on to a career of public appearances as "General Tom Thumb." When public interest waned, Barnum found another midget, George Washington Morrison Nutt, who was exhibited with his own miniature carriage, footmen, and Shetland ponies. Barnum also exhibited a lady of

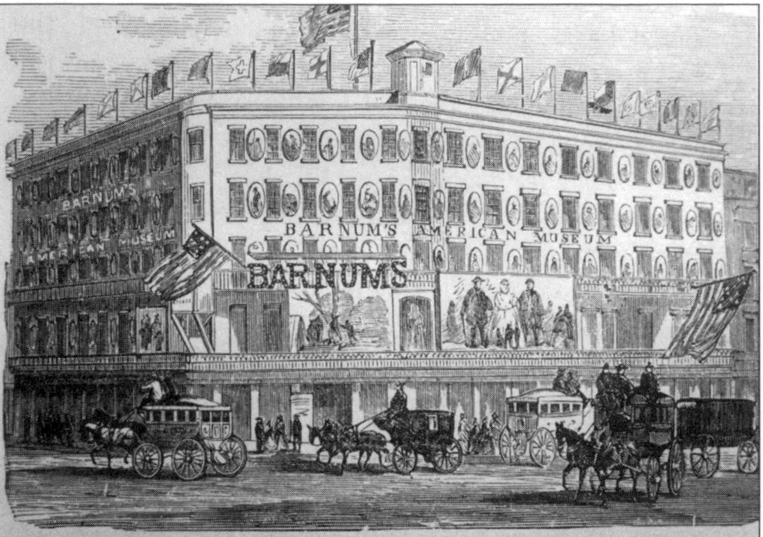

BARNUM'S MUSEUM, 1860.

diminutive size named Mercy Lavinia Warren Bumpus. Both General Tom Thumb and Commodore Nutt fell very publicly in love with Lavinia and competed for her hand in a rivalry that fascinated the nation. When General Thumb, a wealthy and sophisticated owner of yachts and horses, won the heart of Lavinia, Barnum arranged for the marriage ceremony to be held in 1863 at the city's fashionable Grace Church. Guests joining in with the national amusement included General Ambrose Burnside, Mrs. John Jacob Astor III, and Mrs. William H. Vanderbilt. Barnum alone would have made the corner of Broadway and Ann Street one of the most famous locations in the city.

Near the corner of Broadway and Park Row stood the venerable Park Theater, opened in 1798. It was a very plain, three-story stone building, with a frontage of 80 feet and a depth of 160 feet. An azure dome with clouds and celestial shapes formed the ceiling of the Park, decorated with a large standing portrait of President Washington. A canopy of green and gold hung over the stage, with the motto: "To hold the Mirror up to Nature." The stage of the Park was larger than that of any other American theater. But, as one impresario after another learned, New York was not London and could not hold to an aristocratic standard of theatrical productions. Even the crudest productions failed to sustain a large audience. The audience wanted diversions, novelties, and cheap amusements; they would not pay to watch serious plays. Attempts to stage the glories of the operatic canon, such as a luxurious production of *Fidelio* in 1839, failed as much due to the theater itself as to the inadequacy of the taste of the New York audience. "Its boxes were like pens for beasts," remarked Richard Grant White. "The floor was dirty and broken into holes; the seats were bare, backless benches. Women were never seen in the pit…" The atmosphere at the Park was disturbed by unseemly yells and whistles from the gallery and a regular "discharge of apples, nuts & ginger-bread" rained upon the "honest folks in the pit." Men brazenly watched the local belles through spy-glasses. The women of New York took a lead in objecting to the language and suggestive by play of some productions, while the indecorum of juvenile leads being played by actresses and young actors playing female characters drew a particularly provincial disapproval. There was talk of respectables organizing boycotts of performances judged to be risqué. With its "gallery for colored persons" and seating capacity of over 2,000, the Park was the city's pre-eminent place of public entertainment until the opening of the Academy of Music in 1853.

Impresarios drew from the failure of the Park Theater several stark lessons. The first was that you would never hold the affection or loyalty of wealthy New Yorkers in a dingy theater. And the second was that even a large and handsome structure like the Academy of Music on East 14th Street or the old Metropolitan Opera building on Broadway between West 39th and West 40th Streets, could not overcome the fact that the wrong location was as fatal as a scruffy decor. The entertainment district was moving uptown, and the public was unsentimental enough to insist that cultural institutions kept pace.

In John William Hill's panorama of the city, as seen from the steeple of St. Paul's, there were few monumental public buildings and no particularly striking monuments in view. City Hall lay in the opposite direction, to the north of St. Paul's. Familiar as we are with the thousands of images that celebrate the New York skyline, and the tall buildings which assert its wealth and commercial importance, it is interesting to register how far the city was in 1848 from the way it looked even a half century later. John William Hill's New York was an industrious city of three-, four-, and five-story buildings and a population of 515,000. Canvas awnings, some boldly carrying advertising slogans ("Havana Segars") gave pedestrians on Broadway some relief from the summer sun. Beyond the prominent spire of Trinity Church was the harbor. The East River was crowded with ships' masts. It was the largest city in America, and showed every sign of knowing how important it was going to become.

City Hall

"The interior should not be missed by the visitor to the city"—*New York Panorama* (Federal Writers' Project, 1938)

Not so long ago, in a more tranquil age, City Hall was open to the public. Visitors could wander, within limits in the rotunda and visit the Governor's Room. Access was restricted to the working offices of the mayor and other figures in the administration, but there was general access by the public to open sessions of the City Council, oddly intimate for such a raucous democracy, and Board of Estimate. No more. In 1998 Mayor Giuliani imposed restrictions on the public use of the steps of City Hall and upon use of the plaza for meetings and demonstrations. Events not sponsored by the city are restricted to 50 people. A first attempt to impose a limit of 25 people was thrown out in Federal District Court. Members of the public are no longer able to walk directly through the park to the entrance of City Hall. The building is closed to the general public for the indefinite future, and there are uniformed guards controlling access to the area directly in front of City Hall. All we can do is to admire it from a distance.

Used to large and imposing civic buildings erected across America, one's first reaction to City Hall is one of astonishment—at its modest size, its architectural charm, and at its survival in this most restless of cities. After decades of neglected maintenance and civic indifference after the Civil War (the "tobacco juice period"), the appearance and physical condition of the building had so deteriorated that in 1893 the city concluded that it was necessary to erect a new civic building. The proposed demolition of the rundown City Hall was to be followed by the construction of a larger building, occupying virtually the entire remaining area of the City Hall

Park, to provide accommodation for the hall of records, courts, government offices, and council chambers. An architectural competition was held, but ended in farce when the award panel judged all of the entries to be so mediocre that it refused to select a winning design. After that fiasco, no further talk was heard of design competitions for a new City Hall. By that happy outcome, City Hall was spared.

"City Hall is a splendid little palace," wrote Paul Goldberger, architectural critic of the *New York Times*, "a bastard born of French Renaissance and Georgian parentage; it is both delicate and self-assured." The design for City Hall, a "petit palais" of the age of Louis XIV, is the work of a Frenchman, Joseph François Mangin, and a native New Yorker of Scottish descent, John McComb, Jr., who together won a design competition for the structure. Mangin, the architect of other important New York structures such as the State Prison in Greenwich Village and the Park Theater on Park Row, was the principal designer of City Hall. But it was McComb, the master builder who had St. John's Chapel on Varick Street among his major achievements, who was appointed supervising architect for the construction, for which he was paid the handsome sum of $6 per day. And he managed to secure the lion's share of credit for the building as a whole, doing nothing to ensure that Mangin's contribution was acknowledged. Their collaboration is poorly documented, and like similar issues raised over the relative contributions of Frederick Law Olmsted and Calvert

Vaux to the design of Central Park, the clear establishment of their individual contributions has proven impossible. Construction began in 1803 and City Hall was officially dedicated on July 4, 1811. The building cost the city $538,734, an immense sum in that day. To put it in perspective, the annual expenditure on City Hall was equal to nearly half the annual revenues of New York. Until the development of Central Park in the 1850s, it was the largest public works project in antebellum New York.

To trim costs the city fathers insisted in 1803 that plans be revised to reduce the size of the building. It would seem that Mangin was unwilling to agree to this, and McComb was. Their collaboration probably ended then. Famously, the rear of the building, looking north, was faced in a cheaper material (brownstone quarried at Newark) than the white Massachusetts marble used for the south-facing front and sides. The calculation—perhaps legendary—was that it might take many years before anyone took much notice of the rear of a building that was already in 1803 located beyond the main built-up area of the city. In reality, the city had already begun to open streets to the north of City Hall, and the commissioners' 1811 plan strengthened the uptown move of population. It is possible that the large Almshouse, which blocked the view of City Hall from the north, encouraged this celebrated instance of penny-pinching. Time, weather, and pollution took their inevitable toll on the original building materials, and the structure was re-faced with durable Alabama limestone and granite in the 1950s.

Mangin's symmetrical design for the 216-foot-wide building (it is just 105 feet deep) balances two wings on either side of a central portico and its Ionic colonnade. There is a copper statue of "Justice," erected in 1910 after the design of the original wood sculpture of 1812. The dome was erected in 1858 to replace the original cupola, which was destroyed during an overly ambitious fireworks display to celebrate the laying of the first transatlantic cable. That fire destroyed much of Mangin's interior. The reconstruction was not sensitive to Mangin's original plan.

The interior of City Hall is dominated by the double-curve of the self-supporting stairway in the rotunda, making what Goldberger regards as "one of the city's finest public interiors." It was at the head of the stairway, in front of the Governor's Room, where the catafalques stood bearing the coffins of President Lincoln in 1865 and President Grant in 1885. Mangin's wrought-iron railings and columns supporting the upper gallery show a sophisticated attention to detail remarkable in a public building.

The Governor's Room, a triple reception room or suite on the first floor above the front entrances, was established in 1814 as an office for the governor of New York when he visited the city. Until the 1920s the mayor's traditional New Year's Day reception was held in the Governor's Room. The city's collection of historical portraits hangs here in civic dignity. In 1908 the city proposed to redecorate the suite. Despite its shabby appearance, there was widespread expectation that aldermanic taste would complete the ruin of the room as Mangin and McComb envisaged it. A wealthy benefactress, Mrs. Russell Sage, offered to pay for the restoration, brought in her own architect, and with the aid of Mangin's annotated original drawings in the New York Historical Society, many of the missing design features were restored. The success of the restored Governor's Room did much to alert preservationists that City Hall was an architectural gem, well worth defending against municipal jobbery.

New York's art collection, exhibited in the Governor's Room and throughout City Hall, consists principally of portraits of presidents, vice-presidents, governors, mayors, military and naval heroes, American statesmen, the occasional city clerk, and foreign leaders commissioned from artists working in the city. City Hall is far from an ideal location for an important art collection. It lacks the kind of temperature and humidity controls that curators prefer. The portraits do not have fixed locations in the building, and a considerable part of the collection is not on view at any given time. But it is a pleasure to see this wonderful collection of portraits in their intended physical setting. The tradition of commissioning portraits of each of the city's mayors began with the city's first mayor after the Revolutionary War, James Duane, who served from 1784 to 1789, and continued to Fiorello La Guardia, whose term as mayor ended in 1945. (More recent mayors have been photographed.) The artists are an impressive roll call of leading American portraitists, including John Trumbull, John Wesley Jarvis, Charles Wesley Jarvis, Henry Inman, Rembrandt Peale, John Vanderlyn, and Samuel F. B. Morse. From this rich collection highlights include Trumbull's George

Washington, Vanderlyn's Andrew Jackson, and Morse's spectacular Marquis de Lafayette. The collection of sculptures includes David d'Angers' Jefferson, and Jean Antoine Houdon's Washington. George Washington's writing desk, on which it is said he penned his first message to Congress, is located in the Governor's Room.

The collection is under the care of the Art Commission of the City of New York. With a small professional staff and a minuscule budget, the 11-member board of the Commission, which by regulation is required to include a painter, a sculptor, an architect, a landscape architect, and representatives from the New York Public Library, the Metropolitan Museum of Art, and the Brooklyn Museum of Art, serves an unusual role in the city as a guardian of Good Taste. The Commission sits in judgment over all proposals for statues, lighting fixtures, architectural ornaments, and anything else proposed for parks and city-owned property. Visitors to the city's parks, including Central Park, are looking at park "furniture" that has been vetted and approved by the Art Commission. Conflict with the Parks and Recreation Department and its headstrong commissioner, Henry J. Stern, led in 2000 to an all-out attack on the Commission ("We are dealing with a combination of arrogance, elitism, and a patronizing attitude," complained Stern, not perhaps himself the most modest and humble of New Yorkers) and a proposal to abolish it altogether. Politicians with pet projects such as dismal statues celebrating one national hero or another, donated by politically important constituents, disliked the Commission's powers of review and delay and happily joined in Commissioner Stern's campaign to abolish Good Taste and its guardians.

Behind Stern's remark lay a very New York sort of conflict, over 100 flagpoles with nautical yardarms, which Stern's department installed in parks and cemeteries without Art Commission review. A lawsuit filed by the Commission's president in 1999 forced an obviously furious Stern to back down and submit the yardarms for review. At the time of writing, the outcome of the attack on the Art Commission is unresolved.

City Hall Park

The curious wedge-shaped park in which City Hall stands is a surviving fragment of the common land of the colony of New

Amsterdam. Designed as a park and first enclosed in 1792, it has been redeveloped several times. City Hall Park occupies a place in the public life of the city far in excess of its modest size. "The park is the center of New York," wrote an anonymous contributor to *The Ladies' Garland* in 1839, "and its two most thronged and finest avenues form the two sides of it." The park provided a focus for public display, leisure, and a setting for many important public events. The design of the colonial city, and the grid mapped by the Commissioners in 1811, omitted the kind of large public spaces where the citizenry might gather, and that was what by default City Hall Park came to provide.

City Hall Park was a place where citizens could exercise First Amendment rights of political speech in public places, but marches, speeches, waving banners and impassioned oratory were not always to the taste of nervous mayors and the police. The city's magistrates did their best to suppress disorder, imposing severe sentences for rioting. But New York was an unruly community, where drunkenness, rowdy behavior, and rioting were well-established civic traditions. The many saloons and brothels close to City Hall Park (and the theaters lining Park Row) made it a natural home for a floating population of protesters, revelers, and drunks. Prostitutes strolled in the park, and a youthful crowd of homosexuals, notable—as one contemporary remarked—for their "feminine appearance and manners," added to the general sense that this was indeed a public space without parallel in the city.

The multiple functions of City Hall as home of the city council and courthouse in the antebellum period drew crowds of black protesters to the park when cases involving escaped slaves were tried. Attempts were made by main force to rescue recaptured slaves. In 1857 there was a memorable riot in City Hall between the Municipals, a police force loyal to the Democratic mayor Fernando Wood, and the Metropolitans, created by the state legislature and tasked with serving a writ and arresting the mayor. When the rioters spilled out into the park, soldiers of the Seventh Regiment of the National Guard arrived, with fixed bayonets, to disperse the rioting policemen.

The park was also a place where important public celebrations could be staged. At the intersection of Broadway and Park Row, and along the Broadway side of City Hall Park, there is a natural space well suited for parades and events attended by large numbers of people.

A reception in honor of General Lafayette was held at City Hall Park in 1824. Enormous rallies were held in 1860–1 as the secession crisis deepened, and even larger rallies when the Civil War began. When the first northern soldiers departed from New York on April 29, 1861 to defend the nation's capital, the saluting platform was in City Hall Park. The march down Broadway of the 11th Regiment New York State Volunteers, the famous "Fire Zouaves," was one of the premier spectacles in an age of military parades. Led by their colonel, Elmer Ellsworth, and dressed in the style of Algerian mountain tribes, with loose tunics in gray, scarlet, and blue, billowing trousers and fez, the Zouaves had been recruited from the city's patriotic volunteer fire companies. (New York's love affair with fire fighters began long before the events of September 11, 2001.) A sum of $60,000 was raised by the public to equip the regiment with Sharp's rifles. Despite a reputation for rowdy conduct, the Fire Zouaves were heroes of the day when they put out a fire at Willard's hotel upon their arrival in Washington. The dashing Ellsworth, New York's first military hero of the war, was killed trying to cut down a southern flag flying from the Marshall House in Alexandria, Virginia.

The huge crowd that joyously filled Broadway at the news of Lee's surrender at Appomattox Courthouse in April 1865, and the solemn masses assembled in mourning after President Lincoln's assassination a few days later, again showed that City Hall Park had become the focus for national acts of celebration and grief. When ticker-tape parades began in 1886, celebrating the dedication of the Statue of Liberty, it was City Hall Park where the mayor and the city received the honored guests. Radical groups were sometimes obliged to make do with parades and mass meetings ending at Union Square or Tompkins Square Park, to celebrate May Day, demand the eight-hour day or to protest against military interventions abroad. We see Jimmy Herf, the "Bolshevik pacifist and I.W.W. agitator" who figures so centrally in John Dos Passos' *Manhattan Transfer* (1925) watching the unemployed shovel snow at City Hall Park, and feel in the winter wind the harshness of the workers' struggle to survive in the city:

> *The smell of the presses still in his nose, the chirrup of typewriters still in his ears, Jimmy Herf stood in City Hall Square with his hands in his pockets watching ragged men with caps and earflaps pulled down over*

> *faces and necks the color of raw steak shovel snow. Old and young their faces were the same color, their clothes were the same color. A razor wind cut his ears and made his forehead ache between the eyes.*

Marches of the unemployed in February 1936 ended in a mass meeting here, and when the protests over the Vietnam War were at their peak in 1970, rival demonstrators for and against the American involvement converged on the park.

The southernmost point of City Hall Park was occupied from 1878 until just before the Second World War by a five-story federal building. This enormous structure was an extravagant Second Empire wedding cake. Designed by A.B. Mullett, it served as the city's main post office and was inevitably called the "Mullett Post Office." With façades between 130 and 340 feet, the Post Office dominated the park and obscured the view of City Hall from downtown. Its demolition was one of the happier events of 1938. Happier still was the restoration of the park in the late 1990s, which saw the return of the original fountain designed by Jacob Wrey Mould (who contributed so many handsome features to Central Park), which had been banished to Crotona Park in the Bronx, and the installation of thoughtfully designed park furniture, benches, lighting, and planting. When the guards who currently separate the park from City Hall are gone and the barriers and chains are dismantled, the real restoration of this important public space will be complete.

Fashionable Ladies, Dandies, Hotels, and Shops

Visitors to New York in the nineteenth century describe a city with long stretches of quiet empty streets, lined with handsome dwellings of brick and brownstone. It was on the commercial avenues, and especially on Broadway, where the life of the city was on display. However disagreeable, over-crowded, and noisy, one visitor after another talked about Broadway as a unique public space. It was a scene of motion and deafening noise. The yellow and scarlet omnibuses ran on double rail lines laid in the middle of Broadway above 14th Street. Heavy "stages" lumbered downtown between the large hotels and shops; elegant hackney carriages pulled by two horses carried private passengers. A bystander at St. Paul's Chapel in 1850 might watch fifteen omnibuses passing uptown and down, every minute. For most of the day they would all be full. "Each stage makes ten trips a day," noted George Foster, "and takes in an average of twenty passengers, up and down. Here are 70,000 six-pences, or 4,375 dollars per day, paid for omnibus riding in the City of New York—amounting to over a million and a quarter per annum. How these six-pences count up when added together by thousands!" The unceasing, noisy stream of carts and wagons, piled high with merchandise, were driven by teamsters with thunderous voices who scattered any pedestrian who dared step off the sidewalk. "How well I remember them," wrote Walt Whitman in *Specimen Days* (1892).

> *How many hours, forenoons and afternoons—how many exhilarating night-times I have had—perhaps June or July, in cooler air—riding the whole length of Broadway, listening to some yarn (and the most vivid yarns ever spun, and the rarest mimicry)—or perhaps I declaiming some stormy passage from Julius Caesar or Richard, (you could roar as loudly as you chose in that heavy, dense, uninterrupted street-bass.) Yes I knew all the drivers then, Broadway Jack, Dressmaker, Balky Bill, George Storms, Old Elephant, his brother Young Elephant,... Tippy, Pop Rice, Big Frank... and dozens more; for there were hundreds. They had immense qualities, largely animal—eating, drinking, women—great personal pride in their way—perhaps a few slouched here and there, but I should have trusted the general run of them, in their simple good-will and honor, under all circumstances. Not only for comradeship, and sometimes affection—great studies I found them also.*

Whitman claimed that those long omnibus jaunts up and down Broadway, declaiming at the top of his voice "enter'd into the gestation of 'Leaves of Grass.'"

The sidewalks were every bit as crowded. It was, wrote a contributor to *Putnam's Monthly* in 1854, "altogether the most showy, the most crowded, and the richest thoroughfare in America . . . collected into one promiscuous channel of activity and dissipation." On Broadway, noted James D. McCabe, Jr. in *Lights and Shadows of New York Life* (1872), "fine gentlemen in broadcloth, ladies in silks and jewels, and beggars in squalid rags, are mingled in true Republican confusion." It was something to write about in guidebooks, travel books, and letters home. "On Broadway again," wrote a visitor from Sweden, Fredrika Bremer, "there is an endless tumult and stir, crowd and bustle, and in the city proper people throng as if for dear life." Broadway was not only crowded with the usual miscellaneous inhabitants of the city, but as early as the 1820s it had acquired a reputation as a fashionable thoroughfare, where the latest female fashions of the day were on permanent show. "The monstrous new Hats of the Ladies," wrote John Pintard, "take up so much space, that wide as the footwalks are, hardly can walk abreast. To look up & down they appear like flocks of Sea Gulls with expanded wings sweeping along the surface of creation. Positively it requires some management for them to introduce themselves hats & all into a Coach." New York belles and matrons were notorious in the United States for their passionate insistence upon the latest fashions from Paris and London, and their vivid display—a subject gently mocked in William Allen Butler's verse satire "Nothing to Wear" (1857), whose heroine, Miss Flora M'Flimsey of Madison Square, was the shopaholic incarnate, turning the shops upside down in search of

...bonnets, mantillas, capes, collars, and shawls;
Dresses for breakfasts, and dinners, and balls;
Dresses to sit in, and stand in, and walk in;
Dresses to dance in, and flirt in, and talk in;
Dresses in which to do nothing at all;
Dresses for Winter, Spring, Summer, and Fall—
All of them different in color and shape,
Silk, muslin, and lace, velvet, satin, and crape,
Brocade and broadcloth, and other material,
Quite as expensive and much more ethereal...

The effect, according to George Augustus Sala, an English author who visited New York in 1865, was to make Broadway the greatest of spectacles:

How they come, trooping, tripping, sailing, flouncing, and flaunting,—and, whenever they chance to meet a stray male animal, flirting with the most desperately delightful energy! Here they come, decked out in all the

> *colours of the rainbow, and in many other hues undreamt of in the solar spectrum! They float in flocks down the stately stream of Broadway, like swans; and, oh! the delightful sport to go out swan-hopping!*

Fashionables judged the avenues of New York by how many ladies in full skirts were able to walk side by side. Fifth Avenue was particularly highly regarded as having a three-skirt sidewalk.

Broadway was also the showcase of a new species of New Yorker, the Dandy. Flamboyant figures, they expressed a spirit of hedonism and style in the sober capital of American commerce. At a time in the 1840s when men's fashions were changing, with darker and heavier fabrics used, when trousers looked baggy and cravats dwindled into narrow strips of dark ribbon—and when the gloomy look of Mormon patriarchs accompanied the straggling beards that all respectable men were wearing—the Dandy reminded New Yorkers of a resplendent vision of slim elegance and bright colors. Many Europeans visitors had doubts about American manners and sneered at the pretensions of Americans to "society." The omnipresent spittoon seemed to stand for everything that was inferior about American manners. But on Broadway there was a daily expression of a different America, far from the raw, whiskey-swilling, tobacco-chewing frontiersman. Women wore glorious fashions—sometimes too glorious for fastidious Europeans—but it was quite a surprise to find Regency rakes and bucks strolling along the western side of Broadway. What is more, there were lots of them. One estimate in the 1830s suggested that there were 3,000 Dandies in New York.

Dandies announced themselves by their dress, their highly-polished patent-leather boots, tight-fitting striped pantaloons, white Marseilles vests, faultless silk neckties, white shirt with tiny gold studs and immaculate primrose-colored gloves. Eyes turned. That was indeed the point. Social analysts soon offered a field-guide to the kinds of Dandies in New York. They were differentiated by a prominent item of display: the watch chain, the "quizzing glass" (lorgnette) and the cane: "The switched, or caned, dandy is so denominated from a slender cane, or switch, about the size of a pipe-stem, made of whale-bone, or of steel… of a shining black, neatly polished, with an ivory head, a brass foot, a golden eye, and a tassel of silk; which cane or switch, he constantly carries and switches about him..." The dandy was a professed connoisseur of fashion and beauty, instantly ready to whip his glass from his bosom, and with an exaggerated gesture apply it to his eye whenever he was introduced to a stranger of either sex, and as often as he saw a female who had any pretension either to youth or beauty.

The Broadway Dandies had their enemies, who were often uncertain whether to denounce them as simpering and effeminate fops or to warn unsuspecting women that there were swaggering "blackguards" infesting Broadway:

> *One fine days... you will see them on the steps of the Astor, the Howard, the Franklin, City, and other hotels... If you have time and patience to stand by St. Paul's, you may see some of these automatons pass and repass fifty times between Leonard and Rector-streets in the course of three hours. They generally hook arms, and as they grin, look and talk in one another's faces...They have beards like the goats on Mount St. Gothard—their slender waists... are squeezed up and pressed up with whalebone, cord and buckram...Now these insignificant simple sons of silly women do nothing but go about among the weaker sexes seeking whom they may devour.*

Not every walker in the city admired Broadway and what it stood for. Where there were crowds there were likely to be drunks, pickpockets, and worse. George Templeton Strong, a New York lawyer in the mid-nineteenth century whose social circle included some of the wealthiest old families in the city, was an acerbic critic of what Broadway had become. "It's a pity we've no street but Broadway that's fit to walk in of an evening," he wrote in his diary in 1840. "The street is always crowded, and whores and blackguards make up about two-thirds of the throng. That's one of the advantages of uptown; the streets there are well paved, well lighted, and decently populated." A respectable person walking on Broadway could hardly avoid "meeting some hideous troop of ragged girls, from twelve-years old down... with thief written in their cunning eyes and whore on their depraved faces." Nor did the fashionable ladies and Dandies constitute more than a highly-visible fraction of the copyists, clerks, milliners, salesmen, Irish immigrant laborers, and other "democratic plodders" in Whitman's vivid phrase who would crowd Broadway in the morning and evening. Fashion was reserved for the middle of the day.

Promenaders along Broadway could enjoy one of the city's most distinctive features: its luxury hotels and shops. The famous City Hotel, located on the west side of Broadway between Thames and Cedar Streets, was no more, but the tradition it represented—of luxury accommodation in the heart of Broadway—endured. The City Hotel opened in 1794 with 137 rooms, bar, coffee room, concert hall, and ground-floor shops as well as a large Assembly Room used for public dances. It was bought by John Jacob Astor in 1828 for $101,000. But with the opening of the Astor House, also on the west side of Broadway from Barclay to Vesey Street in 1836, the venerable City Hotel was largely superseded by the newer establishment and was finally demolished in 1847. The Astor House was a granite structure six stories high, with 300 rooms, offering accommodation for 600 guests. The $400,000 spent by Astor on the hotel set new standards for ostentatious expenditure—something that Astor alone among the city's millionaires could imagine. He also understood the value of ground-floor real estate on Broadway. The entire ground floor of the Astor House was taken up by shops, and the hotel was entered up a flight of stairs. Visitors were impressed that every floor contained toilets and a bathroom. They were perhaps less pleased to note that on Church and Chapel Streets, within easy reach of the hotel, lay some of the city's up-market brothels. That became the New York pattern: around the large hotels and places of amusement were to be found on adjacent streets gambling dens, brothels and saloons.

Although the Astor House remained open until 1913 and was redecorated and modernized with the installation of elevators, its dominance of the luxury trade was challenged in the 1850s when two new hotels were built farther uptown (the Metropolitan and the St. Nicholas, and then, far uptown, the Fifth Avenue Hotel at 23rd Street, opposite Madison Square, in 1859), eclipsing the older establishment in size, comfort, and luxury. These new hotels were created with press headlines in mind. There were 13,000 yards of deep carpeting at the Metropolitan (located on Broadway between Prince and Houston Streets) and a unique "sky parlor" where ladies could watch the busy scene on Broadway. The mirrors at the St. Nicholas (located on the west side of Broadway between

Broome and Spring Streets—a part of the original structure has survived at 521–3 Broadway) cost about $40,000 and the silver service and Sheffield plate another $50,000. The competition between hotels for ever higher levels of luxury and expenditure—the Donald Trump syndrome—is deeply rooted in the city's commercial life.

"The display in the windows of the Broadway stores is rich, beautiful, and tempting," wrote James D. McCabe, Jr. "Jewels, silks, satins, laces, ribbons, household goods, silverware, toys, paintings, in short, rare, costly, and beautiful objects of every description greet the gazer on every hand." Shopping on Broadway had not yet, in the nineteenth century, completed the transition from specialized shops to the modern department store. But it was heading in that direction. The fancy dry goods store, like that opened by Rowland H. Macy in 1858, specialized in ribbons, laces, embroideries, artificial flowers, feathers, handkerchiefs, hosiery, and gloves. Over the next two decades, Macy expanded into men's furnishings, furs, housekeeping goods, books, and kitchen utensils, as well as French and German fancy goods. In 1870s, he added a soda fountain, Bohemian glassware, ice skates, and a wide range of china, silver, chairs, mats, and rugs.

Goods were set out on counters where they could be examined by customers, and prices were clearly marked. Placing a plainly marked price on each item was an innovation of the Philadelphia merchant John Wanamaker, and the practice was adopted widely in New York. It replaced the older pattern of individually negotiated prices. Large display windows put a range of goods within view from the sidewalks. Entrances were inviting and the sales floors were well lit. Merchants learned that an atmosphere of excitement was good for sales.

The Haughwout store at 488–92 Broadway at the corner of Broome Street—it is currently occupied by Staples—where Eder V. Haughwout sold china, silverware, cut glass, and quality chandeliers, had the first practical steam-powered Otis elevator in New York. (The cast-iron façade of 1857 was fabricated by the New York firm of Daniel Badger Architectural Iron Works.)

Tiffany's, located in the nineteenth century on the corner of Warren Street and Broadway, symbolized the distinctive Broadway mix of luxury goods and go-ahead commercialism: "Tiffany's is a fashionable pleasure-lounge already," wrote the noted Dandy N.P.

Willis, "his broad glass doors and tempting windows being at one of the most thronged corners of Broadway. It is better than a museum, in being quite as well stocked with surprises, and these all ministering to present and fashionable wants."

Above all, Broadway was synonymous with the commercial affairs of Alexander T. Stewart. At five foot tall and with a strong Belfast accent, Stewart carved out an unprecedented career in American business. His

A. T. STEWART'S WHOLESALE STORE.

reputation for probity, a lifetime policy of paying in cash for his goods, and a deft feel for ways to create goodwill and valuable newspaper publicity (by offering discounts to the wives and children of clergymen) made Stewart the city's greatest merchant. He was also notorious for the low wages he paid and the harsh disciplinary rules he imposed upon his staff. Cultural historians have often praised the pragmatism of American life, and the adaptable American entrepreneur has played a large role in national mythology. But there was another spirit in American business, of a domineering rigidity and imperiousness, every bit as representative, and as successful: "One of the principal reasons of his success," wrote a contemporary of A.T. Stewart, "is the rigid system with which he conducts his business. He has a place for every thing, and a time for every duty, and requires the same regularity from his subordinates. His salesmen and managers are thoroughly versed in their duties, and the more important of them are selected with great care. Every thing works smoothly under the master's eye, and there is a penalty for each and every delinquency, which is rigidly exacted."

In 1846 he opened a wholesale store on the "wrong" side of Broadway at Chambers Street. Immediately called a gleaming "Marble Palace," Stewart's was New York's first commercial Italianate building in the *palazzo* style. (Later occupied by the *Sun* newspaper, the building survives in a heavily reconstructed form in the block above City Hall.) The luxury jewelry shop of Tiffany & Young opened next door. To the ex-mayor and indefatigable diarist, Philip Hone, the meaning of Stewart's store lay in the triumph of commerce on Broadway, which had within living memory been the finest residential street in the city. It was an ominous portent of the future of the city, which would, he feared, be decided by "money-changers" on Wall Street and merchants like Stewart. "The mania for converting Broadway into a street of shops," Hone wrote on May 31, 1850,

> *is greater than ever. There is scarcely a block in the whole extent of this fine street of which some part is not in a state of transmutation. The City Hotel has given place to a row of splendid stores; Stewart is extending his stores to take in the whole front from Chambers to Reade Street; this is already the most magnificent dry-goods establishment in the world. I certainly do not remember anything to equal it in London or Paris; with the addition now in progress, this edifice will be one of the "wonders" of the Western World. Three or four good brick houses on the corner of Broadway and Spring Street have been leveled, I know not for what purpose,—shops, no doubt.*

Such a store carried multiple meanings for New Yorkers. The more farseeing might have wondered if it meant that consumption, and not manufacturing, was to become the shaping force in the city's future. It was also a powerful sign of the growing ascendancy of commerce, and its frankly mercantile values, and perhaps the waning of the deference and gentlemanly hierarchies that underlay the colonial city. Money talked, and Stewart had lots of money. Stewart's handsome store seemed also to some observers to look toward a threatening Roman future in which the city was to worship at the false gods of luxury and in which demand for luxury goods was likely to be insatiable. Stewart purchased the entire block near Grace Church between Broadway and Fourth Avenue, between 9th and 10th Streets, for a five-story retail outlet. With 200 feet of Broadway frontage lit by several thousand gas jets simultaneously ignited by electricity, Stewart swept all before him. He was the nation's greatest merchant, and the largest importer, averaging $30,000 in duties paid per day. The "meaning" of Stewart for New York lay in consumption, money values, and luxury.

Stewart died on April 10, 1876 and was buried at St. Mark's graveyard. Two years later his remains were stolen for ransom. His distraught widow Cornelia paid the grave robbers $25,000. After that grotesque event there was a vogue at Green-Wood and Woodlawn cemeteries for mausoleums that looked like banks or fortresses. F.W. Woolworth's Egyptian-Revival mausoleum at Woodlawn was sarcastically described as "the pyramid" by his granddaughter Barbara Hutton. After the death of his widow, Stewart's much-admired mansion on Fifth Avenue was sold to a gentleman's club. The store at Broadway and Ninth Street was bought in 1896 by John Wanamaker.

Chinatown

Broadway, like all New York's crowded avenues, imposes a staccato rhythm upon pedestrians. Waiting for the traffic lights to change, and then the rush across the street, reminds you that this is not the Ramblas in Barcelona, designed for easy strolling. The pleasures of a walk on Broadway must be earned and require close attention—avoiding crates piled on sidewalks, people staring into store windows, bags of uncollected trash, skateboarders, in-line roller skaters, distracted tourists looking for the subway, fast-talking men standing behind little trays selling "Rolex" watches for $40 (if you are persistent, they'll bring the price down to $25), and panhandlers sprawled on the sidewalk, looking miserable and shaking a paper cup to catch your eye.

There is another rhythm encountered on a Broadway walk: the major cross streets each mark a shift in the life of the street. Chambers Street, Canal, Houston, Astor Place, Union Square, Madison Square, and then 42nd Street are bustling with life, but each possesses a different life, a different feel, which is one of the chief delights Broadway has to offer. At Chambers Street the downtown financial world ends. There are fewer really tall buildings north of City Hall. The wholesale dry goods establishments, occupying five- and six-story nineteenth-century commercial buildings on Broadway between Walker, Franklin, and White Streets, belong to the city's commercial past, when the manufacture of clothing was done in sweatshops and small factories on Broadway and in the Lower East Side. Rolls of fabric, often far from the colors one sees at the Gap or J. Crew, stand in bins. The windows are dusty and reveal fabrics, ribbons, and laces more piled upon each other than displayed. Walk-in trade, catching the pedestrian's eye, plays no role in the wholesale dry goods trade.

Where Canal Street crosses Broadway, Chinatown unmistakably announces itself. East of Broadway, on the north side of Canal Street, are dozens of jewelry stores, one of the most important forms of retail trade in Chinatown. "Old" Chinatown was traditionally located east of Broadway, north of Worth Street, west of the Bowery and south of Canal Street. The presence of other well-established and sizable communities in the ethnic jigsaw of New York defined the territory of Chinatown. Little Italy (above Canal), Hester Street, and the formerly Jewish and now largely Hispanic Lower East Side, were on the traditional borders of Chinatown. The city had its first Chinese residents in the 1850s, an all-male population of sailors, cooks, and keepers of boardinghouses. When agitation against the Chinese increased in California after the Civil War, the New York community grew with the arrival of newcomers from the West Coast. The Chinese Exclusion Act of 1882 prevented Chinese New York from developing as any other immigrant enclave. The denial of citizenship confined the Chinese to political impotence, and the absence of marriageable women inevitably created a social life built around bachelors. Laundries and restaurants provided areas of Chinese entrepreneurship requiring little knowledge of the English language and involving the least face-to-face contact with New York's population.

In other ways Chinatown evolved in isolation, and nothing was quite what it seemed. Chinese cultural practices persisted, side by side with public observance of Christian faith. During the years of exclusion, Chinese men adopted Americanized versions of their names ("paper names") as a way of disguising Chinese identity and avoiding some of the worst forms of prejudice (Chew Dip thus becoming Joseph Tape, Jee Mon Sing becoming J.M. Singleton). The American effort was designed to stamp out the practice of "picture brides," women who had been married by proxy to Japanese men legally in the United States. The Japanese, who were excluded from emigration by the Root-Takahira Treaty in 1907, created "paper sons," immigrants with false identities who claimed to be related to legal immigrants. At entry hearings, which could last several days, every effort was made to trip up the applicants and to find inconsistencies in their stories:

What is your living room floor made of?
Where is the rice bin kept?
Where is your village temple?

The Chinese passion for gambling, opium "dens," the "white" slave trade and the Chinese associations (*tongs*), which to outsiders looked alarmingly like gangs, provided opportunities for the embroidery of strong prejudicial stereotypes in the wider community and also encouraged Chinatown to develop as a more closed-off world than any other immigrant community in the city. As with so much in Chinatown, it was always hard for outsiders to tell the real thing from the performed and staged. Tourists could pay a small sum to look at the notorious opium dens. Taken into a small room, they would peer into a poorly lit, smoky area. Upon rows of beds lay the forms of stupefied opium-smokers. Alas, most of the smokers were on an hourly wage to provide a show for out-of-town visitors. There were real opium dens, but they were not put on public display, and Chinatown played an important role in the national drug trade as far back as the late nineteenth century.

The repeal of the Exclusion Act in 1943—a gesture to the important role played by the Chinese in the war against Japan—opened the door for a resumption of direct immigration. The abolition of the old quotas in 1968 enabled 20,000 Chinese a year to enter the United States. The floodgates opened between 1982 and 1989, when 358,119 Chinese immigrants entered America, and of that number 71,888 settled in New York. Only the Dominican Republic and Jamaica provided more immigrants to New York in that period. The impact on Chinatown, which had numbered 20,000 in the mid-1960s, was dramatic, changing a community previously dominated by bachelors and traditional fraternal societies. New areas of Chinese settlement appeared in Brooklyn, the Bronx, and Queens (where the Chinese population grew from 80,000 to 139,820 in the 1990s and now makes up over 17 percent of the total population). New York became the most populous Chinese community in North America and the fastest growing (expanding by 40 percent in the 1990s). It was also becoming increasingly diverse, with newcomers arriving from Vietnam, Malaysia, and Korea, bringing capital and new entrepreneurial energy. There has been substantial investment in Chinatown by Hong Kong capitalists, and it now makes more sense to talk of Chinatown as Asia City, for the new arrivals have transformed the "old" Chinatown of even two decades ago. The explosive population growth in Chinatown has redefined borders with Little Italy, which in the absence of fresh migration in the 1980s and the steady move of Italian-Americans into the suburbs, has become a shell of its former self.

The impact on New York of Korean migration has been even more dramatic. Since mass migration became possible in the 1960s, the Koreans have brought a productive and entrepreneurial flair to dying neighborhoods across the city. There is now a "Koreatown" on West 32nd Street. The figures are impressive: Koreans now run 1,400 produce stores, 3,500 grocery stores, 2,000 dry cleaners, 800 seafood stores, and 1,300 nail salons. The common belief that Koreans have a monopoly on the city's 24-hour grocery stores is close to being accurate. Numbering perhaps no more than 250,000 in the region, they have made an ascent into the city's commercial life comparable with the Jews a century ago. There is a consciousness of similar family values, work ethic, and devotion to education, which has sent Koreans flocking to Harvard. The current estimate is that Korean Americans make up five percent of the student body at Columbia, Yale, and Harvard.

Being a Korean in New York has not always been a friendly experience. In 1990 there was an ugly boycott of Korean groceries by African Americans in Flatbush, which turned violent and threatened briefly to spread across the city. Similarly, Koreans have found themselves competing face to face with older and better-placed ethnic groups. In the garment district, there are at least 300 Korean-owned sweatshops (some estimates place the number as high as 460), and most of them are non-union shops that employ a largely Latino immigrant workforce. Where labor struggles are conducted within the context of ethnic community values, and in the glare of ethnic community public opinion, a "community" strategy has given the International Ladies' Garment Workers' Union some successes. But attempts to organize the sharply divided workforce of the Korean sweatshops have proved difficult. As has always been the case, the sweatshop contractors are at the bottom of a food chain controlled by the big Seventh Avenue manufacturers. The younger generation of Koreans have become impatient with the way their parents have avoided public confrontations in New York. There are no Korean Al Sharptons, and the children, hungry for a more assertive style (there are so many lessons in assertiveness to be had every day in New York!) are asking why.

With its density of occupation, crowded streets, open-fronted shops, and profusion of goods sold directly on the sidewalk, Chinatown has retained the "street" feel of Old New York that has disappeared from a great deal of downtown. But much of that was lost in the aftermath of September 11. Chinatown—less than a half mile from the World Trade Center—was sealed off from the rest of the city. With restricted subway communications and briefly no phone service, a community geared to a high volume of tourist visitors found itself with empty restaurants. Salesclerks in crowded tourist shops, ordinarily hectic with business, sat drumming their fingers in boredom, awaiting the next customer. Chinatown was left in limbo. The streets were quieter. Sidewalks seemed less crowded. Employment in Chinatown was wounded: in food, service and retail business, as well as traditional industries such as the garment trade, 6,000 jobs were lost. A reporter for the *New York Times* remarked how curious it was that waiters seemed "unfailingly patient, even solicitous."

SoHo

A block or two above Canal Street, and we are in SoHo—that is, south of Houston, an area that in the nineteenth century had included some of the most fashionable New York stores. When the stores moved uptown in the 1870s, SoHo became an important manufacturing and commercial district. (The name "SoHo" is a post-Second World War creation of the real estate market, but it is too useful for us to ignore it when talking about the earlier life of this part of the city.) There are only a few reminders of that retailing majesty, like the old Lord & Taylor building at the corner of Broadway and Grand, and the cast-iron Haughwout Building one block north at the intersection with Broome Street. The façade of the remaining sections of the St. Nicholas Hotel at 521–23 Broadway, which was from the 1850s to the 1870s the largest, most luxurious and commercially successful hotel in New York, is another relic of its vanished importance. Ernest Flagg's elegant "Little Singer" building (1907) at 561 Broadway is worth a closer look.

Bordered by Canal Street, Broadway, Howard, Crosby, East and West Houston, and West Broadway, the SoHo Historic District is, architecturally, the most unified area in New York. It contains the largest remaining group of cast-iron structures in the world (there are fifty on Greene Street alone). Many of the cast-iron structures were fabricated nearby at James Bogardus' factory below Canal Street. The use of cast-iron building components allowed maximum daylight, and because the molds for cast-iron were far cheaper to make than cut stone and required less skilled labor to assemble, builders were able to decorate what were quite utilitarian structures with a richness of design (Italian Renaissance motifs were highly popular) visible on Broadway and the side streets in SoHo.

After fashionable life moved further uptown, SoHo was taken over in the 1870s by manufacturers recognizing the opportunities created by a neighborhood in commercial decline. The small SoHo factories were badly hit by harsh conditions in the 1920s. Garment and fur manufacturers wanted to relocate their showrooms to midtown, near the hotels favored by out-of-town buyers. SoHo manufacturers were then lured away by custom-built factories offering more space and improved road access in the outer fringes of the city. The empty space in the cast-iron buildings was filled with smaller shops run by sub-contractors, and the surviving SoHo textile industry concentrated on inexpensive apparel. The sharp decline from the days of the St. Nicholas and Lord & Taylor was clear everywhere in SoHo. Rents were low, and many of the tenants were marginal. And as conditions changed again in the 1950s and 1960s, these small workshops in turn went out of business or moved away, further lowering occupancy levels.

Into this failing neighborhood came artists, looking for lofts and studios with low rents, good light, and a central location. As the number of artists grew, the area attracted dealers and small galleries, which were followed by bigger galleries (the Guggenheim/SoHo at 575 Broadway, the New Museum of Contemporary Art at 583 Broadway, and the Museum for African Art, with galleries designed by Maya Lin, at 593 Broadway), boutiques, coffee shops, smart clothing shops, and much more, transforming SoHo by the 1970s into one of the most sought-after places in New York. There are some 200 art galleries in SoHo, and more photography galleries than anywhere else in the city—perhaps anywhere in the world. Some are hopeful transients; others, like the established Pace and Gagosian Galleries, are big players in the art market. Alternative spaces are a particularly important feature of the SoHo art scene.

There is an entirely different commercial spirit in SoHo—smarter, more brand-focused, with more than a hint of North Beach. The shops cater to a younger and smarter-looking clientele, which is largely comprised of well-heeled NYU students.

The dividing line between West and East Houston, and the dividing line between SoHo and NoHo* (north of Houston) comes at the intersection with Broadway. On the left side of Broadway is the behemoth of New York University, Washington Square, and Greenwich Village. On the east side of the street is the Bowery and the East Village. In the narrow wedge of streets between Broadway and the Bowery, above Bleecker Street, lies what was once the city's most exclusive and aristocratic neighborhood.

Begin an exploration of that patrician enclave with a visit to the Seabury Tredwell House, erected in 1830 on East 4th Street between Lafayette Street and the Bowery. Open to the public, this miraculously preserved structure is one of the very few surviving private residences of the period when this was an unruffled center of fashionable life. Development began on Bond Street in the 1820s, and the earliest inhabitants were drawn from the city's most distinguished citizens.

* In June 1999 the New York City Landmarks Preservation Commission designated "Noho", a new historic district running between Broadway and Lafayette Street from Houston Street to Wanamaker Place. Regulations make it virtually impossible to raze buildings included in this area, and all external changes and structural work must be cleared with the commission. Also in Noho is the Bayard-Condict Building at 69 Bleecker Street, the architect Louis Sullivan's only New York building.

At 5 Bond Street lived Albert Gallatin. He had been secretary of the treasury and minister to France and to the Court of St. James. Gallatin's house was later occupied by Major-General Winfield Scott. Bond Street also included some of the leading figures among merchants and importers. The ship's chandler Abraham Schermerhorn lived at 36 Bond Street from 1839 until his death in 1850. His daughter Caroline ("Lina" in the family) spent her early years in Bond Street before becoming *the* Mrs. Astor when she married William Astor, grandson of John Jacob Astor, in 1853. The social tone of Bond Street was set by the mansion standing on the northeast corner of Broadway and Bond Street, which was later the home of Brooks Brothers. Built in 1831 for Samuel Ward, partner of the banking house of Prime, Ward, and King, it was by common consent the finest private house in the city. In a colonnaded extension at the rear of the house was the first private art gallery in the city. Among Ward's art collection were the four canvases of Thomas Cole's "The Voyage of Life" (though they were unfinished at his death).

Lafayette Place was fully an equal of Bond Street in the wealth and social prominence of its inhabitants. Colonnade Row—428–34 Lafayette was a symbol of everything worth boasting about. In nine Greek Revival townhouses erected in 1833, unified by 27 massive Corinthian columns, lived some of New York's wealthiest families. John Jacob Astor and an assortment of other Astor relations and other families of equal distinction (if not wealth) like the Delanos lived in Colonnade Row. The Astors left a permanent mark upon Lafayette Place (the name was changed to Lafayette Street when the street was cut through from Great Jones Street to City Hall in the 1880s) when the will of John Jacob Astor in 1848 made a bequest to establish a library. His son and heir, William B. Astor, donated land and paid for a building on Lafayette Place where the young library was housed. (It was later incorporated into the New York Public Library.) The red brick and brownstone structure, at 425 Lafayette Street, is today the home of the New York Shakespeare Festival.

What made Bond Street and Lafayette Place an aristocratic neighborhood was the building of the Opera House, which opened on Astor Place in November 1847. With the strong support of the city's wealthiest families, the Astor Place Opera became a battlefield between the patriotic "Bowery B'hoy" supporters of the actor Edwin Forrest and the English tragedian Macready, whose slighting comments about Forrest were taken to offer insult to all true-born Americans. There were violent protests at the Opera House in May 1849, designed to drive Macready off the stage. The militia was summoned, and 22 rioters were killed, many wounded, and even more arrested after the Astor Place riot was violently suppressed. It was the first occasion since the revolution that the militia was used to suppress a rioting mob. After the 1849 riot, the charms of Lafayette Place began to fade when the illusion that it could sustain itself as an aristocratic enclave ended. The mob that attacked the Opera House was not an *imaginary* threat to life and property. The wealthy felt increasingly alarmed at the deepening levels of social disorder around them.

After three further and unsuccessful seasons, the Opera House was sold to the Mercantile Library Association. In 1859, when Peter Cooper gave the Cooper Union to the city to provide free non-sectarian and co-educational education, the changing meaning of the neighborhood became clear. With the flight of the rich to Fifth Avenue and the opening of Lafayette Street to the full force of the city's thunderous traffic, the hope that Bond Street and Lafayette Place might remain an aristocratic neighborhood faded from memory.

Grace Church

In 1843 the vestry of Grace Church, which since 1809 had occupied a plain, box-like building at the corner of Broadway and Rector Street

facing the rather grander structure of the second Trinity Church, decided that it, too, must follow the procession uptown. The structure was sold for $65,000 for conversion into retail stores and a museum of Chinese curiosities. Henry Brevoort was approached about a plot of land on Broadway at the intersection with 10th Street. The stolid Dutch Brevoort family, who had farmed on Manhattan for some two hundred years, accepted $35,000 for the land sought by the vestry. James Renwick's Gothic limestone structure, topped by a wooden steeple (rebuilt in marble in 1883), was erected at 800 Broadway, on the corner of East 10th Street, and was consecrated in 1846.

The precocious Renwick was given the commission at the age of 23, and had, it is said, never even seen a Gothic church before embarking on this, his first commission. He was able to construct his design from what architectural pattern books could be found and from the sketches his father James Renwick Sr., an engineer and professor of natural philosophy at Columbia College, had made when he accompanied Washington Irving on a walking tour of England in 1815. Upjohn's much-admired Trinity Church had made Gothic Revival a natural design for an Episcopal church in New York, but Renwick departed strikingly from the massive brownstone used by Upjohn. Working in white marble and using substantial clear glass windows, the effect of Grace Church was light, airy, and stylish. George Templeton Strong, who was later to be married in Renwick's structure, deplored the architect's "unhappy straining after cheap magnificence," but visitors to Grace Church responded to its decided elegance. "Already its aisles are filled," wrote the sarcastic Philip Hone in his diary in 1846,

> *with gay parties of ladies in feathers and* mousseline-de-laine *dresses, and dandies with moustaches and high-heeled boots; the lofty arches resound with astute criticisms upon* Gothic architecture *from fair ladies who have had the advantages of foreign travel, and scientific remarks upon acoustics from elderly millionaires who do not hear quite so well as formerly. The church is built of white marble, in the extreme form of the florid Gothic, in the form of a cross. The exterior is beautiful, and its position at the commencement of the bend of Broadway, which brings it directly in view from below, striking and prominent.*

The present stained-glass windows were not in Renwick's original structure, but were donated by wealthy parishioners in the 1880s. Renwick's Grace Church was (in the judgment of William H. Pierson, Jr., the foremost student of Renwick's work) "an outstanding achievement of the early Gothic Revival." Ferdinand Joachim Richardt's painting of the church and its elegant parishioners (seen on an imaginary day when there was only the briefest hint of traffic on Broadway) is on display in the church offices in an adjoining building on the site. Of his surviving later work, Calvary Church, on Park Avenue South and 21st Street, was finished in 1847. His masterpiece, St. Patrick's Cathedral (50th Street at Fifth Avenue), a far more complex structure than Grace Church and on a far greater scale, was commissioned in 1853 and completed in 1879, at a vast cost of $1.9 million. It made Renwick, despite the intervention of the Civil War, the successive meddling of Archbishops, the financial constraints of the archdiocese, and the problems created by a difficult site, the leading New York advocate of Gothic Revival architecture.

With the appointment of Henry Codman Potter as fifth rector in 1868, Grace Church arrived at the full flowering of its distinctive mixture of fashionableness and social gospel. Potter aggressively expanded the role of the church in reaching out to the immigrants who were increasingly inhabiting the neighborhood, and when he became Bishop of New York in 1887 he began construction of the Cathedral of St. John the Divine, which has proceeded at a medieval pace on the upper West Side ever since. Potter's successor as rector, William Reed Huntington, drew the church closer to the progressive spirit of the Social Settlements. The construction of a Chapel on 14th Street and First Avenue in 1896 was perhaps the high-point in Grace Church's mission to the immigrant East Side, but important educational work continues, especially the Grace Opportunity Project of summer remedial classes begun in 1968. When the Chapel was closed and sold in 1943, there was a tacit recognition that the fortunes of the "downtown" churches were themselves in precipitate decline.

It was the "beadle-faced" Isaac Hull Brown, sexton of Grace Church from 1845 to 1880, a vast figure of a man who joked that his usual weight was the same number as his Masonic lodge (he was first master of Puritan Lodge, No. 399), who imprinted his memorable visage upon the whole institution. To the old families of New York—the Stuyvesants, Van Rensselaers, and Livingstons—he was a devoted servant, a model of respect and deference. On the north wall of Grace Church a bronze plaque bears an inscription:

To the memory of Isaac Hull Brown
Born Dec. 4, 1812 Died Aug. 21, 1880
For thirty five years the faithful Sexton of Grace Church.
This tablet is erected by members of the Congregation who gladly recall his Fidelity, his Generosity, and his Stainless Integrity.

He was appointed sexton when Grace Church was consecrated in 1846. The congregation included families of distinction and great wealth. What Grace Church represented to Brown was "quality," wealth, old families, breeding, and tradition, and he allied himself unreservedly with their values and social perspectives. The social parvenus and "shoddyites" filled him with scorn and indignation. The sexton's supreme accolade was the description of a social occasion as being "thoroughbred." To the novelist and author of etiquette books, Mrs. Sherwood, he remarked after a ball at the Goelet's or Gerry's, "Ah, Madame, this has been an aristocratic assemblage; *no mixture here.*" He prided himself in his ability to recall family relationships and the complex cousinage underlying the city's elite. Edgar Fawcett recalled Brown in his satire of social climbing, *The Buntling Ball* (1884):

Poor Brown (peace rest him!) knew with searching ken
The grades of difference in all families
Whose carriages for half a century
He had called at weddings, funerals, and balls.

Celebrated in poems and recalled in memoirs, Brown was a memorable figure. Herman Melville wrote a satiric sketch of him and Grace Church, "The Two Temples," which he submitted to *Putnam's Magazine* in 1854. The editor gently advised Melville that jabs at Grace Church were unwise, however "exquisitely fine" and "pungent" the execution: "my editorial experience compels me to be very cautious in offending the religious sensibilities of the public, and the moral of the Two Temples would array against us the whole power of the pulpit, to say nothing of Brown, and the congregation of Grace Church."

Union Square

Union Square, at the intersection of Broadway and 14th Street where Broadway and the Bowery met, was created a public space in 1832. It became a residential district in the 1840s, and in the decade before the Civil War was transformed into the greatest single concentration of theaters, nightclubs, restaurants, fancy hotels, and luxury shopping in America. The Academy of Music, built in 1854, ensured that 14th Street was at the heart of the leading theatrical district until the emergence of Broadway at the turn of the new century. "Ladies' Mile," including Fifth and Sixth Avenues and Broadway, became the true home of fashionable New York in the nineteenth century. In 1854 the exclusive Union Club occupied a brownstone on Fifth Avenue and 21st Street. "Elegant mansions are rising rapidly around it," noted a reporter, "in all the splendor of recent Metropolitan improvements." It was the site of the Fuller Company's Flatiron Building (see Chapter 1). R.H. Macy had opened his "dry goods" establishment at 204–6 Sixth Avenue, near 14th Street, before the Civil War, and as the post-war drive uptown got underway Lord & Taylor moved to 20th Street and Broadway in 1867, to be followed by Hugh O'Neill, B. Altman, and Sterns in the 1870s. Brooks Brothers, W.& J. Sloane, and the Ehrich Brothers Emporium were opened along "Ladies Mile" in the 1880s. The opening of Delmonico's restaurant on Fifth Avenue and 26th Street in 1876 put the cherry on this very appetizing cake.

After the turn of the century one after the other of the fashionable shops (Macy's, Saks, Cartier, Tiffany's, Gimbels, Altman's, Bonwit Teller) relocated to sites above Madison Square to 52nd Street along Broadway and Fifth Avenue. With the move uptown of fashionable shopping, the old "Ladies' Mile" went into steep decline. The formerly fashionable Union Square became a run-down center for workers in the needle trades. Union Square had been the focus for the May Day parades held from 1890 by the city's trade unions and was an important place for demonstrations against unemployment, police brutality, and other political protests. The reputation of Union Square for political radicalism deepened in the 1930s. The editorial offices of *The New Masses* were located on Union Square West in the early 1930s. The offices of the Communist Party Yiddish-language paper, the *Freiheit*, and the Cooperative Cafeteria, rented space on Union Square East.

The extensive renovation and reconstruction of the square between 1928 and 1936 made it less suitable for mass demonstrations. The park bed was elevated by five feet to permit the construction of a mezzanine for the Sixth Avenue subway. By disrupting the visual relationship of the park to the sidewalk life around it, things were made worse.

The most important sign of change was the emergence of Samuel Klein's bargain women's wear empire on Union Square. Klein's story sounded as though it had been written by Horatio Alger. Klein was a poor tailor working in a Union Square loft when he opened a little store on Bleecker Street. He moved to Union Square in 1912. In a series of deft purchases in a declining real estate market, he acquired buildings that had housed departed or failed businesses. By 1928 he owned much of the real estate on Union Square East and his clothing store was breathing new life into Union Square. There, during the Depression, he sold good quality clothes to middle-class women who were watching their pennies. An annex located a block away captured the national imagination: Klein's bargain basement, "Klein's on the Square." It was almost entirely without the usual service offered to New York shoppers: you rooted around, checking sizes and prices, with regular shakes of the head at the astounding bargains. Albert Halper's novel of radicalism and class struggle, *Union Square* (1933), described the scene:

> *Traffic swept around the square. Long before the doors of Klein's Dress Store opened, crowds of women and girls had gathered. Private policemen in gray uniforms tried to keep order at about nine-thirty, because at that time all the doors were unlocked and the women swept forward in a powerful surge, grabbing at the dresses on the racks, searching and clawing for bargains. It was cash down here, "on the Square," each women held her money in her fist.*

Artists whose studios were located in the Union Square area in the 1930s (Kenneth Hayes Miller, Reginald Marsh, Raphael Soyer, and Isabel Bishop) found Klein's customers and the chaotic scenes in the communal changing rooms while customers tried on clothes, an irresistible subject.

The downturn of Union Square as a shopping area was signaled in 1954 when Orbachs moved to 34th Street and Fifth Avenue. The closing of Klein's in 1975, at a time when the city's fortunes were on a downward spiral, seemed to mark the death of downtown shopping and the triumph of the suburban mall. Two decades later, in the same way that Klein's found new uses for the large buildings left behind on Union Square, Old Navy, Filene's Basement, T.J. Maxx, and other national chains have occupied the surviving old commercial palaces of "Ladies' Mile."

When the Square was at a low ebb in the 1970s, mainly occupied by winos and drug-takers, an urban planner named Barry Benepe conceived of the idea of recruiting struggling Hudson Valley farmers to set up stalls selling dairy products, vegetables, and fruit four days a week. Farmers are allowed to sell only what they produce or grow, a restriction which has kept the Greenmarket "real" and in the hands of the producers and customers. The Greenmarket, which is managed by the Council on the Environment, is an imaginative idea of how urban renewal might be approached. Over the 25 years since it was first opened, the Greenmarket at Union Square has earned an important place in the life of the area. Modestly, it is described as the best farmers' market in the United States, and leading chefs are regularly seen among the chatting lines of customers. On a typical Saturday, 40,000 shoppers might call at the Greenmarket, with considerable benefits for the local shops. It inevitably became a tourist attraction, and in the weeks before Christmas a large craft fare takes over the space normally occupied by the market.

The Parks Department and its czar Henry Stern plan a reconstruction of the southwest corner of Union Square in 2002. The $6 million redesign, which involves new tree plantings, has raised concerns that some of the farmers will be edged out. As the area around Union Square has improved, the relations between the Parks Department and the Greenmarket have deteriorated. "I don't think one farmer or any farmer will be forced out," remarked Stern, but the promises of planners and commissioners, like fresh vegetables, have an alarmingly short shelf life. An imposing group of top chefs has written a public letter in support of the market, and the (inevitable) Friends of Greenmarket have begun to mobilize public support.

Madison Square

Madison Square (named in honor of President James Madison) stands upon 6.8 acres of land purchased by the city in 1837 and opened to the public in 1847. The surrounding area only became a fashionable residential district in the 1850s. Anchored by Amos Eno's white marble Fifth Avenue Hotel (with a theater built as an adjunct) at the intersection of Fifth Avenue and Broadway at 23rd Street, an important hotel district was created in the 1850s in the streets between Union Square and Madison Square. The Everett House, Clarendon House, and the Hoffman House—where Bouguereau's fleshy *Nymphs and Satyrs* adorned the bar, and where no woman was ever admitted—were noted for luxury and comfort, offering patrons unparalleled levels of service and accommodation. It remained primarily residential long after Union Square had succumbed to commercial use, and it was only in the twentieth century that the Metropolitan Life Insurance Company (designed by Napoleon LeBrun), and New York Life made Madison Square primarily the home of large office buildings. Among their number was the Fuller Company Flatiron Building (see Chapter 1), facing the southern end of the park. The campanile of the Metropolitan Life building rose 700 feet above Madison Square. When it was erected in 1909, it was the tallest building in the world—and one of the most foolish, for the upper floors were too small for commercial rental and were mainly used for storage. Within four years the Woolworth Building at 792 feet assumed the mantle of the tallest building. The campanile remained a readily identifiable commercial logo for Met Life. In the early 1950s, before the preservation movement had properly come into existence, everything but the tower was demolished and replaced by a larger, more modern limestone structure. The elaborate marble quoins, arcades, balconies, and other decorative details were stripped away. In 1996 the reconstructed building was cleaned. The private homes that once surrounded Madison Square had all been purchased and demolished and on their sites stood tall commercial buildings.

A sign of the increasing importance of Madison Square was the transformation of the area to the north and east of the square, which is today the home of the New York Life Company. In the block above 26th Street, between Madison Avenue and Fourth Avenue (Park Avenue today) stood the Union Depot, the railroad sheds of Commodore Vanderbilt's New York and Harlem Railroad. When the Commodore decided to move his terminal to Park Avenue and 42nd Street (Grand Central Terminal), the depot was used variously for prize fights and the circus of Phineas T. Barnum. With the very influential backing of J.P. Morgan, the property was purchased in 1887 by the Horse Show Association and a new structure, a "Palace of Pleasures," was erected as a venue for the annual Horse Show in November. The architectural firm of McKim, Mead, and White designed a main amphitheater capable of seating 8,000 for the Horse Show and as many as 17,000 for prize fights. There was a theater seating 1,200, the largest restaurant in the city, and an arcade of shops along Madison Avenue. An open-air theater was included in the design of the roof garden, and along the 26th Street side, with the best view from Madison Square, stood Augustus Saint Gaudens' nude statue of Diana, a spectacular weathervane that rotated with the wind. White claimed that he drew inspiration for the design, which used yellow brick and terra-cotta for the exterior walls, from the Giralda Tower in Seville.

The venue was spectacular, but like the Metropolitan Opera House, which opened on Broadway in 1883, proved a financial disaster. The murder by a jealous husband in 1906 of the architect Stanford White (the murderer's wife, Evelyn Nesbit Thaw, had been White's lover and the model for Diana), in the roof garden, and the slow-motion commercial failure of the Garden led to its demolition in 1925. The present Madison Square Garden, west of Seventh Avenue at 31st Street, was erected in 1968.

42nd Street and Times Square

Between 1883, when the Metropolitan Opera opened at Broadway and 40th Street, and the 1970s, when 120 sex joints and porno cinemas and countless bars were thriving in the district (which includes 32 blocks, from 40th to 53rd Street, between Sixth and Eighth Avenue) one narrative might be written about the city's premier entertainment district: decline and fall. It was a district, from the 1960s onwards, increasingly avoided by women. The bums, winos, pimps, and hookers made it into one of the most sexually segregated urban areas in America.

Since the 1970s, there is another story. The scores of porn shops in the 1970s had shrunk to just 13 by 1996 and what remained was much less conspicuous. The transformation of 42nd Street is in part due to the city's most sustained jihad against sex—or at least against visible sex—since the days of Petrus Stuyvesant. Had someone other than

Rudy Giuliani been mayor in the 1990s, the onslaught against porn shops might have been pursued with less energy and less success. But it would be misleading to award the combative ex-mayor the sole credit for this successful policy. It was, in truth, a strategy that began in the 1970s, continued in the 1980s, and turned on the city's using its legal powers in innovative ways. Noise-abatement laws were invoked, for example, to close down locations where gambling and prostitution had brought forth repeated complaints. Health statutes were used to shut down massage parlors. A new zoning law, passed in 1994, banned "adult entertainment" from within five hundred feet of a residential district. In the case of Eighth Avenue north of the Port Authority Bus Station, the proximity of Clinton, a tree-lined residential district that had collectively mobilized to block several attempts at high-rise development on the West Side, provided the legal basis for an attack on the sleaziest of Eighth Avenue businesses. As perceptions began to change about Eighth Avenue, other retailers were prepared to outbid the sleaze-merchants for new commercial leases. The real estate market, in other words, which accepted the porn shops when things were hard in the 1970s and 1980s, was happy enough, when rental values rose in the 1990s, to replace them with more salubrious tenants. The calculations of the midtown real estate market were integral to a successful outcome of the reform of 42nd Street.

There have been many such campaigns against saloons, prostitutes, homosexuals, abortionists, lewdness, immorality, sexually-transmitted diseases, public corruption, Masons, Communists, and speakeasies, each in turn likely to peter out when the offenders dropped below the city's moral early-warning radar or when another issue seemed more urgent. Interest in moral crusades against vice, as with child labor, illegal gambling, organized crime, and so on, has seldom been sustained over time. There are few conclusions to be drawn from New York's long and interesting history of moral campaigns, or from the equally long story of the city's voracious appetite for sex, drugs, pornography, alcohol, and gambling. The campaigns and the customers, the bodies of the sex workers and the police who accept the brothel-keepers' bribes, are linked in a centuries' old social waltz. We can safely say that New York will never arrive at a state of civic virtue, a home for smiling families and the Disney Corporation; nor, if the recent history of the porn industry in midtown is anything to go by, is the reign of vice and wickedness likely to prevail unchecked. It is only the scale of the "vice," its visibility, and the amplified indignation of the moral reformers, which make New York different from other large cities with equally large appetites.

One of the key elements in the resurrection of 42nd Street was a development company owned by the Walt Disney Corporation. David Malmuth, vice president of the company, was sent with a video camera in hand to look at the porn shops, massage parlors, cheap souvenir stores and boarded up retail space that made 42nd Street such an eyesore. "It was dead," he remarked. "It was this odd street in the center of the city where there was almost no life." Within five years, the old 42nd Street had vanished. It was a small investment by Michael Eisner, then chairman of Disney, of $8 million into the New Amsterdam Theater that triggered a cascade of development money into 42nd Street. Disney's investment signaled to the financial and real estate markets that there was going to be another outcome for 42nd Street, and everyone except the Mayor wanted to hop aboard. "New York cannot and should not become Disneyland," remarked Mayor Ed Koch. "That's for Florida. We've got to make sure we have seltzer instead of orange juice."

Disney knew very well the value of the company's name and extracted more than $30 million in low-interest loans from the city and state. It was nonetheless a bargain for Governor Cuomo and Mayor Dinkins. Both the governor and the mayor left office at the end of 1993, and the deal they hurriedly signed with Disney laid the foundation for the successful rebirth of 42nd Street, which yielded so much credit to Mayor Giuliani. It was at Disney's insistence that the peep shows on 42nd Street were closed down *before* they signed a deal with the city.

For more than fifteen years, while 42nd Street sank to ever lower depths of commercial turpitude, planners had been at work on schemes to reinvent the whole area. Four tall office buildings on each of the corners of the intersection of 42nd Street and Broadway were planned to anchor the area's recovery. The idea was to make Times Square respectable. Each successive real estate white knight (including some of the largest firms in North America) turned away. The stock market collapse in 1987 seemed the final straw on the load of municipal impotence and economic decline. In 1991 the development project was refocused to re-emphasize the area's traditional links with popular entertainment. Respectability was junked, or at least postponed. The agreement to build the four regal towers was delayed for a decade, and developers agreed to invest in upgrading the theaters and filling the retail space with bright, attractive tenants. The revival was possible, wrote Marian Heiskell and Cora Cahan, chairman and president of New 42nd Street Inc., "because enlightened state and city officials, past and present, shared the belief, pioneered by preservationists, that the historic theaters and their adaptive re-use were the heart of the reclamation of 42d Street. Although it was anticipated that the planned office buildings at the four crossroads sites would spur the redevelopment of 42d Street, it turned out that the abandoned theaters led the parade. The lineup of legitimate theaters, built at the turn of the century, made 42nd Street the most famous block in the world. Once again the theaters light the way."

If Mayor Giuliani is not quite the hero of the story, the refurbishment of Grand Central Terminal in the 1990s and the facelift and reconstruction of Bryant Park began a process that drove away the hustlers, muggers, and drunks, and created a benevolent ripple effect reaching east to Eighth Avenue. As the improvements were brought in, there was renewed interest in the office space around Grand Central and in tall buildings lining the north side of 42nd Street, facing Bryant Park. Increasing real estate values and higher occupancy rates made landlords more willing to improve their buildings. The commercial prospects for the restaurants and retail tenants improved with the changing feel on the street. When the indications arrived that Disney and Warner Brothers were going to put stores into the "new" 42nd Street, the buzz around Times Square connected with the East Side renewal at Grand Central. Rundown 42nd Street was transformed in the 1990s into an almost unrecognizable place. The process touched even the notorious "Minnesota Strip" on Eighth Avenue north of the Port Authority Bus Station, where young women from out of town, proverbially Minnesota (a state that apparently possesses a symbolic nowhereness in the eyes of New Yorkers), were to be found experiencing the bright lights of the big city as streetwalkers. Crime rates fell across the city. There was a lot of talk about the new economy, and occupancy rates at city hotels were dizzyingly high.

Light and Air

The traditional entertainment industry in midtown was linked to the theater district and the traffic it generated. The Interborough Rapid Transit Company (IRT) and Brooklyn-Manhattan Transit Corporation (BMT) subway stations at 42nd Street were the hub, made busier still by the opening on New Year's Day 1905 of the corporate headquarters and editorial offices of the *New York Times*. The office, at the intersection where Broadway crosses Seventh Avenue at West 42nd Street, gave Times Square its name and much of the popular energy it possessed. The tall, triangular-shaped skyscraper bore a resemblance to the Flatiron Building on Union Square (see Chapter 1). By the 1960s it had descended into low-rent shoddiness, well matching the sleazy environment of Times Square itself. In 1964 the building was purchased by Allied Chemical and given a new skin. In the stinging words of the architecture critic Ada Louise Huxtable, it was given "a no-style skin of lavatory white marble with the look of cut cardboard."

It was a building that had known better days. In 1928 a great bank of 14,900 electric lights was installed on the four sides of the Times Tower, creating the first moving electrical sign. This was the heart of the "Great White Way," the Times Square illuminated by giant electrical lights, which established in the most vivid way that the meaning of this part of town was pleasure, entertainment, and consumption. The route to what the historian Howard Mumford Jones called "the Age of Energy" was marked by the first retail department store fully lit by electricity (John Wanamaker's in Philadelphia, 1878), the first streets illuminated by carbon-arc lamps (Cleveland, Ohio, 1879), the introduction of incandescent electric light (1880), and the first public lighting system (New York City, 1882). Light and illumination offered ready metaphors for changes that were taking place in American society. The large, brightly-lit windows of department stores provided a dramatic showcase for goods from all over the world. The city's role as pacesetter in conspicuous consumption was effectively unchallenged. The use of steel frame construction for skyscrapers meant that office windows in the new buildings could be larger. Increased amounts of natural light would enable office workers to be more efficient, to work harder. It was indeed the land of Hurry-Up. The strip of lights around the Times Building brought the world's news to the city. The New Year was greeted by the fall of a ball of light. Reformers, meanwhile, sought to uncover and illuminate the dangerous conditions and exploitation of sweatshop labor. Photographers carried flashbulbs into the city's notorious tenement "dark" rooms without access to light or ventilation. The pictures they brought back of dank hallways and moldy rooms gave reformers powerful images of neglect. But the brightly-lit modern world carried, for some at least, as much threat as promise, for the light was put to the service of the rich, of capital, and was an instrument of their needs. "There is a terrifying abundance of light in this city," wrote Maxim Gorky in 1906 of his visit to New York.

> *At first it seems attractive, it excites and delights. Light is a free element, the proud child of the sun. When it comes to a luxuriant flowering,… it can destroy all that is outworn, dead and foul. But in this city, when one looks at light, enclosed in transparent prisons of glass, one understands that here light, like everything else, is enslaved. It serves Gold, it is for Gold and is inimically aloof from people…*

In 1997, when Mayor Giuliani proposed to reshape the zoning laws to allow "development rights" or "air rights" to be sold by theater owners to allow expanded development elsewhere, a large windfall of millions of dollars would flow into the calculations of the theater owners. Air rights in New York refers to space above landmark buildings. Prevented from using that space due to their landmark status, the owners were able to sell development rights to property in the immediate vicinity—next door or across the street. By widening the terrain where those air rights could be sold, to encompass the district between 40th and 57th Streets, from Sixth Avenue to Eighth Avenue, some 25 theaters were able to benefit. The mayor's plan included what was estimated to be $100 million of air rights. Other concessions were designed to support the theater industry. Developers in the district who included a new Broadway theater in their building would not have to count the floor space occupied by that theater as part of their overall permitted size. Owners who accepted the mayor's proposals and sold their development rights would have to make a commitment to maintain their theaters to a high standard and use them exclusively for stage productions. Twenty percent of the money from the sales of air rights would be paid to the Broadway Initiative, a nonprofit organization that would make loans to producers of dramas and small musicals suitable to the least profitable theaters. There were plenty of opportunities for the mayor's plan to be derailed, and the national recession that began in 1991, followed by the near-complete collapse of the tourist trade after September 11, left virtually all developments frozen in mid-air. The memory of Broadway as it was in 1999 and 2000, bustling with tourists, new plays, new musical theaters and plenty of new or prospective tenants, including the giant Virgin music store (which opened a 75,000 square-foot store at Broadway and 45th Street in 1995), Condé Nast Publications, and ABC's "Good Morning America" television program, broadcast from a ground-floor studio at 1500 Broadway, has become, with astonishing quickness, a vanished golden age when everything seemed possible and a lot of money was being made.

But with rents rapidly pushed up to $300 per square foot of prime ground-floor space, the casualty rate on Times Square was high. Restaurants and traditional retailers like bookstores and clothing stores could not afford such premium rentals. When the Gap opened at the southeast corner of Broadway and 42nd Street, it was the first major retailer to open a store in the area. The company was paying $100 a square foot for ground-floor space. Theme restaurants, already falling out of favor, did not long survive. Even before 2001 there were dark theaters and landlords turning down deals in hope that rates were ever skywards bound.

Something inevitably should be said about what was lost with the end of the old Times Square. It's easy to be nostalgic over the old Broadway names, about Damon Runyan, "Guys and Dolls," Ethel Merman, and Irish bars patronized by gangsters and prize-fighters—and quietly to regret the passing of Nathan's. Corporate America and the assorted sharks in the real estate market cannot quite give us what a Nathan Handwerker did, in Brooklyn, in 1916. Egged on by two show business unknowns (Eddie Cantor and Jimmy Durante), Handwerker opened Nathan's Famous on the corner of Surf and Stillwell Avenues in Coney Island. He sold hot dogs for 5¢, at a time when the going price in Coney was 10¢. To reassure the public,

Handwerker hired several local unemployed gentlemen (the term for them in 1916 was bums) to wear white lab coats and stethoscopes and reassure potential customers. If doctors ate at Nathan's, it must be OK. Show business types, politicians, visiting celebrities, and countless tourists ate hot dogs at Nathan's. In time the name was franchised and Nathan's appeared in suburban malls. But Nathan's could not survive the new Times Square, and closed their large restaurant (it was not really a restaurant, just a place to grab a hot dog, and it was a good idea not to look too closely at the other customers) at Broadway and 43rd Street in 1996. As much as the peepshows and massage parlors, Nathan's was a victim of what Disney wrought.

Times Square became the city's theatrical center in the 1890s, when Oscar Hammerstein built the Olympia Theater on Broadway between 44th and 45th Street. But it was not until 1900 that work began on the city's first subway line running beneath Broadway from City Hall to 145th Street. The bridges connecting Manhattan to Brooklyn and Queens and the tunnels under the Hudson River opened up rapid transportation from New Jersey. The massive passenger terminals erected by the Pennsylvania and New York Central railroad lines made midtown Manhattan a transportation hub like no other in the United States. When the last of the horse-cars were retired during the First World War, the infrastructure was in place for the extraordinary expansion of theatrical life in the city. In 1904, when the *New York Times* erected its tower at the southern end of what had formerly been called Long Acre Square, the area acquired its modern name, Times Square, and witnessed the construction of just under eighty theaters in the immediate area. Behind this development lay the creation of the Theatrical Syndicate in 1896, which led to the control of between seven and eight hundred theaters across the nation. The Syndicate made Broadway productions profitable because traveling companies were sent to virtually every city in the nation. The disintegration of the Syndicate in 1916 was followed by the rise of the Shubert brothers as theatrical entrepreneurs. By the 1920s, Times Square theatrical productions were big business, and the major producers, agents, booking agencies, and theater periodicals were based in the city. It was one of the ways New York exerted its cultural dominance over the rest of the nation. In 1927–8 some 257 productions were played in New York. But the rise of the Los Angeles film industry, as well as over-expansion in the Times Square theatrical industry, led to a sustained contraction beginning with the collapse of the stock market in 1929. "Legit" theaters and vaudeville were converted into moving picture houses, or demolished. As the value of the land sharply increased in the post-war boom in the 1940s, theaters were demolished to make way for tall office buildings; some were used for television studios. The decline that began in 1929 reached its low point in the 1970s. Ironically, it was the Disney Corporation, with its Hollywood empire created by animated movies, whose intervention at a crucial moment saved 42nd Street.

CHAPTER SEVEN

Harlem

The Italian presence in Little Italy is largely a thing of the past. The Jewish Lower East Side and the Jewish Grand Concourse in the Bronx are now predominantly Hispanic. There are no Germans in *Kleindeutschland.* (And thus no *Kleindeutschland,* either.) The Chinese may soon become a minority of the Asian inhabitants of Chinatown, and the formerly dominant Puerto Rican population in New York is now one among several large Hispanic communities. The aristocrats don't live in mansions on Fifth Avenue, but in apartments on Park Avenue and elsewhere in the Upper East Side. Bohemians can't afford the rent in Greenwich Village.

It is an old, familiar story of change. The movements of immigrants into the city and the constant shifting of distinct communities within it are reflected in the constant process of building and rebuilding. To Philip Hone, writing in his diary on April 7, 1845, the enthusiastic demolition of all traces of the past that had overtaken the community was nothing less than a form of mania: "Overturn, overturn, overturn! is the maxim of New York. The very bones of our ancestors are not permitted to lie quiet a quarter of a century, and one generation of men seem studious to remove all relics of those which preceded them." The communities—defined by race, class, ethnicity, or place of immigrant origin—which gave such vivid meaning to certain neighborhoods in the city, turn out not to have been permanent presences in specific locations, but a more fluid part of the urban mix, and thus a lot harder to map than we thought. Harlem has, over the course of a century and a half, possessed such a rapidly changing identity.

Old Harlem

The area of northern Manhattan, beginning on 110th Street and reaching its northern edge at 155th Street, which lay between Morningside Heights on the west and the East River, had been a rural village, Nieuw Haarlem, settled by Dutch farmers in 1637. The rural calm of Harlem was much prized by aristocratic New Yorkers. John Jacob Astor's country estate at Hellgate, on the East River at 88th Street, was not quite in Harlem, but part of a stately procession of mansions and fine estates, owned by some of the oldest and wealthiest families in New York, which stood along the banks of the East River from Kip's Bay (where the United Nations stands) to the northern tip of Manhattan. It was at Hellgate that the writer Washington Irving stayed in 1835, as Astor's guest, to work on the millionaire's papers for *Astoria*, an account of Astor's failed trading settlement along the coast of Oregon.

The inhabitants of old Harlem had been white, Protestant, and of sober Dutch and Yankee (that is, from New England) origins. Real estate investors assumed that the future of Harlem lay in the transforming of the old colonial farmhouses into estates for the city's aristocratic wealthy, or at least those who aspired to an elegant lifestyle. As the population of Manhattan grew, thoughts of country estates were forgotten, and developers concentrated upon three-story homes modeled on the look of brownstones like "Astor Row" on West 130th Street, which were erected in the 1890s. Richard Croker, the boss of Tammany Hall, and the railroad lawyer Chauncey M. Depew were Harlem residents. There were private academies for the daughters of the Harlem elite, and the local school, Grammar School 68, was known as the "Silk Stocking School" because so many of its pupils were drawn from leading families.

There was a late nineteenth-century construction boom in Harlem. The limestone Renaissance Revival State Bank (1897), at the corner of Fifth Avenue and 115th Street, is now the Brewster Apartments. Ornate synagogues and churches like the St. Paul's Evangelical Lutheran Church (1897–8), now the greater Metropolitan Baptist Church, at 147 West 123rd Street, and Congregation Shaari Zadok, now the Bethel Way of the Cross Church of Christ, at 25 West 118th Street, are particularly striking examples of the exuberant self-confidence with which the late nineteenth-century inhabitants of Harlem viewed the future. As these examples suggest, there is a long tradition of ethnic succession in the use of such large buildings. Perhaps the most interesting of such transformations, recording successive layers of Harlem life, was the Lenox Avenue Unitarian Church, at the corner of Lenox and 121st Street, which was built in 1889–91. When the Unitarians left Harlem, the structure was used as a Jewish synagogue and today is the home of the Ebenezer Gospel Tabernacle.

Harlem was at last connected to the commercial city downtown in 1881, when the Second and Third Avenue elevated railways reached the Harlem River. Cross-town travel was still difficult, but the "el" made it possible for workers in downtown offices and factories to live in the far more salubrious uptown environment. Travel on the el was a new form of social exploration. Passengers looked directly into the second and third stories of the city's small apartments and could clearly see the tenement sweatshop workers. Things which had been formerly written about in newspapers, magazines, or with books like Jacob Riis' *How the Other Half Lives* could now be seen in unmistakable clarity. For those, like Basil and Isabel March in William Dean Howells' novel *A Hazard of New Fortunes* (1890), much taken by the sheer picturesqueness of the city, the el was one of the greatest free shows in town: "At Third Avenue they took the Elevated, for which she confessed an infatuation," Howells wrote.

> *She* [Isabel] *declared it the most ideal way of getting about in the world, and was not ashamed when he reminded her of how she used to say that nothing under the sun could induce her to travel on it. She now said that the night transit was even more interesting than the day, and that the fleeting intimacy you formed with people in second and third floor interiors, while all the usual street life went on underneath, had a domestic intensity mixed with a perfect repose that was the last effect of good society with all its security and exclusiveness. He said it was better than the theatre, of which it reminded him to see those people through their windows: a family party of work-folk at a late tea, some of the men in their shirt sleeves; a woman sewing by a lamp; a mother laying her child in its cradle; a man with his head fallen on his hands upon a table; a girl and her lover leaning over the window-sill together. What suggestion! what drama! what infinite interest!*

The rush to buy real estate along the line of the el, and to build brownstones and apartment buildings, was one of the key elements in the construction boom of the 1880s. The newcomers, however, did not, as expected, principally come from the wealthy who lived on Fifth Avenue but were drawn equally from the Irish and German immigrant communities. The Irish had settled along the route of the Eighth and Ninth Avenue el, and the Germans had colonized the East Side area of Yorkville. In short order they were joined in Harlem by a flood of Jews, at first from the well-assimilated and prosperous German community. For assimilation-minded, upwardly mobile Jews, Harlem held the promise of a new and better way of life. The Russian Jews settled in increasing numbers in East Harlem, south of 110th Street and east of Fifth Avenue, and by 1910 as many as 50,000 Jews lived in that neighborhood. Then the first Italians arrived, looking for an escape from Little Italy and the Lower East Side, where the housing conditions were notorious and where population densities were among the highest in the world.

As the numbers of Germans and Jews living in Harlem increased, a distinctive neighborhood social life developed. People still went downtown for the big occasions, but with the opening by the music-loving Oscar Hammerstein Sr. of the Columbus Theater on 125th Street and his Harlem Opera House (opened in 1889), with its large gilded foyer, Harlemites could legitimately claim the beginnings of a distinctive cultural identity of their own. Theirs was a *gemütlich* world of comfortable *Weinstuben*, a profusion of social organizations, choral societies, debating societies, and *Turnvereine.* There were good German and Jewish restaurants, lots of knackwurst and sauerkraut, as well as busy department stores. The first of the city's ornate movie palaces was opened in 1913 at the corner of Seventh Avenue and 116th Street in German-Jewish Harlem. The Regent, a failing vaudeville house, was closed down, gutted, and rebuilt, with an electric fountain on stage. The whole theater was illuminated with rose-tinted lights.

Harlem offered opportunities for a quality of life fast disappearing from the crowded city downtown. Its appeal soon extended beyond those in white-collar employment, and as the population increased the social mix of East Harlem changed. The proportion of white-collar workers declined steadily, and many inhabitants embarked on something like a white-collar "flight" to less crowded and better neighborhoods elsewhere. It was into this rapidly expanding semi-suburb that the city's blacks turned, when it became clear that their position on the West Side was deteriorating. Harlem truly exemplifies that topsy-turvy process of change, decline and renewal that is, in short, the city's true story.

Toward San Juan Hill

Just over six decades, no more than the life of a single person, separates 1799, when New York State passed its (very) gradual emancipation act, and the outbreak of the notorious draft riots in 1863. As expected by the promoters of emancipation, knowledge of eventual freedom was to bring about a natural decline of the institution of slavery. The slave population of New York State in 1800 was 2,868, and by 1820 shrank to 518. Over the next four decades the city's free black population remained essentially static, hovering between 12,000 and 16,000. In the 1850s the black population stood at 12,574, and ten years later it was virtually the same size as it had been in 1820. In this period, the white population grew dramatically from 54,133 in 1800 to 801,088 in 1860. The black community of New York was shrinking as a proportion of the total population. Although the city contained some of the largest and most influential black churches in America, there was little economic opportunity in New York to attract black people from other regions. There were a handful of successful black entrepreneurs led by Thomas Downing, whose oyster bar on Broad Street was a city institution, but blacks were losing their foothold in areas of employment when they came into conflict with newly arrived immigrants from Ireland. When combined with the effects of deep-rooted racial bigotry, the weakening economic position of black New York made it increasingly hard for blacks to climb the stepladder of social progress. The research of Graham Russell Hodges has revealed that in the 1850s blacks were ten times more likely to wind up in jail than whites. The experience of blacks in New York was shaped by prejudice and poverty, and the diseases of the poor, especially pulmonary illness (tuberculosis, pleurisy, and pneumonia), remained leading causes of death.

Driven out of the "respectable" trades, blacks found opportunities mainly in prostitution and gambling. When Charles Dickens visited lowlife New York on his celebrated visit in 1842, he saw something of the world that black New York had created in the saloons and dance halls of the Five Points, a degraded slum located a few blocks north of City Hall. The landlord and landlady of "Almacks" (the name of a most fashionable dancing venue in London) were black, as were the musicians in the orchestra and the dancers. This was not the Broadway world of black-face minstrelsy, in which white performers portrayed blacks as "Jim Crow" in an exaggerated and comic fashion, but the real thing, blacks vividly performing before a mixed race audience:

> *Single shuffle, double shuffle, cut and cross-cut; snapping his fingers, rolling his eyes, turning in his knees, presenting the backs of his legs in front, spinning about on his toes and heels like nothing but the man's fingers in the tambourine; dancing with two left legs, two right legs, two wooden legs, two wire legs, two spring legs—all sorts of legs and no legs—what is this to him? And in what walk of life, or dance of life, does man ever get such stimulating applause as thunders about him, when, having danced his partner off her feet, and himself too, he finishes by leaping gloriously on the bar counter, and calling for something to drink, with the chuckle of a million counterfeit Jim Crows, in one inimitable sound!*

A study of the position of blacks in New York City appearing in the *New York Herald* on January 25, 1861 suggests why the city was proving to be so hostile a terrain. The principal cause was immigration. The Irish and Germans who came to New York in the two decades before the Civil War drove blacks out of the employment fields where they had formerly had a presence, such as domestic service, barbering, and shoe blacking. Immigrant artisans and mechanics excluded black competitors from their trades. The Irish were determined to keep longshoring work "all-white." Employers were willing to use blacks as scab strikebreakers, and this deepened tensions across racial and ethnic lines. Blacks were left with the least remunerative employment as servants and waiters. The 1860 census revealed that in the black workforce there were 1,165 servants, 666 washerwomen, 515 laborers, 252 cooks, 243 porters, 226 sailors, 137 laundresses. But there were only 2 black midwives, 2 plasterers, 1 wigmaker, 1 mason, and 1 soap-maker. Another feature of the demography of the black community was the small proportion of black New Yorkers who had married and formed families, and—by comparison with the white population—the far smaller number of children being born. The *Herald,* pointing to the inevitable decline of the black population, was brutally frank about the meaning of these statistics: "There is no room in this city for the negro." The draft riots served to underline this message.

The black population of New York slowly climbed back from the disaster of 1863, and if taken as a proportion of the growing population had actually made a small but meaningful increase in numbers. In 1890 there were 23,601 blacks living in New York. While white America celebrated the beginning of the twentieth century with fireworks and much patriotic rhetoric, marking a victory over Spain in the brief war of 1898 and the extension of American power across the globe, black Americans reeled before an onslaught of riots and beatings. There were 1,665 lynchings across the southern states in 1899. A New York City policeman, searching for suspects in a Hell's Kitchen tenement, was killed by a black gangster in August 1900. When the news of the murder got around, there was a race riot in which the police either participated in the brutal beatings or failed to intervene to halt the perpetrators. The 1900 riot flowed up and down Eighth Avenue between 27th and 42nd Streets, on the western border of the Tenderloin, and was followed by a protest meeting held at Carnegie Hall at which the Citizens' Protective League was formed. In this case, it was protection from the NYPD that was wanted. Public opinion strongly supported the protest, and membership of the League shot up to 5,000 within weeks. The police investigation eventually and inevitably produced a comprehensive whitewash, but the 1900 riot was to have long-term consequences for the black population in New York. Most importantly, it triggered a move north, to Harlem.

Relations between the Irish and the blacks on the West Side had been marked by violence and bigotry at least since the New York draft riots in 1863. Economic rivalry, a determination by immigrant Irish longshoremen to exclude competition from "cheap" black labor, and a demand for an "all-white" waterfront (by which the Irish also meant the exclusion of German, Italian, and Polish workers) lay at the heart of the entrenched hostility between Irish and blacks on the West Side. What was not so readily explained was the visceral racism of the Irish, or the sheer murderous brutality of the attacks on blacks during the 1863 riots. When black veterans returned from the war with Spain and moved into shanties in the traditionally Irish area west of Amsterdam Avenue, between 57th and 64th Streets, the neighborhood acquired a new name ("San Juan Hill") and the old conflict with the Irish was re-ignited.

Nonetheless, it was in San Juan Hill where a proto-Harlem was briefly created, with the opening of black vaudeville theaters, restaurants, hotels, and saloons on West 53rd Street. In the clubs west of Amsterdam Avenue ragtime was heard and the first jazz music played. There was also another black New York that looked to 53rd Street for leadership: it was the location of three important churches, major fraternal societies, the YMCA, and home of the leading political clubs of black New York. The performers, singers, and musicians provided one form of social leadership for the black community in the Tenderloin; the pastors, editors, and political leaders sought to provide another. The community they aspired to lead was increasingly Southern-born and typically worked as manual laborers or servants in New York, for a wage of $4 to $6 a week.

By the 1950s and 1960s San Juan Hill was a decaying neighborhood lined with working-class bars and cheap housing. The rundown housing and low rents made it attractive for immigrants, and a large Puerto Rican population settled at San Juan Hill in the 1950s. Press attention to crime and racial violence inspired the idea of a rewriting of *Romeo and Juliet* in the language and music of contemporary New York. *West Side Story*, composed by Leonard Bernstein with a libretto by the 27-year-old Stephen Sondheim, opened to strong reviews in 1957.

Enter Robert Moses, the city's planning czar, who selected the site, between Columbus and Amsterdam Avenues, from 62nd Street to 66th Street, for classy redevelopment. More than 1,500 families, mostly blacks and Puerto Ricans, were evicted by the city to make way for the Lincoln Center for the Performing Arts, which was constructed in the 1960s. Other developments, such as a branch of Fordham University, completed the social transformation of San Juan Hill into a leading national cultural center.

The Migration North

Of all the harsh years in African-American history in the United States, the end of Reconstruction in 1876 is among the most resonant. The vast rural black population of the Southern states was left to the mercy of a white population that scarcely a dozen years before had been their owners, overseers, and masters. At gun-point, or with the threat of a hangman's noose, blacks were driven out of public life. Laws were passed to deny blacks the franchise, and a code of laws was entrenched that placed the African American in a position of abject civic inferiority. The policing of inferiority was overseen by the harsh Southern legal system, and, in the hands of the Ku Klux Klan, by a terror well worthy of comparison with the dreaded Black Hundreds in Czarist Russia, and with similar covert and overt patronage from the highest social levels in the South. Discrimination was a well-maintained way of life. Some whites may have sympathized with the grim plight of African Americans, but no American white in the 1880s, except perhaps Jews who had fled from Russia, had ever themselves experienced systematic discrimination enforced with the creative brutality of an implacable and hostile social order. The end of Reconstruction confirmed African Americans in inferiority and unfreedom.

Of course, no system of brutality was brutal every day and in all of its guises. There were ideas that connected Southern whites and blacks—from Protestant Christianity to a profound commitment to a life on the land. Individual kindnesses and charity in some measure leavened the general social oppression, and the old distorted Southern history of black–white sexual relations continued to play itself out. In the South bigotry was less faceless than in the North. But however well-meaning, such kindnesses were of little consequence for blacks. What they needed, what kind of future they should aspire to, was strongly debated within the black community. It was a debate that took place far from New York, but which was to have striking consequences for New York and Harlem in particular.

At the turn of the century Booker T. Washington, founder of the Tuskegee Normal and Industrial Institute in Alabama and author of *Up from Slavery* (1901), assumed a unique position of national leadership. Born a slave from a broken family, Washington was set free at Emancipation and grew up in illiterate poverty. He was accepted as a spokesman for his people by the white power structures in the South and generally held the affection of the rural black masses, who took inspiration from Washington's self-made success, his eloquence, and the gospel of work and self-improvement that he expressed in his celebrated Atlanta speech in 1895. "In all things purely social," Washington argued, "we can be as separate as the five fingers, and yet one as the hand of all things essential to mutual progress." Washington wanted to turn away from the older forms of racial protest and to leave aside the question of suffrage and full citizenship rights. There was a need for industrial education, a practical and pragmatic education for blacks to enable them to improve themselves in work. Critics described Washington's message as simply "the old attitude of adjustment and submission" and were particularly resentful that Washington's program accepted the "alleged inferiority of the Negro races." The doubts Washington expressed about the value of "academic" higher education for blacks were particularly unacceptable.

In the name of raising the level of African-American horizons, and to overcome bigoted assumptions of black inferiority as well as to encourage black people to assume a rightful place in the national community, W.E.B. DuBois, a Harvard-educated professor at Atlanta University, called for a *cultural* revolution against backwardness, poverty, and isolation. DuBois was a New Englander, whose family had resided in Great Barrington, Massachusetts for three generations. "When he began active life," wrote James Weldon Johnson, "it was with greater intellectual preparation than any American Negro had yet acquired." In a collection of essays entitled *The Souls of Black Folk* (1903), DuBois called for community leaders to face the necessity of breaking with such an honored leader and to reject the position of permanent inferiority which, he argued, was the natural consequence of Washington's program.

The African-American population, approximately ten million strong when Washington's *Up from Slavery* was published, overwhelmingly lived in rural poverty in the "black belt" of former slave states, which stretched from Virginia to Texas. Within a generation, the great migration of blacks was underway. Between 1910 and 1920, half a million African Americans left the South to settle in the Midwest and northeastern cities. Of these, New York City was a principal magnet for migration. Between 1900 and 1940, the white population of the "Greater New York" of five boroughs, created by the amalgamation in 1898, rose from 2.1 million to nearly 4.9 million. In the same four decades, the black population of the city rose from 58,142 to 418,857. It nearly doubled again between 1940 and 1960.

The newly-arrived Southern blacks in New York shared with the immigrants from Europe the experience of self-exile from their homes in distant lands. Like the immigrants, they had come to New York in hope of betterment, and out of a wish to escape the effects of Jim Crow laws. Jewish immigrants spoke with similar indignation at the anti-Semitic "May Laws" in Czarist Russia. Migration to northern cities was, in effect, taking sides in the dispute between Booker T. Washington's vision of a contented black population devoted to the agricultural South and the aggressively modernizing vision offered by blacks in the North. There was a choice, and blacks overwhelmingly chose to redefine themselves as an urban people.

The brownstones and apartment buildings of the northern Manhattan district of Harlem, which had been an elegant residential neighborhood in the mid-nineteenth century, were opened to black residents from 1905. The arrival of blacks in Harlem steadily changed the population mix, which itself had been newly created. The Irish and German inhabitants, who in 1900 made up half of the Harlem population, by 1910 represented less than one-fifth of the total. For approximately a decade after 1910, Harlem was one-third Jewish, one-third Italian, and one-third black. Sharp black real estate operators, led by Philip A. Payton, John E. Nail, and Henry C. Parker, spotted a speculative over-build in apartments north of Central Park. Payton and others bought apartment buildings and, according to James Weldon Johnson, dispossessed the white tenants and installed black ones. A black Episcopal congregation bought a row of thirteen buildings on 135th Street and rented them to black tenants. A row of 109 elegant brownstones on 139th Street, between Seventh and Eighth Avenues, designed for elite Harlemites by Stanford White in 1891, were sold to black purchasers in 1919. They attracted the sardonic identity of "Strivers' Row," a nickname that has stuck.

The reaction of the displaced white tenants may be imagined, but the wider impact of the arrival of blacks in Harlem was marked by hostility, fear, and open opposition. Every social anxiety, from the feared decline in property values to anxieties at the changing tone of the neighborhood, combined with anti-black prejudices. The departure of upper-class Jewish residents at the arrival in Harlem of large numbers of working-class Jews was, so to speak, an internal matter, turning on the role of class in American-Jewish culture. The emotions aroused by the arrival of blacks served to unite the white residents, who in near unanimity concluded that if they could not resist the arrival of blacks, they should leave. A panicky "white flight" followed. Johnson in *Black Manhattan* (1930) described the sequence of arrival and flight. "The presence of a single colored family in a block, regardless of the fact that they might be well-bred people, with sufficient means to buy their new home, was a signal for precipitate flight. The stampeded whites actually deserted house after house and block after block. Then prices dropped; they dropped lower than the bottom, and such colored people as were able took advantage of these prices and bought." The extra burden of high rents led rapidly to the old New York evil of subletting, and from early in its history Harlem was heavily overcrowded. New arrivals from the South increased the demand for cheap sublets and caused the boundaries of Harlem to expand steadily in the 1920s.

All of the city's major black churches moved to Harlem in the decade after 1911, followed by fraternal organizations, political clubs, the black YMCA, theaters, and nightclubs. The leading black newspapers, the weekly *Age* and the *Amsterdam News*, moved their editorial offices and printing plants to Harlem. Journalists, entertainers, doctors, preachers, lawyers—the entire class of leading blacks in New York—moved uptown to Harlem. There were newly-created business opportunities for African-American entrepreneurs, but the *Age* repeatedly called attention to the lag between the growing black population and the low proportion of black-owned businesses in the main area of black settlement on 135th Street and Lenox Avenue. The *Age* was a supporter of the conservative business community in black New York and urged the value of investment and enterprise for the community as a whole. In editorials the *Age* deplored teenage gangs, streetwalkers, and the other signs of the breakdown of community values in the city. There were racial restrictions in the hiring policy of department stores, corporations, large hotels, restaurants, and theaters in Harlem, but when compared to conditions in the rural South, mired in segregation, poverty, and backwardness, Harlem was heaven indeed.

The growth in African-American numbers in Harlem created a certain critical mass of self-awareness, of *consciousness*, which in turn made possible that great "cultural revolution" the "modernizers" within the African-American community had long anticipated. The impulse behind the "Renaissance"—or Renaissancism—was a growth of self-confidence among the younger and better-educated generation of blacks. Theirs was a project of middle-class aspiration and modernization. Spokespersons and community leaders—the group that DuBois referred to as "the thinking classes of American Negroes"—encouraged blacks to attend universities, called for the emergence of black entrepreneurs, and looked forward to the day when black professionals, politicians, and public figures might represent the highest ideals of the community.

But the culture of African America in 1905 was shaped less by the ancient traditions of a people than by the imperatives of survival in a racially charged and hostile environment. Learning and then mastering the white man's culture was an obviously attractive goal. Yet throughout America the traditions of minstrelsy, with its racial stereotypes (Sambos, Uncle Toms, and Topsies), and its legacy of masked performance, irony, dialect, and nonsense routines, engaged with the popular or vernacular culture of America—and scarcely at all with the white, European Protestant "high culture" that found its custodians at Yale and Harvard and whose genteel grip on the publishing industry was largely unchallenged. "I have sometimes fancied," wrote William Dean Howells of the poetry of the African-American poet Paul Laurence Dunbar, "that perhaps the negroes *thought* black and *felt* black; that they were racially so utterly alien and distinct from ourselves that there never could be common intellectual and emotional ground between us…" It was the poetry of Dunbar that convinced Howells that he had been wrong. This was a small victory in the course of a cultural revolution: culture reaching across entrenched racial lines. Culture was also, as David Levering Lewis has argued, "the *only* area in America—from an Afro-American perspective—where the color line had not been rigidly drawn."

The Harlem population was not wealthy enough to become patrons of their own culture. Without a tradition of aristocratic *noblesse oblige* in the black community, the makers of high culture (sculptors, ballet dancers, poets) could not support themselves as writers or artists or find an audience for their work within Harlem. (Of course, a version of the same was true for the majority of white sculptors, ballet dancers, and poets in New York and every other American city.) There was no real possibility that a Black Nationalist movement like Marcus Garvey's Universal Negro Improvement Association, which had broad support in the streets of Harlem in the 1920s, could generate and sustain an autonomous, oppositional culture. (His critics, led by DuBois, saw Garvey as a dangerous demagogue, whose methods were "bombastic, wasteful, illogical and ineffective and almost illegal.") But the humble, conservative, and practical aspirations of Booker T. Washington, which in effect abandoned altogether the idea that African Americans might seek to shape their own cultural identity, seemed more than ever a counsel of despair. There was hunger for a new intellectual and artistic leadership and also for a new politics. Somewhere, between Garvey and Washington, Harlem would have to find a new leadership and a new direction for the black community.

UNIA convention parade through Harlem, 1920.

The New Negro

Between the passivity of Washington's response to the plight of African Americans in the rural South and the grandiose schemes of Garvey, amidst the bubbling, optimistic mood on the streets of Harlem the great Renaissance of the 1920s was born. The publication of Alain Locke's *The New Negro* in 1925 provided a cultural and artistic framework for the movement. Locke's book, an anthology of creative work, essays, and art, had appeared as a special issue of *Survey Graphic* and was designed to represent black life not as a social problem, but as Harlem's energetic urban refutation of the old stereotypes about black culture and the rural South.

The New Negro was published by Albert and Charles Boni from their offices on Macdougal Street in Greenwich Village. There was no "black" publisher able to issue and sell such a book to white America. Few New York publishers were interested in Harlem and African-American writing, but the Jewish firms of Alfred A. Knopf (publisher of Langston Hughes' first book, *The Weary Blues* in 1926) and the Boni Brothers were an exception. Relations between Harlem and the rest of the city, and between blacks and Jews, was an important dimension of the Harlem Renaissance, though one perhaps easy to misinterpret. The role of whites in the founding of the National Association for the Advancement of Colored People (NAACP), organized in 1909 by Mary White Ovington, is well-known, as is the role of white supporters like J.E. Spingarn, professor of literature at Columbia University, and philanthropists led by Julius Rosenwald. The enthusiasm for black art and culture on the part of Carl Van Vechten, music critic of the *New York Times*, did much to alert white audiences to Harlem and its cultural life, though his popular novel of 1926, *Nigger Heaven*, is best left undisturbed wherever it presently gathers dust. The title itself, referring to the inexpensive balcony seating reserved for black patrons in semi-segregated theaters, also alluded to the uptown location of Harlem. Van Vechten was not without supporters in Harlem for the book, but the literary community was deeply divided and friendships were broken over Van Vechten's fictional portrayals of the leading figures of the "Renaissance." The Jamaican writer Claude McKay, who emigrated to New York in 1914, encountered a warm welcome in the radical Greenwich Village magazine *The Masses* and from its editor Max Eastman. Even in

Greenwich Village, however, and among the liberal and radical readers of *The Masses* and its successor, *The Liberator*, there were limits to the amount of space that could be devoted to black subjects.

Harlem benefited from the interest and the connections of white supporters, as the nightclubs were happy to see white customers who came uptown for an evening's slumming, but the agendas of the "Renaissance" writers and artists were not necessarily those of their downtown white allies. That is not to suggest that the existence of liberal white admirers of black writers and of Harlem was irrelevant, but that the most important debates about the meaning of the "Renaissance" and the changing ideas about the racial identity of black people took place between blacks themselves. Whites were always an important, sometimes overwhelming, part of the problems facing blacks. But race was not the only problem the Harlem Renaissance authors and activists were wrestling with.

The African Americans who appear in Locke's anthology aspired to the broadest transformation of a people. Some, perhaps only a radical minority, but an influential minority, linked their concerns for black opportunity in employment to the struggle of organized labor against union-busting American capitalists, and their "national" aspirations to anti-colonialist struggles across the world. Indeed, the notion of "The New Negro" first emerged in the struggle by radicals like A. Philip Randolph in *The Messenger* to wean blacks from their old conservative Southern loyalties. "The Old Crowd enjoins the Negro to the conservative," wrote Randolph in *The Messenger* in 1919, referring to the established black leadership in politics, religion, and education. In reality, the black in America had nothing to conserve. "Neither his life nor his property receives the protection of the government which conscripts his life to 'make the world safe for democracy.' The conservative in all lands are the wealthy and the ruling class. The Negro is in dire poverty and he is no part of the ruling class."

The New Negro was, in reality, a complex and contradictory cause. There were "Renaissance" demands of the most radical political, economic, and social kind. But there were other "Renaissance" voices seeking definitions of blackness that rejected the white world and all of its values, and advocated a return to African racial roots and traditions. There were also those seeking cultural expression and a chance to escape from "race" altogether, who expressed a heartfelt desire to enter the American mainstream. What held the New Negro together, as an idea, was the reality of prejudice and disadvantage. The publication of *The New Negro* was a "cultural" act of self-definition; but there were other voices, other forms of understanding of the meaning of being black.

Harlem was a remorselessly cosmopolitan community, where African Americans from the South encountered blacks from the northern states and the West Indies. Out of this diversity, variety of motives, and differing levels of education, no single theme could define a cultural Renaissance. But the contributors to *The New Negro* were not themselves farm hands or hayseeds from the sticks; the culture they offered to the world was not a folk or "proletarian" culture. Among the leading contributors was a lawyer, diplomat, and professor (James Weldon Johnson), a poet who had graduated from New York University and who had a master's degree from Harvard (Countee Cullen), another poet with a bachelor's degree from Lincoln University (Langston Hughes). Zora Neale Hurston studied folklore and anthropology with Franz Boas at Columbia and received a research fellowship in 1927 to collect African-American folklore in the South. The editor of *The New Negro*, Alain Locke, had attended Harvard and Berlin and had been the first African-American Rhodes scholar. His anthology represented the formation of the first African-American cultural-intellectual elite. They urged the value of folk materials, which anthropologists had increasingly come to fear were vanishing from their traditional place in Southern black life. But they were not any longer themselves part of that life that they studied and sometimes celebrated. The Harlem Renaissance revealed that a veil of class had been drawn across the black community. And they were not perhaps free from the errors that they scornfully dismissed in white perceptions. When W.E.B. DuBois contemplated Africa, he saw an Edenic world alone corrupted by contact with the "spiritually bankrupt" European imperial powers:

> *Africa is happy. The masses of its black folk are calmly contented, save where what is called 'European' civilization has touched and uprooted them. They have a philosophy of life logical and realizable. Their children are carefully educated for the life they are to lead. There are no prostitutes, there is no poverty.*

Among Locke's collection of stories, essays, and poems could be found a challenge to gradualism. As ever, "progress" across the color line was ambivalent. The old customary view that black and white actors could not appear together on the stage was broken by the stunning run of 490 performances from 1920 at the Lafayette Theatre in Harlem of Eugene O'Neill's *The Emperor Jones.* But the atavism of O'Neill's leading character, and the author's view that beneath the veneer of civilization achieved by blacks there was always a primitive being, certainly reproduced negative stereotypes. The Lafayette Theatre, built in 1912 at 132nd Street and Seventh Avenue, was at the heart of the Harlem theatrical district and was the first theater to desegregate. The Lafayette Players were the outstanding black theater group of the 1910s. A black audience at the Lafayette cheered the triumph of a black cast in O'Neill's play, but were perhaps less pleased with the ambivalent meaning of the play for blacks themselves. Stereotypes remained, like small cancers. Black performers and black writers were inevitably forced to contend with the widespread white expectation that they were all, as James Weldon Johnson suggested, "happy-go-lucky, singing, shuffling, banjo-picking" figures, happiest by long association amid cotton fields or along the levee. Black writers were expected to write in dialect, and when Paul Laurence Dunbar objected he found publishers and readers uninterested. "I've got to write dialect poetry; it's the only way I can get them to listen to me."

Harlem represented for the black writer an escape from the traditional dialect poems of log cabins, possums, and watermelons. DuBois and *The Crisis,* the NAACP monthly that he edited, was heavily in favor of a frankly didactic art, which would advocate race political consciousness, uplift, and open support for the cause of black people. At a time when black writers of America were few in number (they could have been comfortably welcomed in a Harlem apartment), *The Crisis* and the National Urban League's journal, *The Opportunity,* acted as midwives for a new literary age. There were senior statesmen, like James Weldon Johnson, who had written a campaign song for Theodore Roosevelt ("You're All Right, Teddy") and been rewarded with the American consulship in Venezuela and Nicaragua. He was the author of *The Autobiography of an Ex-Colored Man* (1912), and editor of the groundbreaking *Book of American Negro Poetry* (1922). The literary editor of *The Crisis*, Jessie Redmon Fauset, herself a novelist, had to contend with the emergent male vanity of the leading "Renaissance" figures while encouraging the talent of the younger black writers. Fauset's first novel, *There is Confusion* (1924), suggested a new form of escape—far from the old life on the land, and ever farther from the new life in the slums. Seeking to write about the emerging "educated and aspiring classes" of the black community, in the words of Alain Locke she reached both the "heights of respectability" and a "plateau of culture" that provided an alternative to the narrow perspectives of "Race" fiction.

Jazz Age

America fell in love with Harlem in the 1920s. Well-heeled whites went slumming uptown and heard the black jazz bands at the Savoy Ballroom. They crowded into Broadway revues like *Shuffle Along*. Written, produced, and directed by blacks for black audiences, *Shuffle Along* opened at the Howard Theatre in Washington; then played at the Dunbar Theatre, Philadelphia, before opening "downtown" at the 63rd Street Theatre in New York in 1921. Written by Eubie Blake and Noble Sissle, and helped along by hit tunes like "I'm Just Wild About Harry," the star of *Shuffle Along* was Florence Mills, who became the toast of Harlem. Josephine Baker, later the star of the *Revue Nègre* in Paris, appeared in the chorus. Adelaide Hall, a young Harlem singer, appeared with Mills in *Shuffle Along* and in Lew Leslie's *Blackbirds* in 1927. The great success of Blake and Sissle, which was repeatedly copied later in the decade, inaugurated the great outburst of interest in black theater and performers.

The old prejudices were not, as if by some miracle forgotten in the 1920s, but were incorporated into new stereotypes—the pagan, the licentious, free, syncopated, sexually-expressive black—who afforded the Jazz Age New York a new weapon to use in the cultural war against the small-town provincial Babbitts of the American hinterland. The success of Al Jolson's *Swanee*, composed by the young George Gershwin in 1919 (he wrote the tune in ten minutes, and it became a runaway success, selling a million copies in sheet music and two million phonographic records), suggests the enduring popularity of the older traditions of black-face performances by whites. But there were signs of a far more widespread interest on every side in black culture. White writers, led by Van Vechten, wrote about black life, and sometimes, as with Marc Connelly's biblical fantasy *Green Pastures* (1930), achieved considerable popularity. Gertrude Stein's stylized opera *Four Saints in Three Acts* premiered in 1934 with an all-black cast. Gershwin's *Porgy and Bess* (first performed at the Alvin Theater in 1935, with the tap dancer John Bubbles playing Sportin' Life), puzzled some critics. Duke Ellington deplored Gershwin's "lampblack Negroisms." Virgil Thomson called it "crooked folklore and half-way opera." But the folk-opera entranced the public and ran for 124 nights, the longest continuous run by an opera on any American stage. The opera, and the novel upon which it was based (DuBose Haywood's *Porgy*), seemed to represent a new spirit of sympathy in American attitudes toward blacks. Later generations of critics would be uncomfortable about the stereotyping of characters, but Gershwin's music itself has retained its high place in the canon of serious American music.

The geography of Harlem popular entertainment ran uptown along Seventh Avenue (Adam Clayton Powell Boulevard) from 125th Street to 144th. Newly-arrived rural farm workers from the South and elegantly dressed black professionals strolled along Seventh Avenue. "The broad pavements of Seventh Avenue," wrote Claude McKay in *Home to Harlem* in 1928,

> *were colorful with promenaders. Brown babies in white carriages pushed by little black brothers wearing nice sailor suits. All the various and varying pigmentation of the human race were assembled there: dim brown, clear brown, rich brown, chestnut, copper, yellow, near-white, proud yellow matrons, dark nursemaids pulled a zigzag course by their restive little charges…*
>
> *And the elegant strutters in faultless spats; West Indians, carrying canes and wearing trousers of a different pattern from their coats and vests, drawing sharp comments from their Afro-Yank rivals… The girls passed by in bright batches of color, according to station and calling… Twilight was developing the Belt, merging its life into a soft blue-black symphony…*

On every corner of Seventh Avenue in the 1920s was a saloon or speakeasy or nightclub. The heart of Harlem, and the main center of nightlife, was at the intersection of West 135th Street and Seventh

Avenue, where all tastes (musical, sexual, and every other) were accommodated. 140th Street had the best transvestite floor-shows, explicit sex entertainment, and "reefer" parlors. Drag balls were held at the cavernous Manhattan Casino at 280 West 155th Street, and gay revues were staged at the Hollywood Cabaret at 41 West 124th Street.

There was, locally, an invisible line, clearly understood by everyone, that some Harlem nightspots were open to blacks, and some were not. Connie's Inn (1921–40) at 2221 Seventh Avenue was a large nightclub where the top black dancers (Bill Robinson, "Snakehips" Tucker) performed before white audiences. Jimmy Durante called it the "swankiest of all the Harlem places." Louis Armstrong first played New York in 1924, with Fletcher Henderson's band at the Roseland Ballroom. By the end of the 1920s he was the featured performer at Connie's Inn. Jazz bands played at the Apollo Theater (where Ella Fitzgerald's long and illustrious career began with a victory in an Amateur Night contest) and the nearby Alhambra Ballroom, on Seventh Avenue and 125th Street. The Cotton Club at 644 Lenox Avenue (Malcolm X Boulevard) was in a class of its own in terms of national reputation. Latching on to the fad for Harlem and the damage that Prohibition had done to the city's nightclub business, the Welsh-American bootlegger "Owney" Madden opened the Cotton Club in 1923 as an outlet for his illicit booze. Madden had come out of the Kitchen Gopher Gang in Hell's Kitchen to run a company that supplied illegal beer to clubs on the West Side and Harlem. By the late 1920s, Madden had become a senior figure among the city's bootlegging fraternity, fully the equal of Dutch Schultz, William V. Dwyer, and the other big men of the trade, all of whom were to be seen at the Cotton Club. Madden was the "patron" of Mae West, and an associate of the gambler Arnold Rothstein, who had an "interest" in so much of the Broadway and Harlem nightclub world. Along with Connie's Inn (run by the Immerman brothers, who were gamblers), the Exclusive Club (run by Baron Wilkins, a black gambler), Smalls' Paradise, and the Savoy Ballroom, the Cotton Club featured the best bands, the best-looking dancers, and attracted the largest share of the downtown audience. The gamblers and bootleggers led the way in re-making Harlem as a cosmopolitan entertainment world. They catered to downtown whites and offered a mixture of music (jazz), drinks (illegal), decor (jungle and plantation settings) and sensuality (only the most attractive black women were hired to work in the Harlem nightclubs). By 1925, and largely due to the criminal connections of Mayor Jimmy Walker, local enforcement of the prohibitionist Volsted Act had nearly ceased. The political machine of Tammany Hall as well as the local criminals exacted their own taxation upon the nightclubs of Harlem.

Harold Arlen and Jimmy McHugh were among the leading Broadway figures who produced revues at the Cotton Club. Duke Ellington's long connection with the Cotton Club, which began in 1928, was of such great commercial value that he was able to persuade the management to admit black patrons. A new black-owned Cotton Club stands today on 125th Street. Smalls', at Seventh Avenue and 135th Street, probably had the most truly interracial audience of the leading nightclubs, and downtown aficionados prized the waiters, who danced the Charleston with trays of food in their hands.

Billie Holiday, born Eleanora Fagan, wrote in her autobiography *Lady Sings the Blues* (1956) that "Mom and Pop were just a couple of kids when they got married. He was eighteen, she was sixteen, and I was three." She moved to Harlem in 1927, when she was twelve, and boarded in a Harlem tenement, which was actually a brothel. By the age of fifteen, she was earning $18 a week singing in a one-room speakeasy, Pod & Jerry's, at 168 West 133rd Street. At twenty she played the Apollo Theatre for the first time. Known as Lady Day or the Angel of Harlem, Holiday was an instant success. Every nightclub and jazz orchestra wanted Billie. As did every card sharp, conman, drug-pusher, bully, and good-looking drunk. She sang with Benny Goodman in 1933 and worked with Count Basie and Artie Shaw. In the post-Prohibition era, jazz clubs opened on 52nd Street, and the appearance of Billie Holiday on "Swing Street" drew socialites, gangsters, and out-of-towners for the finest jazz singer the city had ever seen. The tradition of great female jazz singers in Harlem, which began with Bessie Smith, Ma Rainey, and Ethel Waters, reached a tragic apotheosis in the difficult life and incomparable art of Holiday.

Harlem Reborn

The long decline of Harlem began with the Depression. The collapse of security prices on the Stock Exchange at first meant little to Harlem, where investors with shares were thin on the ground. Nightlife at the Apollo continued in glittering high spirits, with new stars like Ella

Fitzgerald and Billie Holiday launching their careers. But the consequences of rising unemployment levels, overcrowding, and the deterioration of the economic position of black families were inevitably observed in Harlem. Only the churches did boom time business, and the pastors retained a public prominence and influence more akin to the nineteenth-century city than anything that clergy experienced in the twentieth. The decline that began in the 1930s continued remorselessly. By the 1970s two out of every five stores on 125th Street were vacant and many of those that were occupied were owned by Koreans. The physical condition of tenements had declined in Harlem, as they had done across the city. Many were abandoned or torched for insurance money. Crime and the explosion of drugs turned every resident into a victim, and Harlem became a no-go area for white tourists. The decline began to reverse in the 1980s, when the city climbed out of the deep pit into which it had sunk in the financial collapse of the 1970s. The average income of Harlem residents began to rise, from $18,503 in 1980 to $23,230 in 1990. The number of black college graduates rose in pace with the community's rising levels of prosperity.

There were many other signs of Harlem on the upswing. The Apollo Theater, now run by a nonprofit foundation, underwent an ambitious $20 million renovation in the 1980s. The large, good-looking brownstones facing Mount Morris Park were renovated in the late 1990s. Rents rose across Harlem and vacancy levels reached historically low levels. On 125th Street Ben & Jerry's and the Body Shop opened, visual symbols of the rebirth of the street as potent as the Disney presence on 42nd Street. The Schomburg Center for Research in Black Culture at 144 West 125th Street, a branch of the New York Public Library system, has mounted a string of high-profile historical exhibits concentrating on black life in New York. The Hispanic heritage is celebrated at El Museo del Barrio, at 1230 Fifth Avenue, at 104th Street, and the Studio Museum in Harlem, at 144 West 125th Street collects the art and artifacts of the black African diaspora. Older institutions that once formed the spine of Harlem life, such as the Abyssinian Baptist Church at 132 West 138th Street (led in the last century by two generations of Adam Clayton Powells), have taken on a new lease of life. On Sunday mornings, the streets are crowded with well-dressed people attending the 400 churches in Harlem. During the week, busloads of tourists—white and black—crowd the streets.

CHAPTER EIGHT

More than Manhattan

And so, what about the rest of New York City, the "outer boroughs" where the other seven million New Yorkers live? The balance of attention to Manhattan, or imbalance, largely reflects my own experience of the city. But it is essential to emphasize that there is a lot more to New York than Manhattan.

The hundredth anniversary of the formation of Greater New York was marked, or lamented, by a year-long series of events that ran throughout the whole of 1998. The consolidation of the five boroughs (Manhattan, Staten Island, Brooklyn, Queens and the Bronx—always with the *the*) into one city in 1898 raised the population of the newly-formed urban behemoth to 3.4 million people. New York thus became the world's second-largest city, behind London.

Brooklyn

The issue of consolidation was debated throughout the 1890s, and Brooklyn then, as now, was the borough with the strongest self-identity and the most misgivings about the whole idea of consolidation. Looking at the impressive Greek-Revival Brooklyn Borough Hall, and the beaux-art Brooklyn Museum of Art, it is impossible not to sense the community's civic pride and self-confidence. It was a community characterized by strong neighborhoods, deep-seated provincialism, and wonderful flights of boosterism. "Brooklyn is a borough of great talking," remarked Joe Flaherty. "Politically they'll vote conservative, but in the bars they'll be as wicked and funny and obscene about politicians as Swift." The sense of having an independent history, and of giving it away, is a strong note in Brooklyn patriotism. Until the opening of the Roeblings' bridge in 1882, Brooklyn was a large, self-contained community, which within a generation had made the transition from an agricultural economy rooted in small farms into a major commercial and industrial power. By the 1880s, Brooklyn had become the nation's fourth-largest industrial city.

The mercantile, financial, and industrial elites of all five boroughs favored consolidation, but there were deep problems surrounding the very idea. The expansion of the city would strengthen its political position in relation to the rural power-base of the Republicans who generally controlled the state government at Albany. Manhattan, with its vice, and its large Jewish and Catholic immigrant populations, alarmed the Protestant majority in Brooklyn. The political bosses of the Democratic Party saw in consolidation a plot to deny them the majorities they had come to assume in New York elections. On the other hand, after years of struggling against the state-imposed debt limit for cities, the idea of a consolidated city, with an almost unlimited ability to borrow money, was an appealing prospect. A consolidated city would be better able to finance growth and needed improvements. In response, advocates of consolidation talked about lower tax bills, improved credit ratings, and cheaper transportation, and an end to poverty, unemployment, and wickedness in general. With varying degrees of enthusiasm, the electorate voted in five referenda in 1898 to confirm the decision. Brooklyn was carried by the slimmest of margins: under 300 votes.

The alternative was continued independence and thus competition between boroughs. In the eyes of business leaders and an important sector of urban reformers, the consolidated city could make possible what New York alone had seldom managed: honest, efficient city government. The history of civic corruption, which reached its crescendo during the era of the Tweed Ring after the Civil War, was notorious across the nation. It was Mark Twain who suggested that instead of sending US Marines to occupy and pacify the Philippines in 1899, they would be better directed against the corrupt tyranny managed by Tammany Hall in New York. The social problems of Manhattan, where in 1901 an estimated 70 percent of the population lived in tenements, stretched the resolve of the political system, its collective imagination and the city's resources to the breaking point. Manhattan needed the tax revenues of Brooklyn and the other boroughs. Industrialists hoped that with the strengthened influence of sober business interests and Republican votes, the clamoring poor and the trades unions could be more effectively controlled. Despite widespread misgivings, consolidation made sense, of a kind, to most.

For old-time patriots and Romantic remembrancers, Brooklyn has become the Old Cause, betrayed by its mis-leaders and overwhelmed by economic necessity. Life in consolidated New York has done much, they feel, to degrade the civic identities of the "outer boroughs." One revered civic institution after another went to the wall after the Second World War. The much-admired *Brooklyn Eagle* closed in 1955. In 1957 Walter O'Malley took the Brooklyn Dodgers baseball franchise to Los Angeles. And in 1966 the Brooklyn Navy Yard was closed. To Pete Hamill, celebrated New York journalist, being a Brooklynite meant growing up with a deeply engraved sense of grievance:

> *We learned how to lose things earlier because we were Dodgers fans. Then we finally lost the whole thing. We can really point to things the way Europeans can point to 1917 and say after this the world changed. For us, it was the Dodgers leaving, the folding of* The Brooklyn Eagle *and the closing of the Navy Yard.*

There are other arguments about the way history went for Brooklyn, and for the other boroughs. A consolidated New York as a whole has managed its growth, its decline after the Second World War, and its struggle back in the 1980s and since with remarkable civic stability. For all the rich particularity of its neighborhood life, the evident class and racial divisions in the city, and the astonishing flood of immigrants into every borough (except Staten Island), New York is economically and socially a single market. The process, which gained new meaning with the opening of the Brooklyn Bridge in 1883, and was given powerful momentum as the elevated rail network reached outward beyond Manhattan, was locked in by the subway. By the time the Holland Tunnel opened in 1927, connecting lower Manhattan with Hoboken in New Jersey, there were thirteen bridges linking Manhattan with Brooklyn, Queens, and the Bronx. Long after other engineering marvels claimed the attention of the public and some of the affection that the Brooklyn Bridge once enjoyed, bridges were a powerful symbol of the progressive integration of New York City. A new bridge, tunnel or subway line between Manhattan and Brooklyn or Queens had consequences for the development of housing, shops, and schools in what was until then a rural landscape at the outer rim of the borough. In December 1902 the Pennsylvania Railroad was granted the right to join its western and Long Island lines in a Manhattan terminal. Thus the endlessly lamented Pennsylvania Station, designed by Charles F. McKim. Economic integration is complete, and the public transportation system managed by the Transit Authority is rightly admired as one of the best in the world. The argument that this process and its undoubted benefits would have achieved as much if there had never been a consolidated New York, or a Port Authority, and if there had been many more persons seated at the negotiating table when a road or subway was proposed, seems unlikely.

Visitors to the city's boroughs come in the beginning in search of specific things (Coney Island, Yankee Stadium, Prospect Park, Green-Wood Cemetery) and find many others that invite a more leisurely visit: Plymouth Church, which in the nineteenth century was probably the most famous Protestant church in America; Pierrepont Street, with its extravagant mansions; Fulton Mall; the Brooklyn Academy of Music; the Brooklyn Botanic Garden; the Hassidic world of Crown Heights and the Arab restaurants and shops that line Atlantic Avenue; the restored Weeksville houses and Mrs. Stahl's Knishery on Brighton Beach Avenue. In Long Island City, the cultural tourist will find the Noguchi Museum and P.S. 1 Contemporary Art Center. The American Museum of the Moving Image is in Astoria. In the Bronx visitors seek out the International Wildlife Conservation Park, formerly known as the Bronx Zoo, on Fordham Road and Bronx River Parkway, Woodlawn Cemetery, and the Van Cortlandt House Museum and Park. The New York Botanical Garden, with its conservatory modeled after Crystal Palace in London and the Palm House at Kew Garden, is on Southern Boulevard in the Bronx.

There is little prospect that any of the boroughs of New York will ever seriously rival Manhattan as a financial and cultural center or tourist attraction. History lies far too complexly intertwined in Manhattan for it to be possible to imagine it being overtaken—by anywhere. But after 9/11, history is likely to be filled with surprises.

Further Reading

Place of publication New York unless otherwise indicated.

A Maritime History of New York, compiled by Workers of the Writers Program of the Works Projects Administration for the City of New York (Doubleday, Doran, 1941)

Abbott, Berenice, *Changing New York* (Dutton, 1939; reissued as *New York in the Thirties*, with a text by Elizabeth McCausland, Dover, 1973)

Anderson, Jervis, *This Was Harlem* (Farrar, Straus and Giroux, 1983)

Auchincloss, Louis, *The Vanderbilt Era* (Charles Scribner's Sons, 1989)

——, *J.P. Morgan: The Financier as Collector* (Harry N. Abrams, Inc., 1990)

Auletta, Ken, *The Streets Were Paved with Gold* (Random House, 1979)

Beard, Rick and Leslie Cohen Berlowitz, eds, *Greenwich Village: Culture and Counter-Culture* (New Brunswick: Rutgers University Press for The Museum of the City of New York, 1993)

Beck, Louis, *New York's Chinatown: An Historical Presentation of Its People and Places* (Bohemia Publishing Co., 1898)

Bercovici, Konrad, *Around the World in New York* (London: Jonathan Cape, 1924)

Black, Mary, *Old New York in Early Photographs 1853–1901*, rev. ed. (Dover, 1976)

Boyer, M. Christine, *Manhattan Manners: Architecture and Style 1850–1900* (Rizzoli, 1985)

Buck, James E., ed., *The New York Stock Exchange: The First 200 Years* (Essex, CT: Greenwich Publishing Co., 1992)

Cahan, Abraham, *The Education of Abraham Cahan*, trans. Leon Stein, Abraham P. Conan and Lynn Davison, with an Introduction by Leon Stein (Philadelphia: Jewish Publication Society of America, 1969)

Caro, Robert A., *The Power Broker: Robert Moses and the Fall of New York* (Knopf, 1974)

Charyn, Jerome, *Metropolis: New York as Myth, Marketplace, and Magical Land* (Putnam, 1986)

Clay, Steven and Rodney Phillips, eds, *A Secret Location on the Lower East Side: Adventures in Writing 1960–1980* (New York Public Library and Granary Books, 1998)

Cohn, Nik, *Heart of the World* (Alfred A. Knopf, 1991) on Broadway

Cornog, Evan W., "To Give Character to Our City: New York's City Hall," *New York History*, 69 (October 1988) 389–423

Davis, Allen F., *Spearheads for Reform: The Social Settlements and the Progressive Movement 1890–1914* (Oxford University Press, 1967)

Delaney, Edmund T. and Charles Lockwood, with photographs by George

Roos, *Greenwich Village: A Photographic Guide* (Dover, 1976)
Dickens, Charles, *American Notes for General Circulation*, ed. John S. Whitley and Arnold Goldman (Harmondsworth: Penguin Books, 1972)
Gilmartin, Gregory, *Shaping the City: New York and the Municipal Art Society* (Clarkson Potter, 1995)
Glazer, Nathan and Daniel Patrick Moynihan, *Beyond the Melting Pot* (Cambridge, MA: The MIT Press, 1970)
Goldberger, Paul, *The City Observed: New York* (Vintage Books, 1979)
Gray, Christopher, ed., *Fifth Avenue, 1911, From Start to Finish in Historic Block-by-Block Photographs* (Dover, 1994)
Green, Martin, *New York 1913: The Armory Show and the Paterson Strike Pageant* (Scribner's, 1988)
Gutman, Judith Mara, *Lewis Hine and the American Social Conscience* (Walker & Co., 1967)
Hamlin, Talbot, *Greek Revival Architecture in America* (Oxford University Press, 1944; reissued Dover, 1964)
Hapgood, Hutchins, *The Spirit of the Ghetto* (Funk & Wagnalls, 1902)
Hartman, Sadakichi, *Critical Modernist: Collected Art Writings*, ed. Jane Calhoun Weaver (University of California Press, 1991)
Heckscher, August, *Alive in the City: Memoir of an Ex-Commissioner* (Charles Scribner's Sons, 1974)
Hindus, Milton, ed., *The Old East Side* (Philadelphia: Jewish Publication Society of America, 1969)
Hodges, Graham Russell, *Root & Branch: African Americans in New York & East Jersey 1613–1863* (Chapel Hill: University of North Carolina Press, 1999)
Homberger, Eric, *The Historical Atlas of New York City* (Henry Holt, 1994)
Howe, Irving, *World of Our Fathers* (Simon & Schuster, 1976)
Huggins, Nathan Irvin, ed., *Voices from the Harlem Renaissance* (Oxford University Press, 1976).
Huxtable, Ada Louise, *Classic New York* (Anchor, 1964)
Jackson, Kenneth T., ed., *The Encyclopedia of New York City* (Yale University Press, 1995)
James, Henry, *The American Scene* (1907)
Janvier, Thomas, *In Old New York* (Harper & Brothers, 1894; reissued with an introduction by Edwin G. Burrows, St. Martin's Press, 2000)
Johnson, James Weldon, *Black Manhattan*, with a new preface by Allan Spear (Atheneum 1972). First published 1930.
Kasinitz, Philip, *Caribbean New York: Black Immigrants and the Politics of Race* (Ithaca: Cornell University Press, 1992)
Koolhaus, Rem, *Delirious New York* (Oxford University Press, 1978)

Kouwenhoven, John A., *The Columbia Historical Portrait of New York* (Garden City, N.Y.: Doubleday, 1953)

Lazarus, Emma, *Poems by Emma Lazarus,* with a Biographical Sketch by Josephine Lazarus, 2 vols. (Boston: Houghton Mifflin, 1888)

Lin, Jan, *Reconstructing Chinatown: Ethnic Enclave, Global Change* (Minneapolis: University of Minnesota Press, 1998)

Lockwood, Charles, *Manhattan Moves Uptown: An Illustrated History* (Boston: Houghton Mifflin, 1976)

Maffi, Mario, *Gateway to the Promised Land: Ethnic Cultures on New York's Lower East Side* (Atlanta: Rodopi, 1994)

Morris, Lloyd, *Incredible New York: High Life and Low Life of the Last Hundred Years* (Random House, 1951)

New York Panorama: A Companion to the WPA Guide to New York City, with a new introduction by Alfred Kazin (Pantheon, 1984). First published 1938.

Osofsky, Gilbert, *Harlem: The Making of a Ghetto* (Harper & Row, 1963) *Report of the Council of Hygiene and Public Health of the Citizens' Association of New York upon the Sanitary Condition of the City* (Appleton, 1865)

Riis, Jacob, *How the Other Half Lives* (Scribner, 1889)

Rischin, Moses, ed., *Grandma Never Lived in America: The New Journalism of Abraham Cahan* (Bloomington: Indiana University Press, 1985)

Sanders, Ronald, *The Lower East Side: A Guide to Its Jewish Past with 99 New Photographs,* photographs by Edmund V. Gillon, Jr. (Dover, 1979)

Silver, Nathan, *Lost New York* (Boston: Houghton Mifflin, 1967)

Simon, Kate, *Fifth Avenue: A Very Social History* (Harcourt Brace Jovanovich, 1978)

Smith, Thomas E.V., *The City of New York in the Year of Washington's Inauguration 1789* (Anson D.F. Randolph, 1889; reissued Riverside, CT: Chatham Press, 1972)

Spann, Edward K., *The New Metropolis: New York City 1840–1857* (Columbia University Press, 1981)

Stern, Robert A.M.. Gregory Gilmartin, and John Montague Massengale, *New York 1900: Metropolitan Architecture and Urbanism 1890–1915* (Rizzoli, 1983)

Stokes, I.N. Phelps, *The Iconography of Manhattan Island* (Robert H. Dodd, 1915). 6 vols.

Tauranac, John, *Elegant New York: The Builders and the Buildings 1885–1915,* photographed by Christopher Little (Abbeville Press, 1985)

Tax, Meredith, *Rivington Street* (William Morrow, 1982) [novel]

Taylor, William R., ed., *Inventing Times Square: Commerce and Culture at the Crossroads of the World* (Russell Sage Foundation, 1991; reissued Johns

Hopkins University Press 1996).)
Tomkins, Calvin, *Merchants and Masterpieces: The Story of the Metropolitan Museum*, rev. ed. (Henry Holt, 1989)
Trachtenberg, Marvin, *The Statue of Liberty* (London: Allen Lane, 1974)
Van Rensselaer, Mariana Griswold, *Accent as Well as Broad Effects: Writings on Architecture, Landscape, and the Environment, 1876–1925*, ed. David Gebhard (Berkeley: University of California Press, [1996])
Ware, Caroline F., *Greenwich Village 1920–1930: A Comment on American Civilization in the Post-War Years* (Boston: Houghton Mifflin, 1935)
Watson, Steven, *Strange Bedfellows: The First American Avant-Garde* (Abbeville Press, 1991)
——, *The Harlem Renaissance: Hub of African-American Culture, 1920-1930* (Pantheon, 1995)
Weisser, Michael R., *A Brotherhood of Memory: Jewish landsmannshaftn in the New World* (Harper & Row, 1986)
Wharton, Edith, *The Age of Innocence* (Scribner's Sons, 1920)
——, *Old New York* (Scribner's Sons, 1924)
——, *A Backward Glance* (Appleton Century, 1934)
White, Norval and Elliot Willensky, *AIA Guide to New York City*, 4th ed. (Three Rivers Press, 2000)
Wilson, Sondra Kathryn, ed., *The* Crisis *Reader: Stories, Poetry, and Essays from the N.A.A.C.P.'s* Crisis *Magazine* (Random House, 1999)

Novels, Autobiographies, and Memoirs of Immigrant Life in New York

Asch, Scholom, *Uncle Moses* 1922
——, *East River* 1948
Bullard, Arthur, *Comrade Yetta* 1913
Cahan, Abraham, *Yekl* 1896
——, *The Imported Bridegroom and other Stories of the New York Ghetto* 1898
——, *The Rise of David Levinsky* 1917
Cohen, Hyman and Lester Cohen, *Aaron Traum* 1930
Cohen, Rose, *Out of the Shadow* 1918
Colón, Jesus, *A Puerto Rican in New York and Other Sketches* 1961
Crane, Stephen, *Maggie: A Girl of the Streets* 1893
Di Donato, Pietro, *Naked Author* 1970
Fuchs, Daniel, *Summer in Williamsburg* 1934
——, *Homage to Blenholt* 1936
——, *Low Company* 1937
Ganz, Marie, *Rebels: Into Anarchy—And Out Again* 1919
Gazzo, Michael V., *A Hatful of Rain* 1956

Gold, Michael, *Jews Without Money* 1930
Goldman, Emma, *Living My Life* 1931
Gompers, Samuel, *Seventy Years of Life and Labor* 1925
Hijuelos, Oscar, *The Mambo Kings Play Songs of Love* 1991
Kohut, Rebekah, *My Portion: An Autobiography* 1925
Lewisohn, Ludwig, *Upstream: An American Chronicle* 1922
——, *Mid-Channel: An American Chronicle* 1929
Mohr, Nicholasa, *In Nueva York* 1977
Nichols, Anne, *Abbie's Irish Rose* (play) 1927
Ornitz, Samuel, *Haunch, Paunch and Jowl* 1923
Poole, Ernest, *The Voice of the Street* 1906
Reznikoff, Charles, *Family Chronicle* 1929
Riis, Jacob, *Out of Mulberry Street* 1898
——, *The Making of an American* 1901
Roskolenko, Henry, *The Time That Was Then: The Lower East Side 1900–1913—An Intimate Chronicle* 1971
Roth, Henry, *Call It Sleep* 1934
Soto, Pedro Juan, *Spiks* 1956
Suhl, Yuri, *One Foot in America* 1950
Sullivan, James, *Tenement Tales of New York* 1895
Techla, Georg, *Drei Jahre in New York* 1862
Vetter, Christoph, *Zwei Jahre in New York* 1849
Yezierska, Anzia, *Hungry Hearts* 1920
——, *Salome of the Tenements* 1922
——, *Children of Loneliness* 1923
——, *Bread Givers* 1925
——, *Red Ribbon on a White Horse* 1950

Index of Selected People

Adams, Abigail 44
Adams, Henry 57
Adams, President John 44, 53
Addams, Jane 96, 123
Algonquian tribes 12
Arbus, Diane 114
Aspinwall, Gilbert & John, 10–11
Aspinwall, William Henry 11
Astor, Mrs. William 199
Astor, John Jacob 10, 11, 44, 45, 107, 188, 199, 200, 220
Astor Library 11
Astor, William Waldorf 47

Baez, Joan 126
Baldwin, James 127, 132
Bankoff, H. Arthur 17
Barnum, Phineas T. 9, 173–174, 209
Bartholdi, Frédéric Auguste 48, 68–70, 72
Bayard, Mary 12
Bayard, Nicholas 12
Beals, Jessie Tarbox 113
Beame, Mayor Abe 156
Bellows, George 116
Berkman, Alexander 42, 122
Bernstein, Leonard 226
Black, Harry S. 33
Blackmar, Elizabeth 16
Bloomberg, Mayor Michael xvii, xv
Boni, Albert and Charles 118–119, 233
Bourne, Rudolph 116
Boyer, M. Christine 35
Brace, Charles Loring 100
Bradford, William 47
Brady, Matthew 172
Bremer, Fredrika 185
Brevoort, Henry 202
Bristed, Charles Astor 34
Brown, Isaac Hull 204
Bruno, Guido 117–118
Bryant, William Cullen 109
Brown, Henry Kirke 48
Burgis, William 7–8
Burnham, Daniel 32–33
Burr, Aaron 45, 48, 107
Bush, President George W. x
Butler, William Allen 185

Cahan, Abraham 78, 84, 89–93, 98
Calder, Alexander 167
Carrère & Hastings (architects) 11, 40
Child, Lydia Maria 57
Clinton, Governor George 3, 172
Coit, Stanton 95
Cole, Thomas 199
Cooper, James Fenimore 19–21
Cooper, Peter 32, 70, 200
Corso, Gregory 118, 128
Crane, Hart 23
Crane, Stephen 100
Croker, Richard 220

Davids, Carl 49
Davis, Alexander Jackson 50
Dell, Floyd 117, 119–123
Dickens, Charles 224
diModica, Arturo 166
Dinkins, Mayor David 66, 211
Dodge, Mabel 120
Dongan, Governor Thomas 28
Dos Passos, John 182
Downing, Andrew Jackson 138–140, 151
Dreiser, Theodore 57, 64, 117

Dunbar, Paul Laurence 57, 231, 236
Duveen, Joseph 41
Dylan, Bob 126

Eastman, Crystal 116
Eastman, Max 116, 117, 121–123, 233
Eliot, T.S. 75
Ellington, Duke 239
Evarts, William 72

Fauset, Jessie Redmon 237
Ferlinghetti, Lawrence 129
Fisk, Jim 57
Fitzgerald, F. Scott 57, 64, 75
Ford, Henry 75
Foster, George 163, 184
Fowler, Lorenzo and Orson 172–173
Franklin, Benjamin 48
French, Daniel Chester 165
Freud, Sigmund 117
Frick, Henry Clay 40
Fry, Roger 40
Fulton, Robert 47

Gainsborough, Thomas 42
Gallatin, Albert 48, 112, 199
Garvey, Marcus, 3, 232–233
Gershwin, George 237–238
Gilbert, Cass 165
Ginsberg, Allen 121, 127–130
Giuliani, Mayor Rudy xiii, xiv–xv, 64, 66, 103, 158, 170, 176, 210–212, 215
Glackens, William 113, 116
Gold, Michael 83–84
Goldman, Emma 42, 116, 120, 122
Goldman, Marcus 43
Gompers, Samuel 90, 102, 117, 148
Gorky, Maxim 214
Gould, Jay 57, 142
Gould, Joe 118, 122
Grant, Madison 75
Greeley, Horace 32, 70

Hale, Nathan 49
Halper, Albert 206
Hamilton, Alexander 48, 49
Hapgood, Hutchins 92, 116
Harrison, Mrs. Burton 70–72
Hartman, Sadakichi 34, 117
Hassam, Childe 113
Havel, Hippolyte 115, 120–121
Hawthorne, Nathaniel 50
Heckscher, August 155
Heller, Joseph 100–101
Henri, Robert 116
Herter Brothers 18
Hevesi, Alan G. xv
Hill, John William 172, 175–180
Hine, Lewis 79–80
Hoffman, Abbie 61
Holiday, Billie 240, 241
Holladay, Polly 120, 122
Hone, Philip 191, 202, 219
Houston, Sam 12
Houstoun, William 12
Howells, William Dean 90, 221, 231
Hughes, Langston 232, 235
Hunt, Richard Morris 47
Huxtable, Ada Louise 213

Inglis, Rt. Rev. Charles 46
Irving, Washington 3, 10, 146, 202, 220

Jacobs, Jane 37, 114
James, Henry 25, 27, 40, 41, 111–112
Jefferson, President Thomas 48, 54, 180
Johnson, James Weldon 229–230, 235–236
Kelley, James 13
Kennedy, Archibald 166

Kerouac, Jack 127–130
Kértesz, André 113
Kingsland, Mayor Ambrose 10, 48, 150
Klein, Samuel 206
Knopf, Alfred A. 233
Koch, Mayor Ed 211
Kostof, Spiro 27
Kreymborg, Alfred 117, 119, 123

Lafayette, Marquis de 48, 69, 180
LaGuardia, Mayor Fiorello 3, 102, 141, 179
Lambert, John 9
Lazarus, Emma 68, 71–73
L'Enfant, Pierre 28, 53, 172
Lenox, James 11
Lichtenstein, Roy 167
Lincoln, President Abraham 32, 179, 182
Lindsay, Mayor John 137, 155
Lippard, George 47
Lippis, Gina, xv-xvi
Livinston, Chancellor Robert R. 54
Locke, Alaine 233–237
Loory, Alyssa 17
Lowell, James Russell 71

McBean, Thomas 169
McCabe, James D., Jr. 184, 189
McComb, John, Jr. 145, 177, 178
McInerney, Jay 65
McKay, Claude 233, 238
McKim, Mead and White (architects) 246
MacMonnies, Frederick 49
Macy, Rowland H. 141, 189, 205
Mailer, Norman 131–132
Malamud, Bernard 88
Mangin, Joseph 56, 177, 178, 179
Mapplethorpe, Robert 133–135
Melville, Herman 19–20, 50–51, 56, 57, 142, 204
Morgan, J.P. 37–43, 209
Morgan, Junius Spencer 42
Morgenthau, Henry 33
Mortier, Abraham 44, 45, 107, 108
Moses, Robert 114, 155, 156, 167, 226
Mould, Jacob Wrey 153, 155, 183
Moynihan, Senator Daniel Patrick 156, 160
Mullett, A.B. 183
Mumford, Lewis 27, 116

Nevelson, Louise 167
Noguchi, Isamu 167

Olmsted, Frederick Law 30, 138, 151–155, 177
O'Neill, Eugene 117, 121, 236

Paulding, James Kirke 34
Penn, William 26
Plessmann, Ernst 48
Poe, Edgar Allan 114
Poole, Ernest, 22–23, 117
Post, George B. 32
Potter, Rev. Henry Codman 203
Pound, Ezra 121
Powell, Adam Clayton 3, 241
Pulitzer, Joseph 32, 70–71, 72
Putnam, Robert xvi

Reed, Henry Hope 137, 157
Reed, John 117, 120, 121, 122
Renwick, James 202–203
Ricciardi, Christopher 17
Riis, Jacob 81, 99, 221
Rischin, Moses 91
Rockefeller, John D. 168
Rodman, Henrietta 119–120, 122
Rogers, Elizabeth Barlow 157
Rohatyn, Felix G. 156–157

Roosevelt, President Franklin Delano 4, 73
Roosevelt, Sara Delano 3–4
Roosevelt, Theodore 1–2, 19, 21–22, 83, 86, 236
Rosenzweig, Roy 16

St. Gaudens, Augustus 209
Saarinen, Aline 39
Sage, Mrs. Russell 179
Sala, George Augustus 185–186
Salvo, Joseph J. 65
Sargent, Frank P. 74
Sartre, Jean–Paul 26, 163
Schermerhorn, Abraham 199
Schermerhorn, Caroline *see* Mrs. Astor
Schwartz, Delmore 131
Scott, Major–General Winfield 199
Scott, Sir Walter 3, 9, 39
Scudder, John 9
Scudder, Vida Dutton 95–97
Sennett, Richard 114
Shinn, Everett 113, 116
Silver, Joan Micklin 98
Simkhovitch, Mary 116
Singer, Isaac Bashevis 92–94
Sitte, Camillo 27
Sloan, John 113, 116
Sondheim, Stephen 226
Stedman, Henry Clarence 56
Steffens, Lincoln 91, 116
Steinberg, Saul 67
Stern, Henry J. 157, 180, 207
Stern, Robert A.M. 87
Stewart, Alexander T. 190–192
Stieglitz, Alfred 34, 117
Stillman, James 33
Straus, Isidor 3
Strong, George Templeton 187, 202
Stuyvesant, Petrus 12, 209
Suhl, Yuri 98

Taylor, President Zachary 50
Thomas, Dylan 128, 131
Tilden, Samuel J. 11
Tompkins, Governor Daniel D. 3
Town, Ithiel 50
Twain, Mark 244
Tweed, William M. 51

Upjohn, Richard 43, 47, 140, 202

Vanderbilt, Cornelius x, 6
Van Vechten, Carl 233, 238
Vaux, Calvert 30, 151–153, 155
Veiller, Lawrence 97, 99, 101

Wagner, Mayor Robert F. 157
Wald, Lillian 95, 97, 102, 116
Walling, William English 116
Ward, John Q.A. 48, 49, 60
Ward, Samuel 199
Ware, Caroline 121–124
Warhol, Andy 133–135
Warren, Sir Peter 107, 108
Washington, President George 37, 38, 48, 49, 53–54, 141, 172, 180
White, Richard Grant 175
White, Stanford 49, 87, 113, 209, 229
Whitman, Walt 1, 4–6, 9, 23, 29, 70, 172, 184, 187
Willis, N.P. 190
Wolfe, Tom 56
Wood, Mayor Fernando 51, 181

Zenger, John Peter 52

Index of Places and Institutions

African Burial Ground 8, 14–16, 19, 49
Allen Street 18
American Academy of Fine Arts 9
Art Commission 180
Astor House 188
Astor Library 200
Astor Place Opera House 200

Battery ix, 13, 54, 145–147, 164, 167
Battery Park City xv, 146–147, 171
Bethune Street 3
Bloemendael 12
Bowery 2, 198, 205
Bowling Green 143–144, 166, 168
Broadway 2, 163–217
Brooklyn Bridge 154, 245
Brooklyn–Manhattan Transit Corporation (BMT) 213
Brooklyn Navy Yard 25
Broome Street 3, 189

Castle Clinton 146
Castle Garden 145
Cedar Street 2
Cedar Street Tavern 127
Central Park Conservancy 159, 160
Charity Organization Society 97
Cherry Street 2, 54, 82
Children's Aid Society 100
Chinatown 88, 192–197, 219
Chrysler Building 35
City Hall 12, 55–56, 145, 171, 176–181, 193
City Hall (Wall Street) 52 , 53, 171; demolition 55
City Hotel 188
Clinton Street 3
Columbia University 45, 116, 123, 195
Community Gardens 103
Cooper Union 30–31
Cotton Club 239
Custom House (Wall Street) 50
Custom House (Battery) 165

Dey Street 13
Duke Ellington Boulevard 3

Eldridge Street Synagogue 18
Ellis Island 74–79, 146
Empire State Building xii
Equitable Building 168–169

Federal Hall 50–51, 53
Fifth Avenue Hotel 188, 208
Five Points 224
Flatiron Building 30–35, 205, 208, 213
Fuller Construction Company 32–33

George Washington Bridge 24
Goldman Sachs 13
Grace Church 146, 192, 200–204
Grand Central Terminal 208, 212
Greenmarket at Union Square 207
Greenwich Street 13, 170
Greenwich Village 3, 107–132, 198, 219
Green–Wood Cemetery 140, 142, 192
Ground Zero xiii
Guggenheim Museum 35
Guggenheim/SoHo 198

Haarlem 12, 220
Harlem 219–241
Haughwout Store 189, 197
Henry Street Settlement 94

Holland Tunnel 245

Interborough Rapid Transit
Company (IRT) 13, 213
Irving Place 3

John Street 2

"Kleindeutschland" 86–87, 219
Kleins 206–207

Lafayette Place 199–200
LaGuardia Place 3
Landmarks Preservation Commission
15, 102
Lenox Avenue 3
Lenox Library 11
Liberal Club 119–120
Liberty Street 2, 167
Lincoln Center 35
Lincoln Tunnel 24
Lott farmhouse 17
Lower East Side 2, 3, 81–89
Lower East Side Tenement Museum
104–105

Macdougal Street 118–120, 232
Macy's 3, 205
Madison Square 192, 205, 207–209
Malcolm X Boulevard 3
Metropolitan Forensic Archaeology
Team 15
Metropolitan Life Building 208–209
Metropolitan Museum of Art xv, 11,
39–42, 154, 157, 160, 175, 180
Metropolitan Opera House 209
Morgan Library 39, 41
Municipal Arts Society 27, 33,
Museum of Jewish Heritage 161
Museum of the American Indian 165
Museum of the City of New York 13

Nathan's 215–216
National Arts Club 147–148
New–York Historical Society 54, 179
New York Public Library 11, 180, 200
New York Society for the Suppression
of Vice 39
New York Stock Exchange 13, 35,
38, 57–61
New York Unearthed (museum) 14
New York University 114–115, 198

Park Theater 174–175, 177
Parks
Central Park 30, 137–138, 149–
155
City Hall Park 14, 163, 167,
176–177, 181–183
Gramercy Park 110, 147–148
Marcus Garvey Park/Mount
Morris Park 3
Van Cortlandt Park 2
PATH Trains xii, xiv, 24
Peretz Square 3
Pine Street 2, 48, 167, 168
Plaza Hotel 33
Port Authority xii, xiv, 24–25

Richmond Hill 44–45
Richmond Hill Opera House 44
Rivington Street 84–85
Rockefeller Center 3, 35, 168
Roosevelt, Sara Delano, Parkway 3

St. George's Chapel 46
St. Nicholas Hotel 188–189, 197–198
St. Paul's Chapel xv, 2, 46, 54,
169–176, 183, 187
St. Vincent's Hospital 114
San Juan Hill 223–226
San Remo Bar 118, 127, 131, 132
Schermerhorn Row 10

Seabury Tredwell House 199
Seneca Village 16
Shevchenko Place 3
"Shteeble Row" 90
Slave Market 8
SoHo 196–201
South Street Seaport Museum 10
Staten Island 6,
Stadt Huys (first City Hall) 7, 13, 52, 164
Stuyvesant Street 2

Tammany Hall 244
Tiffany's 189–190, 191, 205
Tompkins Square 3, 148–149
Trinity Church 2, 7, 37–38, 43–48, 164, 170, 176, 202

Union Club 205
Union Square 182, 192, 205–207
University Place 11, 127
University Settlement 95

Wall Street 8, 9, 12, 33, 37, 38, 42, 49–52, 54, 56–61, 75, 89, 102, 117, 139, 163–165, 167, 168, 172
Walt Disney Corporation 211
Washington Square 110–115, 125, 146, 198
Waverly Place 3
Weeksville 16–17
White Horse Tavern 127, 131, 132
Woodlawn Cemetery 141, 192
Woolworth Building 209
World Trade Center viii, x, xii, xiv, xv, 16, 96, 146–147, 161, 165, 167, 169, 197

Yorkville 222